TEACHING OF MORAL EDUCATION

other recent books on similar topic

ENCYCLOPAEDIA OF EDUCATIONAL ADMINISTRATION.
in 5 Volumes
Edited by Paul Monroe

ENCYCLOPAEDIA OF HISTORY OF EDUCATION.
in 4 Volumes
Edited by Paul Monroe

ENCYCLOPAEDIA OF PHILOSOPHY OD EDUCATION
in 2 Volumes
Edited by Paul Monroe

ENCYCLOPAEDIA OF PSYCHOLOGY OF EDUCATION.
in 2 Volumes
Edited by Paul Monroe

INTERNATIONAL ENCYCLOPAEDIA OF EDUCATION
New Edition
in 12 Volumes
Edited by Paul Monroe

ENCYCLOPAEDIA OF SEX EDUCATION.
in 3 Volumes
Edited by A. Bigelow

ENCYCLOPAEDIA OF GREAT EDUCATIONAL THINKERS.
in 4 volumes
Edited by Paul Monroe

INTERNATIONAL ENCYCLOPAEDIA OF HIGHER EDUCATION.
in 10 Volumes
Edited by S. R. Sharma

TEACHING OF MORAL EDUCATION

Edited By
DR. S. R. SHARMA
Director Education Department,
Delhi Administration

Cosmo Publications
2006 New Delhi

TEACHING AND MORAL EDUCATION

First published by COSMO 2005
Edition 2006

Published by
COSMO PUBLICATIONS
for
GENESIS PUBLISHING PVT. LTD.
24-B, Ansari Road, Darya Ganj,
New Delhi-110 002,
INDIA

Printed at
Mehra Offset Press

CONTENTS

1

What Is Moral Education?

"They should be brought to know and love God and to practise in the school community the virtues appropriate to their age and environment." These words from the Plowden Report on primary education (1966,& 572) not only highlight the importance of moral education, they also illustrate very effectively the confusion that surrounds a good deal of thinking about both moral and religious education and especially about the relationship between them.

Any discussion of the theory and practice of moral education must begin, then, by attempting to define in some detail what is meant by moral education and what are its fundamental principles. It will be equally clear, however, that in order to do this we must first endeavour to discover what kind of relationship exists between moral education and religious education and, indeed, whether there is or should be any such relationship. A clarification of that issue might of itself take us some way towards a definition of moral education.

At all events it is a question we should deal with first before turning our attention to the question of what moral education itself is. When we come to that question, it will be helpful to consider it from at least three points of view. To begin with, we must look for some of the reasons for the recent upsurge of interest in moral education. For if we can discover why it is coming to be regarded as so important, we may be able to find out what it is hoped it will provide. Secondly, it will be useful to ask what is implied by calling it moral education rather than moral instruction or moral knowledge, since, as we shall see in the next section, a failure to distinguish these three terms in the teaching of religion is symptomatic of, and perhaps a major cause of, the confusion that has existed or has come to exist there. Thirdly, it may well prove profitable to approach the problem from the other end, as it were, and ask what we would regard as the essential characteristics of a successful product of a process of moral education. Whom would we regard as a morally educated person? If we can produce some answers to that question, we may have found a further source of clues towards our definition of what moral education is. All of these approaches we will explore in turn in an attempt to get some answers to the question, "What is moral education?".

Moral education and religious education

The links between moral behaviour and religious beliefs that have been established over the ages in the traditions of most religions but perhaps especially in the Judaeo-Christian tradition have been so strong that many people still regard the two as inseparable. There is little doubt that the requirement of the 1944 Education Act in the United Kingdom that religion be the only compulsory curriculum subject was prompted as much by a desire to promote the moral education of pupils as by any intention to propagate the Christian religion itself. We have already seen the same attitude and approach reflected in the recommendations of the Plowden Reports published over twenty years later and it can be seen as a major factor in the continuing demands from parents and others that religion should be taught to all pupils compulsorily.

The church and its officials, too, still consider this area of education their own preserve and appear to be of opinion that there can be no proper discussion of morals nor of moral education unless the church is fully represented. This view is usually also supported by those responsible for the media, so that, on the one hand, many "religious" programmc on both radio and television turn out to be discussions of, or pronouncements on, moral questions and, on the other, it is unusual to see a moral issue tackled without reference being made to the "expert" opinion of a clergyman of one denomination or another.

The same confusion is compounded by the practice of many schools, since often the compulsory "daily act of worship" nowadays is replaced by some kind of humanist, secular and non-religious event - the playing of a piece of classical music, the reading of a poem or the telling of some "morally uplifting" anecdote -, the approach to the compulsory period of religious education is often very much, if not entirely, concerned with moral issues and there is still a tendency for many teachers and head teachers to regard moral education as the private domain of the RE teacher.

It is not surprising, therefore, when this kind of link is assumed by those whose thinking on these issues ought to be lucid, that parents, politicians and even the intelligent and educated man in the street continue to regard the two as inextricably linked. Thus there emerges a danger, somc of the results of which we are witnessing today, that when religious beliefs are rejected there appears to be no longer any basis for moral principles and the baby goes down the drain with the bathwater. It is important to consider, therefore, whether such links are necessary or merely contingent.

However, it might be worthwhile in doing so to ponder first of all some of the confusions that have surrounded our understanding and practice of the teaching of religion itself. This confusion is reflected in the fact that schools have used a variety of terms to denote the religious component of their curricula. Religious Instruction, Religious knowledge and Religious Education are all terms quite commonly found on school timetables and they seem to be used almost indiscriminately according to the whims of individual head-teachers or heads of the relevant departments rather than as a result of any awareness of the semantic differences between them. Yet those semantic differences are crucial. To describe this area of study as Religious Knowledge begs all kinds of epistemological questions concerning the status of knowledge in this field; it also makes certain claims about the truth content of what is offered. To call it Religious Instruction, on the other hand, neither begs these questions nor makes these claims; what it does do is to suggest that, regardless of the epistemological status of religious knowledge and of questions concerning its truth, children will be instructed in it and will, one presumes, therefore, be taught to accept it. In contrast to this again, the term Religious Education suggests a more open approach to the teaching of religion. What precisely it implies is, of course, the subject of much heated debate, but in general it does invite such debate and requires that we approach it with an open mind.

It is this latter term that is now most common in schools and this suggests that our approach to the teaching of religion in schools has become over recent years liberal and open ended.

One development that illustrates this is the increased incidence of the study of Comparative Religion in schools and colleges. We no longer regard religious education as concerned to teach only the Christian religion. It is clear that this was the intention of the 1944 Act, since there could be no other reason for allowing parents to withdraw their children from RE lessons. It is also clear from the quotation with which we began this chapter that this was the intention of the Plowden Committee in its approach to RE in the primary school, a point which is emphasized by the refusal of some members of the committee to go along with its recommendations on this issue and the submission of a note of reservation by A.J. Ayer and several others. However, in spite of Plowden and even the 1944 Act, which is still in force, this is not usually any longer the practice of the schools, not least because many of them are catering for the kind of multi-ethnic community for which this sort of approach would be totally unsuitable. The approach to religious education in schools, then, like the approach to religious assemblies, is today far more open.

Two further points must be made about this trend in the teaching of religion in schools which are of crucial importance for moral education. Firstly, it is a trend which reflects a distinction that has come to be made by some theorists, theologians and educationists alike, within religious knowledge. Our attention has been drawn to the fact that all religious utterances are not of the same kind and are not, as a result, subject to the same kinds of verification procedures. In other words, what we call religious knowledge is a body of assertions of several different logical types. We need, for example, quite different methods for testing the truth of such diverse kinds of assertions as "Moses led the Israelites out of bondage in Egypt", "Jesus Christ is the son of God", "God is love" and "Goodness is treating one's neighbour as oneself". A broad distinction can be drawn, therefore, between what might be called "historical" or "factual" assertions, a category which would include statements concerning the history, the social significance and the ritual of a religion, and those that have been called the "parahistorical", a category which includes the doctrinal, the mythological and the ethical (Smart 1968).

Furthermore, not only has it been argued on the basis of this view of religious knowledge that we should adopt the more liberal and open approach to it that we have already discussed (Smart 1968); it is further argued by some that no justification can be found for teaching the second kind of religious knowledge at all (Hirst 1965a). Some would even argue that it is not really knowledge. There are good reasons, it is claimed, for teaching *about* the Christian religion (or any other religion if it comes to that), since it is part of our heritage, has played a major role in the development of our civilization and has the same claims to be included in the curriculum as English literature, history or any of the humanities. There is no justification, however, for teaching its doctrines or for attempting to establish faith or belief in them, since to do so is to discourage that open and critical approach to knowledge which is the essence of education and to offer as "fact" "knowledge" whose bases are highly problematic.

The importance of this for moral education will be clear. For, where links between morals and religion have been claimed, these links are forged with the doctrinal aspects of the religion not the historical. It is because "God is love" that we are urged to love our neighbour, not because Moses led the Israelites out of bondage in Egypt. It is because "Jesus Christ is the son of God" that we are encouraged to follow his moral teachings, not because he lived at the beginning of the first century AD.

This general development draws our attention, then, to the problems surrounding moral assertions as well as those of religious knowledge. It also puts moral education at risk. For it raises the baby and bathwater problem to which we referred earlier. If we cannot justify teaching the doctrinal aspects of religion, then we cannot justify teaching the moral precepts that are based on them. If our approach to the teaching of religion is liberal and open-ended, the implication of this that pupils are to be encouraged to make up their own minds on religious issues, to accept or reject, "to stand on their own feet in such matters"(Smart 1968, p.99). If, however, their considered choice is to reject religion, the result of a linking of religion and morality will be the rejection of morality too. Not only is this undesirable, it is also a logical and psychological impossibility. For, while it is possible, as many people demonstrate daily, to live without religion, it is clearly not possible to live, except at the level of animal existence, without any set of moral values or principles to guide one's behaviour, one's human choices. This in itself must cast the greatest possible doubt on the validity of any linking of morality with religion.

It is for this reason that recent years have seen the development of what has been called "secular morality", an approach to morals that is independent of all religions. This term is used as though it denoted something new and unusual; it also suggests that it represents merely an alternative kind of morality. It is our contention that this is the only approach one can adopt to the problem of morals.

There is no logical connection between morality and religion. Any connection that exists is merely contingent. We have just discussed some of the dangers of this contingent connection, particularly those consequent on any rejection of religious beliefs. There is another danger too, however, which may be of even greater significance. A religious morality must essentially be an authoritarian morality. Our reason for accepting those moral principles that have their basis in religion and for adopting as a consequence certain kinds of behaviour must be that they are recommended, if not demanded, by the godhead. This is true of any religious code of ethics no matter what religion it emanates from. For if our reasons are other than these, then by definition our morality is not a religious one. If, for example, I believe on other grounds that I should treat my neighbour as myself, then my code of morality is not a religious one. If I believe this because God or Jesus Christ demands it of me, then I am tacitly accepting that the only reason for acting in that way is that it is required of me by an authority whose right to make such demands I recognize. Any morality that is based on religion, therefore, is authoritarian in essence.

Further problems will arise if one tries to avoid this difficulty by suggesting that there are reasons for these principles other than the arbitrary commands of God, that God's role is to reveal to us certain eternal moral truths. For if these moral truths exist in some way independently of God's will, then there are important implications for his omnipotence. If loving one's neighbour as oneself is right "independently of God's will, then God in not omnipotent, since there exists something that is beyond his control and to which he may even be subject himself (O'Connor 1957). In any case, to argue thus is to acknowledge that the basis of any set of moral principles is independent of religious beliefs.

Thus the linking of morality to religion either creates enormous theological problems or must lead to the acceptance of an authoritarian basis for one's moral code. It is for this reason that over the centuries religion and theology have inhibited rather than enhance moral debate, since they have focused attention on questions of the interpretation of the word of God rather than on how man could set about thinking for himself on moral issues.

Why is this not acceptable? Primarily it is unacceptable because it denies to the individual the right to choose his own beliefs, moral principles and behaviour on his own terms and in the light of his own thinking. The same arguments that have been put in favour of making up one's own mind on religious questions must apply with at least equal force in relation to moral principles and choices. In order to do this, one must reject any morality that is based on the blind acceptance of any kind of authority.

Secondly, it is unacceptable because it does not allow for the evolution of moral knowledge or understanding. It does not allow for the fact that moral "knowledge", like all other knowledge, will develop and change. Its model for all knowledge is that of a progressive revelation by God to man of eternal truths and such a view would seem to be no longer tenable in any area, least of all that of morality. To put it differently, our moral understanding must be such as to enable us to adjust to changing social circumstances, to meet new moral problems and modify our principles to deal with them. This is not possible with a morality that is based on authority.

For adjustment becomes a matter of interpretation and this is usually difficult and sometimes impossible, as the ambivalence of the church and its slowness to pronounce on such issues as contraception and abortion indicates. To leave such questions to the judgement of the individual is to admit that religion itself can provide no firm basis for moral decisions.

Thus a proper morality has to be seen as independent of religion. If there is a connection it is not that morality is dependent on religious beliefs, it is much more likely that man's religious beliefs are a result of his moral awareness. As Kant said, "Belief in God is grounded in the moral consciousness rather than the moral law on belief in God".

Because of the dangers inherent in the rejection of religious beliefs, therefore, and in the adoption of an authoritarian morality, we have begun in recent times to consider moral education independently of the teachings of religion. This is one of the reasons for the growing interest in moral education. It is our intention in this book to examine what is involved for teachers in facing up to the task of providing a moral education on this basis. In order to do that we shall begin by attempting to discern what moral education is, since we have now established that it is not religious education, and, firstly, what other reasons there might be for its growing importance.

The importance of moral education - in traditional theory and practice.

From earliest times in education theory and practice moral education has been seen as the very core of the educational process, and moral upbringing has been regarded, almost without question, as the central feature of education itself. The truth of this is immediately apparent from an examination of the work of any or all of the great theorists and practitioners of education.

All of the great theorists throughout the centuries have been quite explicit on this point. For Socrates virtue was knowledge of the good and, in Plato's elaborate development of this theme, the role of education, its whole point and purpose, was to help people, those at least who were blessed with the necessary intellectual capacity for it, to acquire the kind of knowledge that would of itself bring virtue in its train and lead to the attainment of that wisdom that comes from knowledge of the good. All other forms of intellectual activity were regarded as means to that end. The coping stone of all knowledge for Plato, that which bound all knowledge together into one unified whole, was knowledge of the supreme "Form" of "beauty, truth and goodness". Not only, therefore, was morality seen as the central feature of education, "goodness" also was regarded as the focal point of all human knowledge.

For the Roman Quintilian, too, the development of virtue was the core of educational practice. Quintilian's concern was with education in rhetoric, the education of the orator, a concern which reflects not only the more practical approach that he himself takes in discussions of education but also the major difference in "the national genius of the two peoples, Greek and Roman"(Rusk 1957, p.38). Nevertheless, the primary aim of this training in rhetoric is the production of the good man rather than merely the good politician or lawyer. "The perfect orator must be a man of integrity, the good man, otherwise he cannot pretend to that character; and we therefore not only require in him a consummate talent for speaking, but all the virtuous endowments of the mind... Let therefore the orator be as the real sage, not only perfect in morals, but also in science, and in all the requisites and powers of elocution." In this way Quintilian attempts to give an educational rather than a purely vocational dimension to the training in rhetoric by introducing into it as a central core the notion of moral upbringing

The Judaeic tradition likewise stresses as the focal point of education an upbringing according to the law enshrined in th Torah and a commitment to living according to its demands. Christianity, as a fusion of these two traditions, similarly regarded character training as the central task of education and even condoned practices that we might be inclined to see as far from moral in themselves if they appeared to be conducive to the establishment of a proper sense of moral rectitude in children. As a result, most of the great educational theorists have seen moral education in one form or another as the hub of any activity that was to merit description as educational. Indeed, the term "Hunanities" as used to designate a very large section of the curriculum (for a long time, infact, the whole of the curriculum) indicates by its derivation that relations between man and man were seen as the central, or even the only, concern of education in the full sense. Moral upbringing, or character training, therefore, was for long the central feature of what education itself was understood to be by the great theorists and, indeed, by the great practitioners.

Thus Comenius tells us that the curriculum should include "all those subjects which are able to make a man wise, virtuous and pious". Locke claims, "T is a virtue, then, direct virtue, which is the hard and valuable part to be aimed at in education." This is echoed in Rousseau's assertion "Life is the trade I would teach him", and taken up by Pestalozzi with his claim that the ultimate goal of education is preparation for life by Herbart who tells us that "the one and the whole work of education may be summed up in the concept - morality", and by Froebel's recommendation that the main purpose of education should be to bring out and develop to the full the innate goodness of the child (Rusk 1957).

It was probably with the development of education for all and the concomitant introduction of a vocational component into the curriculum the moral education lost in part this central role. There was, of course, an element of "gentling" of the masses in the early thinking about education for all, some kind of training for everyone in obedience and good behaviour, but much stronger was the need to provide every member of society with the basic skills that a developing industrial community needed and to tap as efficiently as possible the human wealth of the nation. Most practical decisions in education as elsewhere are made on economic grounds. Thus schooling came to be seen rather less as the eduaction of the cultured gentleman and rather more as a national investment. New subjects came to be added to the curriculum whose prime justification was social or vocational, rather than based on their contribution to moral development, so that moral education or character training lost its central place and was no longer seen as the focus of thc schools's activities, although continuing to be the concern of some aspects of schools life, particularly those extra-curricular activities that most schools have promoted. Within the curriculum, as we suggested earlier, it came to be regarded as the concern almost solely of lessons in religion.

The importance of moral education - in current theory and practice.

Recent years, however, have witnessed a revival of interest in moral education as such, as evidenced by the establishment of several curriculum projects in this area and by the appearance of Moral Education as a subject on the timetable of many secondary schools. There would seem to be several reasons for this. One must be the decline in religious belief or at least in allegiance to institutional religion that has characterized the development of many societies in recent times. If morality is too closely linked to religion, then, as we have seen, a growing tendency to reject religion will raise difficult moral questions and may even suggest *prima facie* a rejection of morality. Hence, faced by an increasing reluctance on the part of many pupils to accept what Religious Education has offered them, especially in the way of moral teaching, schools have been forced to consider other ways in which their responsibility for the moral education of their pupils might be fulfilled. A good example of this process has been the increased secularization of the compulsory daily "act of worship" in many schools at all levels in the United Kingdom.

An equally cogent factor, however, has been the change that has taken place in our view of morality itself. The ideas of the theorists we mentioned earlier are based on a theory of morality that few today would regard as tenable. That theory is one that sees moral precepts as objectively valid and, as a result, regards it as sensible to speak of moral knowledge or knowledge of "the good" and to talk about "right behaviour". It results, therefore, in a view of moral education as a kind of character training and such a view is only tenable if one accepts the theory of morality at its base as fixed and objective. This, as we have seen, is inevitably the kind of view of moral education that emerges when it is too closely associated with religious education, since most religions include a relatively fixed code of morals within their tenets. It is a view, therefore, which leads to the notion that the morally educated person is one who has come to recognize the truth of certain particular moral values and to act on them and that the purpose of moral education (or rather moral instruction) is to instil these values in pupils, to bring them to a "knowledge" of them. Few would now subscribe to such a view of morality, since not only is it based on an outmoded theory of knowledge, it also leads, as we saw in our earlier discussion of religion, to an authoritarian morality.

The conflict between the traditional view of education as essentially concerned with moral upbringing and the change that has taken place in our attitude to morality itself is clearly reflected in the work of John Dewey which must be seen both as a culmination of the ideas that were first proferred by Rousseau and then developed by other theorists in the nineteenth century and at the same time within a new intellectual setting, characterized by such major intellectual advances as theories of evolution and the "revolution" in philosophy. For Dewey the central concern of education is still life or living itself, so that its main purpose is still to provide man with control over all aspects of his environment. But now the environment is seen as a changing one and the prime need is to produce people who can adapt to and control those changes; this they will do by learning to make decisions not in the light of some notion of fixed values and unchanging moral standpoints but from the point of view of moral positions that must be seen as themselves subject to the same process of continuous charge and evolution.

For Dewey, then the central purpose of the education is to enable human beings to make the necessary adjustments to meet a constantly changing environment and the most important (and most difficult) adjustments to be made are adaptations to changing moral values).

Herein lies the major clue as to the changes that have taken place in our view of education and especially of the role of moral education within it. The traditional theory of morality as fixed and unchanging which formed the basis of so many educational theories, as we have seen, is no longer adequate. One reason for this we have also just seen to be an acceptance of the notion of the evolution of all things. However, there have been several other contributory factors and, since they all combine to offer further perspectives on our main question of what is moral education, we must look at each of them briefly in turn.

The first of these is the fact of social change. Not only have we come to recognize evolution as a theory; we have come to see it also as an ever-present reality. Society in every respect has changed dramatically in recent years. Major advances have been made in technology and these have transformed life in all parts of the world to the point where most adults today take for granted features of their daily existence which in their own childhood they would have regarded as science-fiction. Worldwide television networks, landings on the moon, supersonic travel are no longer the prerogatives of Flash Gordon or Dan Dare; they are a part of the lives of all of us.

However, technological change brings social and moral change in its wake; at the very least it raises moral questions for which tradition can provide no ready-made answers and for which new answers must be found. The development of the ability to transplant organs from one body to another, to abort a birth or to prevent conception has presented us with many new moral problems and these are among the more obvious examples of the way in which improved technological skill creates moral and social change by forcing us to adjust our systems of values to meet these changes. This is the reality of the point that we described as central to John Dewey's philosophy. Technological change is a fact and so, therefore, is the social and moral change that it engenders.

Furthermore, it is quite clear that on all of these issues many different stances are possible. There is no single hard and fast answer to them. Even established religions fail to offer solutions to them that all can accept and this must be seen as one factor in the decline of the influence of organized religion. Indeed, many societies now are multi-ethnic and thus contain a variety of religions which often offer a corresponding variety of moral codes. Most advanced societies, therefore, can now be described as pluralist; that is, they can be seen to contain groups and individuals who differ very markedly from each other on certain questions of value. As a result there has grown an awareness that moral issues cannot be dealt with in a once-and-for-all manner by the offering of universal moral answers, but that each individual will reach his own conclusions on most moral questions. This is true at least of most Western societies. If this is so, then it becomes the task of the schools to help children to acquire the ability to engage in the kind of thinking necessary to reach conclusions that are sound.

It should be quite clear by now that we cannot prepare pupils for this kind of world by offering them set answers to those problems we are aware of at that point in time when we happen to be attending to their moral education. A good deal of the moral turmoil and confusion that we have witnessed in recent times is a result of attempts made in the past to offer a moral upbringing in these terms. Even if we think we have the "right" answers to current problems and can persuade young people to accept them, this will not help them when new problems come along. It is for this reason, among others, that people who have had that kind of moral training find it difficult to respond to moral problems for which they have not been prepared. The Crowther Report (1959) suggested that the rapidity of technological change required not a vocational training for young people in specific skills but the development of a "general mechanical ability" that would enable them to cope not only with the technology of the present but also with that of the future. The rapidity of the social and moral change that is a concomitant of technological change requires us to approach moral education from a similar perspective. People need to learn how to adapt, to think for themselves, to be fully autonomous beings. If this is so, if this is the force of current social change, then we cannot, even if we might want to, set about the moral education of our young by trying to teach them what to think in a manner that does not invite their critical appraisal.

However, there are perhaps good reasons why we should not even want to approach moral upbringing in this way. For a second, and closely related, reason why our thinking about moral education is changing is that we have come to take a different view of the nature of man, a different model of man as a basis for our thinking. The pressures for this can be traced to a number of sources. One of these is, of course, the experience of social change which we have just been discussing. Another is the thinking of those philosophers, often dubbed "existentialist", whose view of individual autonomy goes back at least as far as Immanuel Kant and who have stressed the uniqueness of each human being an his consequential right to make his own decisions and thus determine his own "essence". As a result, there has emerged a growing hostility towards any theory, especially within education, which, like the views, of the behaviourist psychologists, for example, is based on a passive view of man, as a being who is acted upon, shaped and guided, like an inanimate object, by forces external to himself rather than on a view of him as an active, dynamic being in charge at least to some extent of his won destiny and therefore responsible for his actions and behaviour.

Certainly in the Western world this has come to be a dominant feature of our way of looking at existence. For it is, of course, closely bound up with ideal of social freedom that is fundamental to the explicit philosophy of what has sometimes been called the "free world". Such an ideal entails the notion of man as an active agent responsible for his own destiny and entitles to make his own moral choices according to his own moral values. Clearly, if acting on such choices, putting his beliefs into practice, is likely to lead unjustifiably to harm or threat of harm or loss of freedom to others, then his freedom of action must be curtailed. But a man's freedom of thought, his right to his own beliefs no matter how unacceptable or even distasteful they may be to others in theory, is not to be denied since it is fundamental to what is seen as the democratic way of life, one of the great freedoms of the Atlantic Charter.

If this view of man is taken, then an authoritarian approach to morality cannot be adopted. A man's values must be his own since he is not free if his behaviour is controlled by a code of values imposed by others. This, as we have already seen, is the source of the great tension that has always existed in Christian theology between the notion of free will, of the freedom of the individual to choose or to reject God, and the idea of an authoritarian code of morality set for man by God. This in turn is the source of some of the moral dilemmas the Christian church has faced - not always successfully in recent times. If an authoritarian view of morality cannot be accepted, then an approach to moral education that derives from it cannot be accepted either. And so we have here a second major reasone why moral education can no longer be viewed as a process of telling children what to believe and how to believe.

We have tried to show, then, that among the reasons for the recent revival of interest in the moral aspects of educatin are, firstly, the changing nature of society and, secondly, consequential changes in our view of what it means to be a human being. In doing so we have begun to discover part of the answer to our question of what moral education is, since we have seen that if it is to be a response to the demands of a changing society and suited to our concept of man as free and active being, then this will to some extent determine the form it must take. Not only, then, must we recognize this as a demand for the freedom and autonomy of the individual; we must also acknowledge that nothing less than respect for that freedom and autonomy can enable us to help people to live in society as we know it. Hence not only are we made aware of an increased need for moral education; we are also made aware of the need for a different concept of what it is, the first aspect of which we have now discovered to be that it must enable people to do their own moral thinking rather than encourage them to conform to an externally imposed moral code.

The concept of education

The same conclusion is forced upon us if we approach this question in a different way and ask what is involved in using the term "education" to denote this process rather than speaking of moral instruction or moral knowledge. We saw earlier how crucial were the semantic differences between these terms for the teaching of religion in schools. There must, then, be similar significance in using the term "education" to denote the school's contribution moral upbringing. Again the implication is that this is not a matter of instruction in certain moral tenets nor is it a matter of being introduced to certain moral values which are fixed and unquestionable and, as a result, the objects of moral knowledge, but that it is a process of learning to think of oneself on moral issues, of becoming morally autonomous.

However, an examination of the implications of the use of the term "education" in this context will take us further than that or, to put it differently, it will begin to reveal in further detail and at further levels of complexity some of the features of this moral autonomy.

Philosophers such as G.E. Moore and Ludwig Wittgenstein have suggested that the meaning of a term is to be discovered by exploring how it is used, and have further proposed that, if we wish to discover the similarities,the differences and the connections existing between related terms, we must do so by looking for significant differences or similarities in the contexts in which they are used. Acts of teaching are described as instruction, training, conditioning or indoctrination as well as education, according to the context in which they are used. Clearly everyone chooses his terms in this area according to some definite criteria. To discover the differences between them, therefore, we need to discover what those criteria are. Our particular concern here is to establish some of the conditions that must apply before we feel it appropriate to use the term "education".

The concept of "education" as it is used in wider contexts has been very well unpacked by Richard Peters (1965, 1966) and it will be helpful if we consider some of the general points he makes in the specific context of moral education.

What are the main features of education that make it different from other processes that teachers put pupils through, processes such as training, instruction, conditioning and even indoctrination? Fundamentally, of course, as we have already asserted, education is concerned with the developing autonomy of the individual as these other processes are not. To set about training or instructing someone in something is to ignore any consideration of that person's autonomy; such considerations just do not arise; in some cases they may even be irrelevant and inappropriate, as in training someone to drive a car. Processes such as conditioning or indoctrinating go even beyond this. For, whatever else is implied by the use of these term, they would appear from their normal usage to be deliberate attempts to stifle the individual's autonomy. A man who has been conditioned or indoctrinated in some respect does not by definition think for himself in that area. Attempts to indoctrinate people into the blind acceptance of particular social and political systems are deliberate attempts to discourage and prevent them from questioning the validity of these systems. If successful, this kind of process will result in what Bertrand Russell, in commenting on Plato's theory of education, once described as "good behaviour with the wrong emotions"(Russell 1908). This provides further confirmation, therefore, of what we have already asserted, namely that to educate someone morally rather than instructing or indoctrinating him is to endeavour to promote in him the ability to think for himself on moral issues.

However, this can be developed further, as Richard Peters shows. For several things are involved here. To begin with, there is implied the development not only of knowledge but, further, of understanding, the acquisition of what Richard Peters calls "cognitive perspective" and the development of critical awareness. For in order to engage in one's own thinking on any issue it is necessary to possess as wide an understanding of that issue, and, indeed, of all relevant and related issues, as it is possible to gain as a basis for a critical analysis and review of the opinions held by others in this sphere. To be educated, then, is not merely to be given autonomy - one has that anyway - it is to be assisted to use that autonomy effectively. What distinguishes an educated man from an uneducated man in any area is that, while both have their opinions and enjoy their freedom of thought, the former's opinions are informed, based on a breadth of knowledge and understanding and thus qualitatively quite different. One of the "aims" of education, therefore, one of the principles that should inform all activities that are to be called educational rather than instructional, indoctrinatory or whatever, is that it represents an attempt not only to develop in pupils the ability to form opinions but also to improve the quality of the opinions they form.

What this implies for moral education, therefore, is that we are committed to promoting in people a desire to achieve the greatest possible knowledge and understanding of whatever kind will help them to reach autonomous choices which are based on careful and informed thinking about the issues involved. Autonomy of itself is of littel values if it results in thinking that is done out of the top of the head or through the elbow. This crucial distinction is well illustrated by the basic pedagogy of the Schools Council's Humanities Curriculum Project, which we shall look at in greater detail in a later chapter. The authors of that project, which is concerned to encourage discussion amongst older secondary school pupils of moral and social issues of current relevance, have stressed that, while on the one hand the teacher must be neutral with regard to the conclusions that pupils reach on these issues, his job is certainly not to remain neutral with regard to the standards of the discussion, "that the teacher accepts the need to submit his teaching in controversial areas to the criterion of neutrality at this stage of education, i.e., that he regards it as part of his responsibility not to promote his own view", but "that the teacher as chairman of the discussion should have responsibility for quality and standards in learning"(Schools Council 1970, p.1).

Thus there is an important distinction to be made between the manner and the matter of education (Peters 1965, 1966). An examination of the concept of education tells us a good deal about the manner in which it is to be conducted. Indeed, this may be the only thing it tells us much about. When we apply this to the concerns of moral education, a crucial distinction emerges between the form and the content of moral education, which makes it clear that the moral educator's job is to teach pupils how to think rather than what to think on moral issues.

There is another aspect of this distinction that also needs to be mentioned here. Not only is it important that we should take care over the manner in which we set about the moral education of our pupils, the form of what we offer them; we must also pay close attention to the manner in which they come to hold their moral beliefs. We shall discuss at some length in Chapter 3 the theories of those developmental psychologists who have studied the stages through which children must pass if they are to reach the goal of moral autonomy. In broad terms, they have suggested that from a state of anomy which is without rules, children pass to the stage of heteronomy at which rules are seen as emanating from others, from people in authority, especially parents and teachers. The next stage is that of socionomy or conventional morality, at which rules are seen as based not on arbitrary authority but on social utility. Only after that can they come to the stage or autonomy of what Kohlberg calls "self-accepted moral principles" (1966).

The important thing to notice at this point in our discussion is that not only do these represent stages of moral development. They also represent qualitatively different levels of response to moral choices or dilemmas, different kinds or definitions of moral behaviour, all of which can be observed at all ages and in all people. In other words, it is an oversimplification to see this scheme as chronological, as tied to age. We must recognize that the point that is being made is epistemological as well as psychological. Few people, no matter how well educated they are morally nor how skilled at moral debate, will not hold some of their moral principles in an uncritical manner, having accepted them unthinkingly from those who have exercised authority over them or from the society in which they live. If moral education is concerned with the manner in which we hold our moral beliefs, then, it must endeavour to ensure that we reflect critically on all of them. This was one of the reasons we gave for arguing the unsuitability of a religious base for moral education. It is a point we will need to take up in greater detail in Chapter 5.

Furthermore, it will soon be clear that among the factors involved in teaching pupils how to think about moral questions, among the criteria we should appeal to in making judgements about the quality of people's thinking in this area will be such things as logical coherence, respect for truth and breadth of relevant knowledge and understanding. A moment's thought will reveal that we do not respect a man's opinion on any issue unless we are convinced that he has given proper thought to the matter and "Knows what he is talking about". If he doesn't, we regard him as "not worth listening to" and certainly "not worth arguing with". Moral education, therefore, should be concerned not only to encourage pupils to think for themselves on moral issues but to help them to do this in an informed and intelligent manner.

Another feature of education to which Richard Peters draws our attention is that it involves bringing the pupil to the point where he comes to care about the activites we have engaged him in and values them; further, that he values them for their own sake, comes to regard them as having "intrinsic value". Again we must note that with other activities that involve teaching this feature need not be present. We can train someone to drive a car or instruct him in motor mechanics without any concern for the question of whether he likes such activities, cares for them or values them at all. From the psychological point of view, of course, our task will be easier if he does enjoy what he is doing and is thus motivated to work hard at it, but, conceptually speaking, such considerations are not crucial. On the other hand, it would be strange and perhaps illogical to speak of a man as educated while at the same time asserting that he places no value at all on any of the knowledge and understanding that he had acquired as part of that process of being or becoming educated.

Again, we must note that this has several implications for moral education. For it will be clear that the moral educator must be concerned to develop in his pupils a conviction of the worthwhileness of moral behaviour, a sense of moral responsibility. It will not be enough to teach pupils how to carry out their moral thinking at a high level if we do not at the same time bring them to the conviction that it matters.

Furthermore moral behaviour above all has a "caring" dimension to it. The man who "goes through the motions" of behaving morally is usually regarded as a pretty cold fish and is unlikely to be considered morally educated at all, not least because behaviour of this kind is prompted by considerations of a purely intellectual kind and can sometimes lead to the sort of "moral rectitude" that does more harm than good. This feature of human behaviour is well illustrated in a number of works of the Greek tragedians, this ability to cause mayhem by inflexibility of values untempered by any kind of human feelings being for them a significant source of truly tragic consequences. Thus Sophocles, for example, in his *Antigone* depicts the conflict between the desire of Antigone herself to act from the heart out of love for her dead brother, Polyneices, and the rigid intention of her uncle, Kreon, to maintain his ruling that Polyneices, who has died in battle fighting against the state, should not be accorded the rights of a proper burial, a conflict which results in the death not only of Antigone herself but also of Haemon, Kreon's own son, to whom she is betrothed. In this way too rigid an adherence to the dictates of the head, to what appear to be the demands of reason, is shown to be productive of harm rather than good. Moral behaviour has to be seen as involving the heart as much as the head

Indeed, it may the case that autonomous moral thinking as such cannot be carried out at a purely intellectual level since, if there is no real valuing of other people and of one's relations with them, one of the principal ingredients of a moral decision would appear to be missing. Every viewer of *Dr. Who*, young or old, knows that Daleks cannot make truly moral decisions and that this is precisely because they are "all head and no heart'. Their leaders make decisions based on purely scientific or utilitarian considerations (usually involving the extermination of various beings who stand in the way of the attainment of their goals) and the others, with loud and repeated emotionless assertions of "I obey!", trundle off to carry these orders out.

This draws our attention, then, to an important feature of moral education which is often overlooked but which reflects what is probably the most complex and least understood aspect of morality, namely the extent to which it involves not just the intellect but also the emotions. As far as education is concerned, this means that it is not just a matter of cognition; there is an important affective dimension too. It thus opens up a new and important area of concern for the moral educator.

A related point emerges from an examination of what we mean by "morality", what counts as a moral action. For a moment's reflection will reveal that one crucial element in this is the intentionality of the agent. There are two aspects of this. In the the first place, we do not regard a man's actions as moral - nor as immoral, if it comes to that -, as subject either to praise or blame, unless we have first established that he acted of his own free will. It must be an act that he is in the full sense responsible for, if we are to make any kind of moral judgment on it. This is the practice of every court of justice, which must establish not only whether a defendant did in fact commit the crime with which he is charged, but also whether he did it knowingly and can thus be held responsible for it and criminally culpable. Aristotle made a distinction between actions performed "willingly" and those done "not unwillingly" and claimed that only the former were moral actions in the full sense. Aquinas too makes a similar distinction between "human acts" and "acts of man".

Secondly, however, when we come to the question of apportioning praise or blame, the kind of motive also becomes important and we do distinguish between actions performed because the agent thinks they are right and those performed because he thinks they will bring certain advantages. It is not only the action that we weigh when making a moral judgement, it is much more the motivation. This is what Kant meant when he said "Nothing can possibly be conceived in the world, or even out of it, which can be called good, without qualification, except a Good Will." Actions can be and usually will be performed out of mixed motives; certainly they are susceptible to a variety of interpretations. Only the good will can be free of any such real or imagined flaws. This is why Kant also distinguished between action is performed *for the sake of* duty and those performed in *accordance with* duty. A grocer in reducing the price of his goods may make them more accessible to the hungry poor but he may do so not for this reason but to boost his sales and thus his profits. If the latter is his intention, then although his action is in accordance with his duty it has not been done for the sake of duty, so that it is not a truly moral act. Crucial to moral behaviour, therefore, is that it should be motivated by the desire to do what is right and not by considerations of expediency.

It has, of course, been argued throughout the ages that morality is only a matter of expediency, that we treat other people properly only because we are frightened of the consequences to ourselves if they were to cease to treat us in the same way, that we do unto others that which we hope they will do unto us and that, as a corollary, we also do unto them that which we think we can get away with. This theory has a long and distinguished history in the annals of Western philosophy. The whole of Plato's *Republic* is an attempt to demolish the view put in the early stages of the dialogue by the sophist, Thrasymachus, that justice or morality is "the interest of the stronger" and the "social contract" view of morality that is also put there. Men create and obey rules only to promote their own interests, usually of self-protection, and, if they do not need that, then they are above morality. This is illustrated in the *Republic* by the story of Gyges, a Lydian shepherd, who, on acquiring the power to render himself invisible, kills the king of Lydia, seduces the queen, becomes king himself and lives happily ever after. The question posed is "Who would be stupid enough to behave otherwise in such circumstances?". The behaviour of the Gods in Greek literature, especially in the early works, such as those of Homer, also supports such a view and one of the major features of the works of the Greek tragedians is an attempt to take up this issue and resolve it in a more satisfactory manner. It is a theme that has reappeared frequently down the ages, in the social contract theories of men such as Thomas Hobbes, for example, and it is a view that is not very far from acceptance by many people today.

What refutes this view (if "refute" is the word) is that it does not fit with the way in which people do behave and the way in which they view moral behaviour. The distinction we are referring here between actions performed from a sense and conviction of their rightness and those done out of considerations of pure expediency, those done for their own sake and those performed as means to some other end, is one that we do make. Some of the behaviour of all of us is prompted by prudential motives, by considerations of expediency, but not all of our behaviour is of this kind. Some actions are performed because of a conviction that they are right and sometimes these are actions that cannot in any sense be regarded as in the interests of the agent. Furthermore, it is only actions of this latter kind, those done for the sake of duty, that are regarded as moral actions.

The relevance of this to moral education will be clear. If we believe that what is called moral behaviour is entirely explicable in terms of self-interest, self-protection or expediency, then we can have no interest in moral education at all; we can have no concept of moral education even. For our task can only be that of any animal mother of providing her offspring with the skills necessary for survival in a world characterized by being, as Hobbes suggested, "a war of all against all", in which there is "continual fear and danger of violent death" and in which the life of man is "solitary, poor, nasty, brutish and short". If we do have a concept of morality and thus of moral education, this must include centrally the notion of actions to be performed because they are felt to be right and not merely expedient. The importance of this to the practice of moral education we must examine later.

Our brief examination of some of the features of what we mean by "education" and "morality", then, has taken us some way further towards answering our question,"What is moral education?"It has provided further evidence of the importance of moral autonomy and it has taken us beyond this by drawing our attention to the need to develop in our pupils the knowledge, the understanding and the respect for morality that will help them to use their autonomy to best effect, to achieve informed moral opinions and values based on a full appreciation of their implications and a critical appraisal of the possible alternatives. It has also drawn our attention to the important role played by the emotions in moral behaviour and has suggested that this cannot be ignored by the moral educator.

Some of the facets of this will become plainer as we now turn to our last angle of approach to the question of "What is moral education?" by considering what might be regarded as the essential features of the morally educated person.

Who is the morally educated person?

So far we have tried to gain some idea of what is involved in moral education, first of all by considering why it has come to be regarded as so important and then by examining what is entailed by the use of the term "education" to denote it. Both of these approaches have brought some results. We must now finally try to discover what can be learnt by approaching the question from the other end, by asking what characteristics we would expect to find in a man or woman we would be willing to describe as morally educated. For if we can discover what qualities would be regarded as essential in a morally educated person, we will have gained a clearer view of the qualities we should be concerned as moral educators to promote and the principles which should, as a result, inform all of our activity in this field. This is an approach that proved very useful to John Wilson and his colleagues of the Farmington Trust Research Unit into Moral Education as a preliminary to the framing of their own proposals for moral education which we will discuss in detail in Chapter 7 (Wilson, Williams and Sugarman 1967).

To begin with, we must note that this approach will emphasize and offer further evidence for the importance of several of those features of moral education that our earlier discussions have revealed. We would be unlikely nowadays to describe as morally educated the person who has had the kind of moral upbringing we referred to earlier as the result of traditional views of the purposes of moral education, the man who has been taught what to believe and how to behave, who has been exposed to character training rather than moral education. For a moment's thought is sufficient to reveal that we would be unlikely to describe someone as morally educated who either was incapable of reaching his own autonomous moral decisions or who reached them without any kind of thought or consideration of relevant factors. The former person we would regard as totally indecisive, the latter as merely prejudiced. Nor would we regard it as satisfactory if a person made such decisions without a high degree of understanding, of awareness of possible alternatives and the ability to review these critically at some depth and in the light of the fullest possible knowledge as a preliminary to reaching his own conclusions. Thus this approach brings further confirmation of what our earlier discussions revealed.

However, it is possible that by asking what other features we would expect the morally educated person to display we may be able to go beyond this. For example, asking this question may be the best method of getting beyond the mere declaration of the need for knowledge and understanding that are needed.

In the first place, we would expect the morally educated person to possess a good deal of factual knowledge or at least to be aware of the kinds of factual knowledge relevant to each issue on which a decision needs to be taken, what A.J. Ayer once called the "non-moral" facts of a case (Ayer 1936, 1946). For, although ultimate choices themselves cannot be deduced by any process of logic from factual premises, this should not taken to imply that factual knowledge has no kind of relevance to these choices. In particular, for example, we need in full the kind of scientific knowledge that will indicate the likely consequences of certain alternative courses of action. The morally educated person, therefore, must be aware of the need to take account of such factual evidence in reaching his conclusions; he must be aware of the need to be as fully in formed on these matters as possible; and, in particular , he must recognize the importance of not basing his choices on actual misinformation. John Wilson offers us the example here of the man who might "through sheer ignorance..... believe that (say) because negroes have less nerve-endings or thicker skulls they do not get hurt so easily"(Wilson, Williams and Sugarman 1967, p.193). It will be clear how that kind of misinformation can, and often does, affect the decisions people make. Thus the morally educated person will recognize that he must be as fully and as accurately informed as possible on the non-moral facts of each situation.

He will also need certain skills if he is to be able to act in a moral way as well as to think things through morally; he will need to know *how* as well as knowing *that*. It will not be enough for him to be able to work out intellectually and theoretically that a certain course of action is right if he lacks the necessary skills to put his decisions into practice. Some of these skills will clearly be social skills, the ability to relate to people, get on with them, even communicate with them. Others will be skills of a rather more basic and practical kind. It is not enough, for example, to decide that you should help the old-age pensioner next door to redecorate his living room if you either make a total and hideous botch-up of it or, worse, lack the social graces to avoid making him feel awkward, ill at ease or patronized all the time you are with him. These are further kinds of knowledge, then, that the morally educated person will need to possess. At the very least he must be sensitive to their necessity and importance.

This leads us, thirdly, to suggest that the morally educated man will also need knowledge and understanding of the feelings of other people. However, this is a kind of knowledge that is of little value if it never gets beyond the intellectual or cognitive level. If we recognize other people's feelings as facts and calculate accordingly what our behaviour towards them should be, there will be a coldness about our relationships that few would wish to characterize as moral. Consideration of the need for this kind of knowledge and understanding, then, takes us, as we suggested earlier, into a consideration of the affective dimension of moral behaviour and the part played by the emotions.

There are several features of this which we must take account of since they would seem to be essential elements in the equipment of the morally educated person and therefore of prime concern to the moral educator. The first of these we referred to earlier when, in looking at the significance of the use of the term "education" in this context, we suggested that it was important not to lose sight of the need to bring pupils to regard moral behaviour as important not to lose sight of the need to bring pupils to regard moral behaviour as important, to feel that relationships with others matter. Clearly, this is a feature that will be equally apparent when we are considering the qualities that should be evinced by the morally educated adult. It would be an odd kind of morality that resulted in decisions being made with no corresponding emotional commitment to them. It would result not so much in good behaviour with the wrong emotions as good behaviour with no emotions at all. This, as we shall see in a later chapter, is one of the criticisms levelled at Kant's view of morality and particularly at the kind of rationalist theory that it led such of his successors as Hegel to produce. In fact, it was this feature of rationalism more than any other that sparked off the existentialist reaction to it.

One aspect of this ability to recognize that moral behaviour is important, of course, is that it involves accepting the significance of other people's feelings. To recognize that other people have feelings like oneself is a matter of knowledge; to regard these feelings as important and as of equal value to one's own in any moral decision one takes is to have an attitude; it is to be emotionally rather than merely cognitively directed towards an acceptance of other people's rights, interests and feelings. The ability to do this, therefore, is not merely an intellectual attainment; it is another aspect of the emotional attitute towards moral behaviour we have just been discussing.

We might, however, take this even further. For it will not be sufficient for us to accept the importance of other people's feelings if we lack the ability at the same time to understand them. It happens quite frequently that people who do recognize the importance of the feelings of others cannot in particular situations appreciate the strength of someone's feelings and, as a result, do not let those feelings weigh with them as heavily as they should. We often "cannot believe he feels that strongly about it". Thus it is necessary in making moral decisions also to be able to see things from the other person's point of view, to get into his or her perspective on the matter at issue.

Thus far, therefore, we have established that the morally educated person will need to have a positive commitment towards the value of morality, towards the importance of other people's feelings, and the ability to understand as well as to recognize those feelings and their significance. There is, however, another way in which the emotions enter moral decision making. For our moral behaviour will be influenced by our own feelings and emotions even more than by a consideration of those of others. This feature of human behaviour has been regarded as of crucial importance at least since the time of Aristotle and it is vital that we do not ignore it in attending to the needs of moral education.

For Socrates and for Plato virtue was knowledge of the good. In other words, they were convinced, because of their total faith in and regard for man's rationality, that God-like quality that raised man above the animals, that once a person knew what the right course of action was in any given context he would follow it through without hesitation. Thus, as we saw earlier, for them moral education was a matter merely of bringing people to an intellectual recognition of the good. Once that was done, they believe, all else would follow, as the night follows the day. Aristotle, however, took a much more realistic view of man. He realized that it was not sufficient to have taken a moral decision at the rational and intellectual level. To do that is in many ways to have done the easy part. Once one comes to carry the decision out, other factors enter into the equation to make this far more complex and difficult than either Socrates or Plato had been willing to concede. These factors he called simply "pleasure", but by this he meant all of those emotional "pulls", those feelings that get between us and the implementation of our moral decisions. He was in fact asserting what St. Paul was later to confess, "The evil that I would not that I do and the good I would I do not". For Aristotle, then, moral education involved not only bringing up children to recognize the "right rule"; it also involved the kind of character training necessary to enable them to act on it once recognized.

This aspect of moral behaviour is clearly very important and it is again something we must discuss more fully in a later chapter. What we must stress here, however, is not merely that this is a feature of moral education that it is neither possible nor desirable to ignore, but further that it is one that we must develop a proper perspective on, a more sophisticated view than that of Aristotle. For it is not satisfactory to regard this emotional dimension, as Aristotle and many rationalist philosophers do, as an unpleasant reminder of human infirmity, as something, therefore, to be stifled and overcome, original sin to be stamped out. It must be seen as an indication of the necessary role the emotions play in morality. The emotional aspect of moral behaviour must be acknowledged and accepted as an essential part of it and not as an undesirable and unfortunate excrescence. As we said earlier, Daleks cannot behave morally since they lack the ability to respond emotionally to anything. Such response is the peculiar privilege of the human being; it is this that constitutes his humanity and enables him to live as a moral being. It is an aspect of moral behaviour that we must come to understand and value, therefore, rather than endeavour to stifle. This must also be the approach of the moral educator, since it is not his task to turn children into Daleks.

We cannot afford, then, to ignore this affective dimension of moral education and its many facets. For the morally educated person must be emotionally as well as intellectually attuned to his relationships with others. We must be concerned with the education of the emotions, helping people to acquire control of their emotion, but by developing an understanding of this aspect of human experience rather than by learning to stifle and suppress it. The message of Freud in this respect is clear and we must examine its precise significance for moral education in a later chapter.

This is another important feature of moral education, therefore, that emerges from an examination of what it means to be morally educated. Not only must we be able to understand the feelings of others; we must also be helped towards the greatest possible understanding of our own, which may, oddly enough, be much more difficult to achieve.

Summary and conclusions

We have attempted in this chapter to obtain a clearer picture of what moral education is so that we can begin to see what teachers have to do in order to plan and attend to the moral education of their pupils. We approached this question from three angles. Firstly, we tried to discover some reasons for the recent revival of interest in moral education and suggested that therein lay certain clues as to what its essential features are. In particular, we suggested that rapid social change has not only caused a revival of interest in moral education; it has also required us to approach it from a different point of view, to see its main concern s being with the development in pupils of the ability to think for themselves morally.

Our second approach led us to a similar conclusion. For this involved us in an attempt to discern what was entailed by the use of the term "education" in this context. We suggested that in addition to reinforcing the need for moral thinking of an autonomous kind, this sort of analysis also alerted us to the need to promote understanding and critical awareness, a concern for the manner rather than solely the matter of education, a respect for truth and knowledge and a commitment to the importance of moral behaviour. Lastly, we tried to discover the main characteristics of the morally educated person, to see if this would add to add to our understanding of moral education. This approach in turn brought confirmation of what our earlier searches had revealed but it also opened up further considerations. It began to reveal in greater detail the kinds of knowledge people need to make moral decisions - knowledge of the non-moral facts, awareness of the likely consequences of their actions, skills of various kinds and understanding of the feelings of other people. This last point took us in turn onto a consideration of that very important but frequently ignored aspect of moral behaviour, the affective dimension, the role of the emotions, and we concluded by asserting the importance of helping pupils to develop not only an understanding and a sympathy for the feelings of others but also, of equal importance but perhaps of greater difficulty, an understanding and an acceptance of their own emotions.

All of these are aspects of moral education that later chapters will consider in greater detail. It is hoped that this chapter has succeeded in creating a clearer picture of what moral education is, upon which subsequent discussions can be based.

2
Moral Philosophy

Those philosophers who are content to define philosophy simply as 'thinking about meaning', tend also to stress that philosophy is easy; it is not a mysterious pursuit suitable only for wise gurus and sages. Anybody can do it, and in a sense everybody does do it some of the time, for everybody at one time or another applies his critical powers to some problem of meaning. There are, however, dangers in stressing the ease with which one may philosophise: the implication is that provided one questions, rather than passively accepts, one is doing the job. Even allowing that this is in some sense true, it is a further question as to whether it is easy to do the job well and whether all spheres into which one might choose to inquire by 'thinking about meaning' in them are equally easy to penetrate.

Certainly the techniques of philosophy do not have to be acquired by most people, as the techniques of building might have to be. The techniques of philosophy are no more than one: that critical examination of meaning already referred to. That is *how* philosophers proceed in any sphere; and most of us have this technique to some degree at our finger-tips. It is therefore not difficult for people to settle down to the task of philosophising. There is nothing particularly exalted about being a philosopher. But it would be a mistake to conclude that the going must therefore be easy in any philosophical inquiry. Whether it is or not will depend upon the complexity and difficulty of the sphere of inquiry.

Irritating as it may be to say it, for those who like easy answers or who believe that they have the answers to moral questions, the moral sphere, is not particularly easy to inquire into. Here, as in any other sphere, anybody can play the philosopher. Anybody can ask what is meant by saying that something is good, anybody can return an answer to this question, and anybody can reject passive acceptance of some traditional view. But going through the motions of philosophy in this way does not get us far. Hitler did these things, and Hitler was a very bad philosopher, if it is reasonable to call him one at all. It is not so easy to cut a coherent path through the many varied approaches and solutions to moral problems that have been offered at one time or another; it is not so easy to arrive at a satisfactory account of what 'freedom' means and to explain why and in what sense people ought to be free; it is not so easy to establish whether a philosopher such as John Stuart Mill did, or did not, prove what he set out to prove in his essay *Utilitarianism*. It is not even all that easy to establish what he did set out to prove.

It may seem silly of me to emphasise the difficulty of the task at the outset. Those who insist that philosophy is easy, may at least hope to hang on to their readers. But nobody need be intimidated or put off by the emphasis, for it remains true that the way in which we have to proceed, the manner of inquiry, is nothing mysterious and can be handled by virtually everybody. All that I am stressing is that the moral sphere is not an art that admits of easy answers and obvious solutions. And this needs stressing at a time when so many people seem so sure that they know the answer. The fact that something is wrong with this state of affairs should be immediately apparent when one reflects that different people apparently know completely different answers.

The moral sphere is complex precisely in that various people, including professional philosophers, have such different accounts to give of it. There is not only sharp disagreement as to what kind of behaviour is morally acceptable and what kind of actions are good; there is an equally great divergence of opinion as to what it means to call something 'good', or who it is about what somebody regards as morally acceptable behaviour that makes it morally acceptable. If I describe a table as square, there is not much room for doubt about what I am doing: I am attributing a specific quality to the table, namely thc quality of squareness. I am telling you its shape, and you are unlikely to be ignorant of what shape the word 'square' signifies. But what am I doing when I describe an action as good?Am I attributing some quality to it? If so, what? What does 'good' signify? All manner answers have at one time or another been put forward, more or less persuasively, to this kind of question. They range from the view that a thing is good, and can only be good if God approves of it, to the view that describe something as good is just a way of saying that one likes it - and that is quite a range.

Given the many quite distinct positions that have been adopted relation to moral values, few of which are so obviously absurd as to merit consideration, it is at least a possibility that it is going to be very difficult indeed to offer some complete and incontestable explanation of the most sphere. However, it is not so difficult to understand these different view points, to see how they gain whatever measure of plausibility they have, and hence to understand the nature of the problems that are to be found in this area.

Understanding the problems, understanding where, in what way and why moral philosophers have been perplexed, and why they have failed to agree on convincing answers to questions such as 'What ought we to do' or 'What does "good" mean?' is an enormous step forward. For practical terms, the problems surrounding the question of moral values are only of interest and importance because different people have such different values, and often these values are mutually incompatible. It is this fact that gives practical urgency to the demand for all to do moral philosophy.

An integral part of what it means to adopt certain moral values is that one feels strongly that other people ought to adopt those same values. If I have certain aesthetic values, such as an admiration for Wagner's music, it does not necessarily follow that I resent the fact that others do not share my taste. But if I adopt a moral value, such as the view that no man ought to take another's life, then it does follow that it matters a great deal to me when others can be seen by their actions not to share this value.

Insofar, then, as people have different and incompatible values, there is an obvious case for looking into the matter in an attempt to see whether some are more acceptable than others. And insofar as the adoption of a moral viewpoint involves the desire that it should be universally adopted, and insofar as some people's moral values may actually be repugnant to others, the exercise of doing moral philosophy may be extremely important, even if it does not lead to a comprehensive and indisputable right answer. Even if ultimately we feel obliged to conclude that there is no way of distinguishing between the correctness of rival value claims, no way of establishing beyond reasonable doubt that certain things ought to be done and that certain others ought not to be done, as some philosophers would claim, it would at least be beneficial in practical terms that people should appreciate this awkward conclusion, rather than assume that they know that other people are wrong.

One prevalent view held today is that there is no real problem about moral values, because the sort of things a particular society values is simply a matter of choice on the part of that society. A problem, it is claimed, is artificially created by those who try to argue that there is some eternal moral truth and that therefore certain things ought to be regarded as good and others not, at all times and in all places, whatever any particular people may think. People who maintain, for instance, that human sacrifice always was and always must be wrong are simply confusing the issue. All they are entitled to say is that *they* would never approve of it. Our society happens to have adopted this particular value, but it might not have done, and it does not make sense to ask whether it should have done or not. According to this view, various factors may be produced to explain why a particular society values some particular code of behaviour, but these factors will be economic or social. They will explain, but not justify. The notion of justification is out of place.

Human sacrifice is not a custom that can be condemned as in some sense always necessarily wrong, any more than a custom such as monogamy or the wearing of long hair can be. All three are similar in that they are culturally induced conventions; the only difference between them in our society is the strength of feeling associated with them. We don't regard length of hair as a moral issue because we do feel very strongly about it. Conversely we do regard human sacrifice as immoral because we disapprove of it very strongly. Perhaps, it may be for the accuracy of this analysis of the situation is indicated by the fact that attitudes to monogamy and related sexual practices are at this moment changing. Fifty years ago,if we may generalise, people felt strongly about marriage and approved of Christian ideals of monogamy and chastity before marriage. They therefore regarded relations between the sexes as moral issue. Today, many people feel that these ideals are questionable, they do not value them so highly, and therefore the issue ceases to be seem as a moral one.

This relativist view - so called because it stresses that moral values are relative to particular societies - is not new. It was around when philosophy as we know it was born. Many of the fifth-century Athenian sophists seem to have been relativists, and it was precisely this view that Plato tried to combat by arguing that, although different societies might adopt different values, that did not in itself show that they were right to do so, or that the values adopted by some societies were not preferable to those adopted by others. According to Plato, regardless of what some societies chose as value, there were nonetheless some things that just ought to be valued and others that ought not. He was therefore the first recorded absolutist; this is to say he believed in certain absolute moral values that were always and would always be binding on all people at all times and in all places whether they recognised them or not. In semi-mystical language, which in the long run has probably done his argument more harm than good, Plato claims that there were eternal Forms of such things as Goodness situated some where, somehow, beyond the material world. An action could only be good if it partook of the Form of Goodness in some way, and since the Form did not change, so the goodness of actions on earth could not vary. Since most people feel that they have no idea what Plato is talking about, his theory of Forms is not of much help. But it is clear that it represents metaphorical attempt to state an absolutist position.

Since that time battle has never ceased to rage between relativists and absolutists, two fairly recent champions of either position being Karl Marx and John Stuart Mill. Ignoring a certain inconsistency in his writing Marx was a relativist. He took the view that moral values were culturally induced conventions and that they reflected the economic structure of the given society: those who had the power, effectively promoted standards of right and wrong that would perpetuate the status quo and therefore the power. For instance, feudal societies tried to maintain the belief that it was morally right for the serf to show loyalty to his overlord. (Marx's view was substantially the same as that attributed to a character named Thrasymachus in Plato's dialogue, the *Republic.*)

Mill, on the other hand, was a utilitarian, which is to say that he believed that the promotion of happiness was, and must always be, the supreme moral consideration. Rules and conduct in a society were good if, and only if they contributed to a greater balance of happiness over misery. If one could demonstrate that a particular custom was in fact promoting unhappiness, then it was wrong, and it was wrong whether people regarded it as wrong or not. It is clear that Mill is not committed to the view that certain actions and customs must necessarily always be wrong or right, as some absolutists have been. For people and conditions might change, so that a practice that once promoted happiness might begin to promote unhappiness. Nonetheless he is an absolutist in the sense that his formula for testing whether something is good or not, is supposed to be absolutely binding on all men at all times.

It is worth drawing attention to the long history of the debate between relativists and absolutists, because some people today who adopt a relativist position tend to talk as if their point of view was obviously correct and as if it is only because previous generations lacked the knowledge of the world that we now have that they failed to appreciate this. They sometimes talk as if until very recently all people were some kind of primitive sheep who believed in nonsensical moral absolutes, but that now man is so knowledgeable, so much master of the world, that he can see that in the past he has merely been a victim of superstition. But the matter is not as simple as that.

The case for some kind of relativism certainly looks strong. This is partly because of the indisputable fact to which relativists draw attention that moral values vary in different societies and even change with time within one society. But this in itself will not substantiate their point of view. After all, different societies have had different opinions about other things besides moral values, and some of them have then been shown to have been wrong. Many people have believed that the world is flat. But the world is not flat, and the fact that some people may think it is does not make it so. In the same way, the fact that some societies have thought that it is morally acceptable to practise cannibalism does not show that it is.

What really gives relativism plausibility and what makes the fact that different cultures have different values look significant is the difficulty of seeing how one could ever *know* that any particular moral viewpoint was the one that ought to be adopted. The relativist's caricature of history as a steady line of development from blind superstition to complete knowledge has at least this much truth in it: it is difficult to see how those who have claimed to know what is good could convincingly show that it is.

Imagine some primitive society, all the members of which are convinced that certain things are good and certain ways of behaving are right. They have a rigid code of behaviour and nobody is in any doubt, for example that paying back one's debts is good and burning one's neighbour's house is bad. In such a society there is no question about *what* is good and to question *that* it is good. Nobody is puzzled about how it was originaly discovered that paying back debts was good. Questions such as 'Why is it good?' do not arise. The world is flat and paying your debts is good. Two facts; two truths. And that, as far as the members of this society are concerned, is all there is to it. They know that these two statements are true.

The word 'know' can be used in a number of distinct ways: one can know that something is the case, one can know why something happened, one can know how to do something, or one can simply know someone. We are clearly concerned with 'knowing' in the sense of 'knowing that'. Normally when we claim to know that something is the case, we are claiming both that it is as a matter of fact the case, and that we can produce, or at least point to, the evidence which shows that it is the case. In other words we claim that the matter is demonstrably true and, by implication, that any body would have to accept the demonstration or the evidence as convincing.

Thus in theory if I claim to know that my wife is at home,you would expect me to be able to produce evidence to support this claim, such as the I have just rung her up and spoken to her . If I am merely assuming the she is at home because she generally is at this time, it would be more a curate to say that I have strong reason to believe that she is at home. When we say that we know that pearls dissolve in acid, we can back up our claim by an appeal to empirical demonstration. In practice, of course, we many use the word 'know' very loosely, but if we really have knowledge that something is the case, we must have access to the evidence that shows that it is. Otherwise we merely have opinion or belief. Knowledge therefore presupposes generally accepted rules as to what counts as evidence. Many people will accept the evidence of their own eyes that pearls dissolve in as convincing; and in normal circumstances people will accept the fact that I have just spoken to my wife on the telephone as good evidence that she is at home.

And so it is that we can show that the members of this primitive society were wrong in their belief that the world is flat. Evidence of various sorts the most immediately recognisable being aerial photographs, is available to support the claim that we know that it is round. There is no convincing evidence to support the claim that it is flat. But when we turn to the most claims of this same society the situation is entirely different. It is not simple that they cannot produce the evidence to support their claim that they know that it is wrong to burn one's neighbour's house down. We cannot produce the evidence to show that they are mistaken either. For it is complete unclear what sort of thing is allowed to count as evidence one way or the other.

Claims to knowledge in any sphere do not make sense without generally agreed standards as to what counts as evidence. What are the criteria for claiming moral knowledge? What sort of evidence is one supposed to produce to show that something is good? Satistical surveys would show us what people think is good, but not that it is good. Demonstrations might indicate that a certain type of action invariably has certain consequences that people like, but that would not show that either the action or its consequences were good. To reach that conclusion one would have to show that what people like is good. And how would one do that?

The question arises as to whether the idea of producing evidence that all would have to accept to show that paying debts is good is not as absurd as the idea of producing evidence to show that cake is delicious. Cake neither is, nor is not, delicious. Such statements are absurd. All one can say is that some people find some cake delicious. Whether a cake is delicious or not is a matter of taste, not knowledge. Is the same true of moral values? Are the relativists right? 'Freedom is good' may look like a straightforward factual proposition like 'Pigs are four-legged', but the more one looks, the less obvious is the parallel. 'Pigs are four-legged' causes no problem. We know what is meant by all the words involved and we know how to test the truth of the statement. We line up all the pigs we can find and we look and see whether they do or do not have four legs. Only the blind could seriously question the evidence. But how do we test the truth of the statement that freedom is good? What is freedom?But far more important:what is 'good'? what are we looking for? One certainly could not establish that freedom is good simply by observation, for at the very best one could only demonstrate something such as that freedom produces results that one approves of . But one normal supposition is that 'good' means something more than 'what I approve of'. Is that merely because, as some would claim, one has been brought up to *assume* that it means more, without having any good reason for so doing?

Once societies, or individuals within them, get as far as questioning their moral beliefs, the temptation to adopt some form of relativism is very great. Once one appreciates the difficulty of talking about knowledge in the moral sphere, what could be more plausible than to say that there is no more to moral values than the adoption of certain rules by a given society that promote consequences that it happens to like? And that, therefore, it makes no sense to talk of certain societies having values that are bad or immoral in any absolute sense?

But in historical terms, the realisation that moral values were open to questioning and that their truth could not simply be taken for granted did not lead to widespread relativism. Once the matter was open to debate, all kinds of solution to the problem were offered. Common to virtually all of them was an attempt to lay down a precise meaning for 'good'. For philosophers rightly saw that if one knew what 'good' meant, if one had definition of the term, as one has a definition of the term 'bachelor', it would be as easy to distinguish between good and bad as it is to distinguish between bachelors and married men. And so out the definitions tumbled 'good' meant 'productive of happiness'; 'good' meant 'natural'; 'good' meant 'pleasing to God'; 'good' meant 'contributory to security'.

But none of these solutions achieved very much. In the first place, the definitions themselves were often as ambiguous and obscure as the term 'good'. What, for instance, is natural? Natural behaviour might mean spontaneous behaviour; it might mean the sort of behaviour that is presumed to have gone on in pre-civilised jungle life; it might mean which people regard as normal (as, for example, when people refer to heterosexuality a natural and homosexuality as unnatural). Or how do we know what is pleasing to God - assuming, that is, that we know that God exists in the first place? Even the suggestion that 'good' means 'productive happiness', which looks a little less complex at first glance, poses the problem of what precisely we mean by 'happiness'.

But secondly, and much more importantly, where would the acceptance of any one of these definitions get us? The assumption of the members the primitive society had been that if something was morally good, then by definition one ought to do it. And this is the assumption of most of us still. Even if we are relativists, we may accept that insofar as somebody in some society does think that something is morally good, then they must feel that that something ought to be done. But in the case of each of the proposed definitions of good it seems quite reasonable to ask why, in the case, one ought to be good. It seems quite reasonable to ask why one ought to behave naturally, why we ought to promote happiness or security, and even why we ought to please God, assuming he exists. The only way which one could hope to persuade people that 'good' actually means of these things is by showing that people must agree that they ought to be one of these things. But it is precisely the possibility of showing that certain things ought to be done that is in doubt.

By the beginning of this century the frustration caused by the apparent impossibility of getting anywhere in the search for moral knowledge was beginning to tell, and impatience beginning to show. G.E. Moore announced shortly, in his book *Principia Ethica*: 'If I am asked "what good?" my answer is that good is good, and that is the end of the matter or if I am asked, "How is good to be defined?" my answer is that it cannot be defined, and that is all I have to say about it.' But Moore was not relativist. He believed that certain things were good, regardless of whether any particular society recognised them as such or not, but he believed that the only way in which one could know that something was good was intuition. He was followed by various other philosophers, who modified his view in various ways, and it is these men rather than Moore himself who are usually meant when the intuitionists are referred to.

Intuitionism was really a rather extraordinary ethical theory to have arisen so late in the history of moral philosophy. The point of the theory was that it was supposed to preserve the idea that there were objective moral truths that were not dependent on the changing tastes of society, and the idea that moral knowledge was possible. But whereas scientific knowledge was acquired and substantiated by empirical demonstration, moral knowledge, on this view, was acquired and substantiated by intuition. As many people have pointed out, the difference between claiming to *know* something on the strength of intuition and simply *believing* something is difficult to see. And it is therefore difficult to distinguish between the members of a primitive society who claim to 'know', without being able to produce any publicly acceptable evidence, that 'paying debts is good', and the twentieth-century intuitionist who might claim to 'know', the same thing on the strength of their intuition. Despite the appeal of this theory for those who wished to defend some notion of absolutism against the relativist, it was in effect a completely pointless theory.

This is not to say that it provided a false account of the situation. It is very important to realise at this stage that one cannot necessarily say that the intuitionists were wrong. It may be the case that there are certain things that ought to be done and others that ought not, whatever most people think at any given time. It may yet turn out that it makes sense to say 'This is good, and everybody ought to do it', even though most people object to doing it. And it may be the case that the only way one can know what, as a matter of fact, ought to be done is by intuition. But in practice the theory is quite unhelpful because different people have different intuitions as to what is good. How are we to decide between these different intuitions? By intuition, presumably, but *whose* intuition? In the last resort, intuitionists are indistinguishable from relativists; for in the face of the adoption of different moral values by different societies, the relativist will say there is nothing to choose between them in terms of being right - it is a matter of taste. The intuitionist will claim that it is a matter of knowledge that some societies have adopted the right values, but this 'knowledge' that he claims to have turns out to be his intuitive feeling - which to most of us looks suspiciously like his taste.

As if in answer to this rather feeble last-ditch defence by certain absolutists, a particularly extreme form of relativism was then launched by A.J. Ayer. This was emotivism. The emotivist theory of ethics has subsequently been modified in various ways by Ayer himself and others. But in essence the theory is nothing more than a view that was hinted at above as being a possibility - namely the view that to describe something as good is simply to my 'I like it'. That, according to emotivism, is really all there is to morality. The reason that nobody can find the moral truth, and the reason it is so difficult to agree on what would count as evidence to support a claim to moral knowledge, is that there is no such thing as moral truth and no such thing as moral knowledge. 'Freedom is good' does not reassemble 'Pigs are four-legged' in any way at all, beyond the similarity in superficial appearance. The latter proposition makes a factual claim that can be tested; the former does not make a factual claim at all, although it may look as if it does. The expression 'Freedom is good' is just a way of saying that, I, the speaker, like freedom.

Emotivism was the straw that broke the camel's back. It was at about the time of the emergence of this theory that most moral philosophers seemed to come to the conclusion that moral values could not be produced out of thin air and convincingly shown to be true. To put it cynically, they lost their nerve. To put it as they would choose to put it, it was appreciated that the moral philosopher's job was not to produce elaborate systems as desirable behaviour nor to prescribe good conduct, but to analyse the way in which we do in fact use moral language, as the motivists had claimed to be doing. His job was not to discover what was good, so much as to show how people use the word 'good'.

Now this redefinition of the moral philosopher's role - it was not something completely new so much as a decided shift of emphasis - did not arise because all philosophers accepted an emotivist position. As a matter of fact, very few of them accepted it in its original stark form which reduce moral judgements to no more than expressions of personal taste. But they recognised that it represented a possible explanation of all that was involved in morality. So too, however, as they saw and as I have stressed did intuitionism. So, if it came to that, did many of the other ethical theories that had been produced at one time or another: perhaps happiness is the only ultimate good; perhaps the ten commandments do represent eternally significant injunctions. Philosophers were not necessarily committing themselves to the view either that any of these theories were false and that they were correct. Nor were they denying themselves the right to adopt specific moral values and to attempt to argue in support of the adoption of these values. What, in general, they had effectively concluded was that was inconceivable that anyone should ever establish one ethical view as the correct view beyond all doubt. Knowledge of ultimate moral principle was impossible. (Belief concerning them, of course, was not therefore illegimate; nor was knowledge related to specific moral rules ruled out, provided that the it was appreciated that one could only talk of 'knowing' that certain rule was a good one in the light of ultimate moral principles that were accepted on the strength of belief. For example, if we agree to value happiness then we may talk of knowing that certain behaviour is best because it promotes misery.) Philosophers, in effect, were simply retreating from what they regarded as an insoluble problem.

Unfortunately, to a great extent the view that emotivism was the correct view seeped into the public conscience and won the day for relativism. Some people, of course, clung to specific moral values and continued to claim that they knew that this, that and the other, ought to be done. From a philosophical point of view, as we have seen, this position is extremely suspect: how do they know? Where is the publicly acceptable evidence necessary to substantiate a claim to knowledge? And from a practical point of view, this position may be dangerous: fanaticism is bred of people's conviction that they know what ought to be done and that people who do not agree are just wrong and can therefore be ignored. But many other people adopted, and still adopt, the view that we now know that emotivism, or some other form of relativism, represents the truth about morality. On this view, we *know* that moral values are simply conventional and arbitrary. It should be clear that this view is equally suspect from a philosophical point of view. And, incidentally, from a practical point of view it may be no less dangerous: fanaticism may be bred of the conviction that there is only one right answers, but the equally insidious feelings of apathy and allienation may be born of the convinction that there are no right answers.

Emotivism is not necessarily the correct view of what morally involves. It gains its plausibility because, in common with other relativist view, it lays stress on two aspects of moral language that it would be difficult to deny. When people describe something as 'good' they certainly do indicate their approval of it; and when they are asked how they know that it is good, it seems difficult - and perhaps impossible - to conceive of an answer that everybody would have to accept as convincing. We certainly do not 'know' that 'freedom is good' in the way that we know that bricks fall to the ground when dropped. We do not see what would count as evidence for knowledge in the moral sphere. This much must be conceded. Equally it must be acknowledged that emotivism can explain without difficulty why it is that different people have different views as to what is good.

But even allowing for its plausibility, emotivism is not without its problems. Am I really *only* indicating my approval of freedom when I say that it is good? Is it true, as another emotivist has put it, that the 'major use' of ethical judgements is simply 'to create an influence'? Is the remark that one ought not to steal no more than an indication of my dislike of the practice and an attempt to create an influence designed to promote that dislike? R. M. Hare, in putting forward the ethical theory known as prescriptivism, has suggested two further features of moral judgements. First, he argues that judgements of the form 'You ought to do such and such' do not just attempt to create an influence, they have the more positive function of attempting to guide people's conduct. They are disguised imperatives that amount to the order 'Do this', but they differ from other imperatives in that one expects consistency of a man who says 'You ought to do this', in a way that we do not expect it of a man who says 'Do this'. Moral judgements on Hare's view, are universalisable. That is to say that if I say that you ought to do this in these circumstances, then I commit myself to the view that I, or anybody else, ought also to do this in the same circumstances. Without going into these suggestions in any detail, is it not possible that they indicate some inadequacy in emotivism? Although prescriptivism does not represent a denunciation of relativist theories, and although it may have its own problems, it surely suggests that emotivism as originally stated was an unconvincingly bald ethical theory.

And then, allowing for such modifications to emotivism as Hare or others might wish to introduce, do we really accept that in saying that Jews ought not to have been treated in the way in which they were treated in Nazi Germany, we are essentially saying no more than that we do not like the fact that they were? Is it totally meaningless to suggest that it was wrong and that it would have been wrong even if we had all decided that we couldn't care less? One can concede all the difficulties already raised in this chapter - the difficulty of showing what it would mean to say that it just was wrong, and the difficulty of seeing how one would set about proving that it was wrong. But all that I ask here is whether we are prepared to accept that 'Exterminating Jews is wrong' *means* simply 'We do not like exterminating Jews'.

To revert to our starting position - the conflict between absolutists and relativists - the point is this: just as absolutist views are suspect because we do not see how people could justify a claim to *know* that something is good so we do no *know* that a relativist view is the correct one to adopt. To claim that relativism is the correct view to adopt involves claiming that we know that there is no more to moral values than the observable fact that different societies choose to adopt different values. But how do we *know* that this is all there is to the matter in the normal sense of 'know'? Where is the evidence to support the claim that a statement such as 'Gassing Jews is wrong' cannot have any objective validity and cannot be regarded as either true or false? What argument has been produced to show that the intuitionists, for example, were incorrect? The answer is none. The truth is that because we have no agreement (no understanding, perhaps) as to what would count as criteria for claiming moral knowledge, we know absolutely nothing about morality. And that means that we do not know that relativism is more correct than absolutism.

All that we have as a consequence of this brief survey of various ethical views is something akin to a number of possible solutions to a murder mystery. At this stage many of the proposed explanations of the moral mystery may seem plausible. It may be that ultimately this mystery cannot be solved, or at any rate not to everybody's satisfaction. However we cannot simply ignore the mystery. And some explanations may turn out on closer examination to ignore certain important features of the case; some may ultimately be seen to be more plausible than others; and conceivably only one explanation will finally prove acceptable.

When Socrates was told that the Delphic Oracle had pronounced him to be the wisest man in Athens, he was at first puzzled.[3] But as he went the rounds of the various experts in the city - the expert politicians, playwrights, carpenters and so on - and heard them pontificating on every subject imaginable, he came to see that he was perhaps the wisest of them all, in that he knew that he knew nothing. To put it less epigrammatically, he knew the limits of his knowledge. And, of course, the notion of a man wise in his ignorance is more than an ingenious paradox. To distinguish between what one actually knows and what one believes or accepts on the authority of others, to know that to talk of knowledge in certain fields is sometimes inappropriate, is a genuine increase in positive knowledge. To appreciate that one cannot glibly assume that various moral truths are known is to learn something and to learn something important.

Nonetheless many people may feel that to have got this far raises the question of whether it is worth going further in moral philosophy. Absolutists and relativists alike merely have to agree that it would be more accurate, by standards of normal usage, for them to state their positions in terms of belief rather than knowledge. The former believe that certain things are good and ought to be done in any society at any time; the latter believe that this kind of talk is meaningless. And that is all there is to it. If it is a question of belief and if knowledge is out of place in this sphere of inquiry, there is not much point in pursuing the matter. So, at any rate, they may feel.

There are, however, two considerations that give considerable point to inquiring further into the matter. First, whether we like it or not, we are continually faced with the need to make decisions that involve moral assumptions - and this, as suggested in Chapter 1, applies particularly to those involved in education. We have to decide whether this or that ought to take place, ought to be encouraged, or ought to be discouraged. At the very least, we have to decide whether teachers ought to make such decisions on behalf of their pupils of whether children should be left free to do what they choose to do. Given this responsibility and the realisation that there are no easy answers in the moral sphere, it surely becomes all the more important to look again, and in much greater depth, at our own moral assumptions. One consequence of abandoning the idea that some of us 'know' what is good is that all beliefs as to what is good have an equal claim to be taken seriously. The absolutist must ask himself whether his beliefs are based on anything other than the influence of those who brought him up, for example. The relativist must ask himself whether, despite his interpretation of morality, there are not in fact some things that it seem more reasonable to regard as morally desirable than others. The alternative to a more thorough going examination of various moral beliefs is to settle for some form of dogmatism or nihilism - to conclude that, since ultimately no belief as to what is good can be shown to be wrong, we cannot justify condemning anything and should settle for a policy of anything goes, 'anything' presumably including dogmatic fanaticism as well as extreme laissez-faire. Are we prepared to accept that?

Secondly, as indicated in the previous paragraph, the fact that something cannot be known to be true does not necessarily do away with a distinction between reasonable and unreasonable belief. One can think of many areas of history, for example, where our lack of evidence rules out the plausibility of a claim to 'know' what was going on, but where we could nonetheless produce reasons for regarding some suggestions as preposterous and others as possible. There is still a distinction to be made between the sphere of history, where there is not much doubt as to the sort of things that would count as evidence in support of a particular view, and that of morality where there is even disagreement as to what would count as evidence. But even in the moral sphere there may be a distinction between what we regard as good reasons for adopting certain moral values and what we regard as bad reasons

As Aristotle pointed out in his Nicomachean Ethics, it is the mark of a rather foolish person to expect to find the same degrees of certainty in all spheres of human inquiry. Certainly the idea of moral knowledge and the proof of moral propositions conceived of on the scientific model has received a nasty shock. But why should we expect to demonstrate moral propositions in the same way and with the same degree of certainty as we demnstrate simple scientific propositions? After all moral proposition are not scientific propositions. But there are all kinds of statements that we may make, that either cannot convincingly be proven or where we are very uncertain as to how we would set about trying to prove them, which may nonetheless be more or less reasonable and even possibly true or false. For example, it might be very difficult to produce agreed criteria for good music; but he probably was, and not many of us would regard the suggestion that he wasn't as very reasonable. It might be difficult for me to prove that my wife loves me, but I have good reason to suppose that she does. I cannot prove that Athenian democracy in the fifth century was shambles, if by 'prove' we mean demonstrate to the satisfaction of all who are interested in the demonstration. In this case, of course, the problem is one of incomplete evidence and disagreement as to how to interpret what evidence there is. But what I can do in this case, as in the others, is expand and clarify precisely what it is I am claiming and put forward may reasons for the claim. As a result of doing this, in conjunction with others who are interested in the question at issue, one may hope to approach that degree of certainty that is appropriate to the case.

In the same way we can consider various suggested moral values, clarify their precise meaning, and examine the reasons that may be put forward in favour of and against their adoption. It may be that at the end of the day there will still be a measure of disagreement, but at least the nature of that disagreement will be clear, and when all is said and done there is difference between agreeing to differ after real consideration of the matter and refusing to agree in blind ignorance.

REASON AND MORALITY

There is far more to moral behaviour than the mere application of reason to moral questions. Reason does play a major role in morality. In fact, we suggested that it is play a major role in morality. In fact, we suggested that it is man's ability to reason, to think rationally, that distinguishes him from the other members of the animal kingdom and it is the resultant ability to act purposefully, while at the same time considering consequences and alternatives, that constitutes in part what it means to be oral. In brief, it is because man can reason that he is capable of moral action, just as it is because animals cannot reason that they are not. It is man's rationality, therefore, that makes morality possible, so that reason must have a central role in the making of moral decisions.

It is the intention of this chapter to endeavour to throw some light on the difficult and contentious question of what that role is. What i the contribution of rationality to moral debate and, in particular, to moral behaviour?

What is rationality?

In order to achieve anything like a proper view of the place of rationality in morals we need first to clarify somewhat what we mean by rationality itself. Obviously, it is not possible to devote the rest of this book to the kind of detailed examination that this most interesting question warrants and requires, but it is necessary to attempt some kind of analysis-no matter how superficial it may have to be-if we are to get a sufficiently clear idea of the essential features of rationality to provide us with a basis for considering its place in moral decision making.

As we have just said, man, unlike other creatures, is capable of purposeful action, of acting deliberately n the basis of his own judgments, decisions choices. He is not a passive creature whose behaviour is totally explicable in terms of instincts and the action of the environment on him (although we must not forget that some human behaviour-and in the case of some people almost all-is of this kind). He has the capability to behave positively, as an active agent rather than a passive recipient, in some respects at least controlling the effects of the environment upon him and even sometimes changing it to suit his own purposes. He has this capacity because of his ability to develop by the use of intelligence an ever growing understanding of his world and a knowledge of the likely consequences of the different courses of action open to him. It is to the development of this kind of knowledge of the likely consequences of the different courses of action open to him. It is to the development of this kind of knowledge and understanding that the use of reason is directed and it is this basic notion of the function of rationality that i likely to offer us the most productive source of clues as to its nature.

For its prime features are essentially those encapsulated in the

Hegelian notion of rationality as a dialectical process of argument and counter-argument, thesis and antithesis, leading to the emergence of the kind of synthesis that will add to our continuously developing understanding of the world. There are no features of this dialectical process and of the bodies of knowledge that result from it that are central to an understanding of what rationality is. For, in the first place, it will be obvious that the knowledge and understanding so developed should satisfy as nearly as possible such standards of truth as seem appropriate to it, so that suitable means need to be devised to test the truth of individual elements in the process. Secondly, we will need to be equally concerned with the validity of the process itself and of the bodies of knowledge it gives rise to. In other words, the process must be coherent and the links between on assertion and another must satisfy certain criteria of logical coherence, clearly, questions of truth and validity are closely interwoven, but both are central features of what we mean by rationality.

We must not assume, however, that the definition of what will constitute truth or validity in any sphere will be easy or straightforward. In fact, the case is quite the opposite, since there are many problems and difficulties over both, especially over the questions of what is meant by truth and what can be accepted as satisfactory criteria for testing the truth of any assertion. There, after all, are the central questions faced by philosophers, and in particular that branch of it known as epistemology or theory of knowledge. For, in the first place, there are also those who would wish to argue that truth and validity, in fact rationality itself, has several forms and that the tests for both truth and validity, in fact rationality itself, has several forms and that the tests for both truth and validity will vary according to the particular form of knowledge or understanding or "realm of meaning" we happen to have under consideration in any given context (Phenix 1964; Hirst 1965b). Mathematics, the physical sciences and the human sciences, for example, represent different kinds of knowledge, it is argued, distinguished from each other not only by the concepts they us but also by their logical structure and the truth criteria appropriate to them. Different verification procedures must be used in proof of Pythagoras' theorem from those appropriate to Boyle's Law or Gresham's Law. It has been claimed that as many as seven such distinct forms of knowledge may exist (Hirst 1965b).

However, while acknowledging the problems that exist, the disputes that rage and the traps and pitfalls that await anyone who ventures into such continues territory, it is possible for us to pick out certain elements of rationality, certain essential characteristics which will be acknowledged by all, to identify certain features other than those that are the objects of disagreement and debate. Furthermore, it is important at least to attempt to do this, since, as we shall see later, it will only be an awareness of these features that will provide us with a secure basis for any conclusions we may come to about the role of reason in morals. Four such features spring immediately to mind.

In the first place, it will be apparent that, whatever views are held as to the precise nature of truth and validity, the exact tests for them or the form of these appropriate to the particular context of any discussion, there can be no doubting the need for any kind of rational process worthy of the name to able to stand up to some appropriate tests of truth and validity. In other words, whatever precise criteria we have adopted, any body of knowledge or understanding to merit the description "rational" must hang together in some way; it must display coherence when measured against whatever tests are regarded as appropriate to those criteria and when viewed in relation to other assertions in the same field. We must all accept that rationally requires that any body of knowledge or set of beliefs we subscribe to must be internally coherent and consistent. For example, one test of any new "discovery" in science must be whether it fits in with other currently accepted theories. If i does not , then either it must be rejected or the theories adjusted to accommodate it is a rational, non-contradictory manner. A claim to rationality, therefore, requires at the very least a respect for the need for internal coherence and logic.

Secondly, the central concern of this process of developing bodies of knowledge and understanding that hold together in a rational way is the production of generalizations or universals, those general assertions without which no kind of prediction, no matter how tentative,would be possible and which must, therefore, be seen as essential prerequisites of purposeful action. For in order to act purposefully as we said earlier, we must make choices and to do that we need to be able to make some calculation of the likely consequences of the different course open to us. These calculations in turn cannot be made by reference to particular experiences we have had; they can only be based on the general conclusions those particular experiences have led us to make. Thus when the world's first streaker, Archimedes, ran though the streets of Syracuse shouting " I've found it!", this was not a comment on the discovery of an exciting and hitherto unnoticed part of his own anatomy nor even of something new about his own bath; it was the discovery of a general scientific law that excited him. Again, the rules by which such universal assertions are reached and the grounds for claiming their truth or the validity of arguments that make use of them may be open to dispute. What is not open to dispute, however, is the need for such universals to be established if any process of rational thinking is to be possible. Thus not only does the notion of rationality demand coherence in our thinking; it also requires that that thinking be productive of generalizations based on our experiences. For what else could "understanding" mean?

Thirdly, if the generalizations we reach and the arguments we base on them are to have any claim to truth or validity, there must be some grounds for them and this implies not only that they must satisfy the criterion of internal coherence we have already referred to; it implies also that reasons of many kinds be produced in support of them. In other word, to make any universal assertion for which one wishes to claim a rational basis is to be able to produce reasons for that assertion and, in some cases, evidence of an appropriate kind in support of it. Again we must stress that there is likely to be in many contexts a good deal of disagreement over what will constitute appropriate evidence or good reasons for any particular claim, but again of the need for evidence or reasons of some kind there can be no question. The ability to produce appropriate evidence or reasons is as crucial a part of what it means in most spheres to claim the truth of any assertion or the validity of any body of knowledge as any criterion of coherence.

Lastly, we must note the need for these reasons or this evidence to be public in nature and for the standards of coherence to be generally acceptable. If we wish to claim that a particular process of argument is rational, we must be prepared to have it tested by public criteria of rationality. For if it only satisfies our own personal criteria it will be an example of rationalization rather than rationality, a distinction the importance of which for morality we will see later. This draws our attention to a further very important feature of rationality, its relation to language and communication. There are those who believe that it is language nd communication. There are those who believe that it is language that makes thought possible, that without the ability to express our thinking in word very little thinking worthy of the name would be possible (Vigotsky 1962). The converse of this is certainly true. For language is essentially a social activity and no kind of communication would be possible without common and shared standards of logic and rules of reasoning. Thus any claims we make for the rationality of our arguments imply by their very nature an appeal to some shared standards of truth, validity and logic, so that reasons we offer and the evidence we produce in support of our claims must be such as to be intelligible to others and seen by them to be coherent within the overall framework of our argument. It is for this reason that those phenomenologists who regard all experience as personal and subjective, believe that everyone's view of the world is unique and, therefore, deny the possibility of shared experience must reject not only the kind of universal rationality we are describing here but also the possibility of any kind of communication between individuals.

Thus what has been revealed by this brief and inevitably oversimplified account of rationality is that, while there are many problems and disagreements over its particular manifestations, over what constitutes truth, validity, logic and rationality itself in particular contexts, certain cerntral features can be picked out and identified of a kind that cannot be denied by anyone who admits the possibility of shared meanings. Among these, we have suggested, are respect for the need for validity of some kind, a recognition of the necessity of producing universal assertions as a basis for decision making of all kinds, an acceptance of the need to give reasons and evidence in support of any claims of truth and validity we wish to make, and an acknowledgment of the requirement that all of these processes should be capable of withstanding the test of public intelligibility.

Our final point which prompted a brief consideration of the importance of communication in rationality brings us conveniently back to our central concern with morality. For it highlights the natural progression from thought through language to social behaviour and reveals these as the central characteristics of man's rationality, the three major aspects of that which differentiates him from other creatures, a threefold notion well expressed in the words of Sophocles. "Many are the wonders of the world and none more wonderful than man; for man has learnt the art of language, the use of thought swift as the winds and the temperament for social living."

These lines illustrate very well the interconnection as well as the importance in human life of both rationality and morality and, now that we have gained some idea of the major characteristics of rationality, we can return to the central question of this chapter, what we can learn from these general considerations that will help us to establish the place of reason in morals.

Rationality and Morality

Throughout the first section of this chapter we have tried to maintain a crucial distinction between what can be said in general about the characteristics and the requisites or requirements of rationality in any sphere of knowledge and the difficulties which arise when we consider in particular contexts what will constitute appropriate criteria of truth and validity. We have suggested that, although it might be possible to reach a fair measure of agreement on the former general issues, many disputes and disagreements arise in almost all particular areas when we come to spell out what kinds of evidence are to be considered appropriate, what theory or theories of truth are applicable, what will constitute an acceptable logic, what criteria will be regarded as offering suitable tests of validity. We also drew attention to the disagreement that exists over the question of whether the same tests for both truth and validity should be applicable in all contexts.

Nowhere is the importance of this distinction more clearly apparent than in the sphere of moral "knowledge". For while it may be possible to achieve agreement over the truth and validity of assertions in the fields of, say, science and mathematics, so that the possibility of disagreement there is less readily apparent, no one can after a moment's reflection fail to recognize the impossibility of this in morals. The process of establishing whether, for example, someone has stolen a loaf of bread is clearly far easier and less problematic than that of deciding whether he was right or wrong to do so, whether there were reasons, excuses, circumstances that should be accepted as mitigating, and so on.

Moral "knowledge", then, provides us with specially difficult problems and this distinction between the general requirements of rationality and the particular problems of its manifestations in any given field are especially relevant to any discussion of the role of rationality in morals. It is also the clue to where so many moral philosophers and others have gone wrong.

Moral "knowledge" provides us with particular difficulties because of the problem of establishing an appropriate logical basis for it and/or discovering its precise logical status. In particular, it is immediately apparent that it is not possible to state with any confidence of achieving general acceptance what would constitute "proof" of any particular moral position or belief, or what criteria would be accepted by all as appropriate Trg appeal to in order to resolve any moral dispute. Thus, although there is no real difficulty in demonstrating the stupidity of filling the bath to the brim if one does not want to be continually mopping up the bathroom floor nor of resolving any dispute one might find oneself in with anyone who regarded this as not stupid at all, there are enormous difficulties in demonstrating the rightness or wrongness of, for example, using contraceptive devices and in resolving those disputes which manifestly do exist between those people who approve their use 2and those who do not, unless of course their approval or possible side-effects. What this amounts to is that whatever "knowledge" or discourse nor, indeed, like mathematical knowledge or discourse.

It is precisely here that traditional moral philosophy went wrong, since its approach failed to recognize the unique problems of moral discourse and treated it as mathematical or as scientific or as analogous to one of these, as a matter of proving certain kind of moral belief to be right or wrong, correct or incorrect. Whether by mathematical methods or by scientific methods or by some new and different kind of approach, the aim was to demonstrate the truth of certain moral positions.

The early rationalists, for example, adopted what is essentially a mathematical approach to morality, regarding it as a matter of deducing particular moral positions from higher order principles. Thus for Plato, as we have seen morality is a matter of " knowing" and recognizing the "form of beauty, truth and goodness" and "applying" it in particular contexts, just as one might know and the "truth" of Pythagoras' theorem and apply that to particular problems of a spatial kind. Indeed, Spinoza's Ethics is set out in the form of a series of theorems "proving" each moral point step by step and thus building up a huge quasi-mathematical edifice of moral "knowledge". Religious approaches to ethics, whether Christian or Judaeic, are also of this kind, as are metaphysical theories generally, since they all attempt, albeit in different ways, to establish "first premises" or "higher order principles" from which particular deductions can then be made.

The other main strand of traditional moral philosophy rejected this kind of rationalist metaphysics in favour of empiricism and took a scientific rather than a mathematical approach. In other words, it attempted to reach its first premises or principles not by some kind of mystical or purely intellectual means but by empirical observation. Thus the firs premise of utilitarian ethics is man's observable tendency to seek pleasure and to avoid pain, so that it is claimed that what is right in any given context is that which promotes pleasure and minimizes pain. Evolutionary theories of ethics too, seeing the "fact" of evolution as the key to an understanding of human existence, deduce from this that what is right is that which will enhance and assist the evolutionary process. Such "naturalistic" theories, then, seek a basis for the proof of certain moral tenets in some empirical observation or other about human character or the human condition, and thus regard moral "knowledge" as analogous to the natural sciences.

Others have tried not to use an overtly mathematical or scientific approach but nevertheless to suggest that the approach but nevertheless to suggest that the approach to moral enquiry has to be seen as analogous to these, that the task is still to establish some basis of proof for certain moral positions, even if such proof cannot be achieved by mathematical or scientific processes as such. This is the approach of those theories that constitute what one might describe as "developed rationalism", theories which, taking their cue from Immanual Kant, endeavour to establish the truth of certain higher order principles by appealing to the nature of rationality itself and developing some kind of metaphysic of morals or, as we might say, peculiar moral logic. We will need to consider this approach again later. It will be sufficient at this juncture if we merely note this as an attempt to do the same job by different methods.

That none of these approaches is satisfactory is clear from several considerations. The first of these is the manifest fact that no such attempt has been successful in producing moral "knowledge" of a kind that is or can be universally accepted. On the contrary, one of the salient characteristics of moral discourse is the degree of disagreement it permits and tolerates. Secondly, it will be clear that one reasons for this is that all of these approaches have perpetrated a logical fallacy, endeavouring to deduce moral conclusions from factual premises, committing what G.E.Moore (1903)called the "naturalistic fallacy" by endeavouring to define "good" in non-moral terms. This is equally the case whether these terms by metaphysical, scientific or logical. Thirdly, these theories do not allow for the fact of social change, to which we have already referred on several occasions. We now realize, as a result of our experience of change of all kinds and the moral issues it presents us with, that no hard and fast rules of a once-and-for-all kind are possible. We saw in Chapter 1 that the work of men such as John Dewey has drawn our attention to the hypothetical nature of all human knowledge so that, when we have come to regard even scientific knowledge as subject to modification, change and even rejection in the light of newly acquired evidence, the possibility of achieving anything approaching certainty in moral knowledge becomes even more clearly remote.

Whatever the role of rationality in morality is, then, it would seem clear what it is not; it is not the production of reasoned "proofs" of particular moral positions; it is to the establishment of a base upon which can be built a corpus of moral "knowledge".

An appreciation of this has led some people to go to the other extreme and claim that, since no particular moral beliefs can be "proved" and no moral dispute resolved in any final way, then anything goes as any other's.

This kind of view takes a number of forms. There are those, for example, who adopt a sociological relativism and argue that all moral beliefs are conventional, relative to the society, that having ten wives (no matter how stupid some of us may regard the practice) in some societies is the accepted thing and consequently right; in short that, since it is not possible to establish universal overriding moral principles, we must accept that what is right is what is in accordance with he accepted tenets of any given society.

One obvious difficulty which many find with such a view is that it makes comparisons between societies impossible; one cannot condemn cannibals nor headhunters nor Nazis; one certainly cannot justify such actions as the trial and condemnation of war "criminals"; nor can one claim that to civilize a primitive society is to improve it. This, however, is a difficulty that has to be faced once one adopts any kind of relativist stance.

The particular difficulty with sociological relativism is that there seems to be no basis for taking this kind of middle position. Once one accepts that there are no universal moral truths that transcend human societies, one cannot claim that there are nevertheless such truths to be found within particular societies which transcend the choice of individual human beings, since it is clear that there is seldom any real consensus and that, in any case, neither consensus nor majority opinion are any guarantee of truth. Furthermore, there is that feature of advanced societies to which we are constantly referring, namely their pluralism, the fact that many shades of opinion are to be found on most issues. Laws, rules and customs may vary from society to society, but values vary not only between societies but also between individuals in every society.

For this reason many have stressed that morality is an individual matter, that we must make our own moral choices in the light of fundamental moral principles which themselves have also been chosen by us. This is a basic feature of existentialist philosophy and of those phenomenological theories, to which we have just referred, which claim that, since everyone's experience of the world is unique and personal, everyone's reaction to that world must be of a similarly unique and personal kind.

Furthermore, many would argue that, although this is true, there are in fact no rational grounds upon which one can make such a choice of moral principles, that there are no reasons for taking one moral stance rather than another. This was the position taken by David Hume in relation to all human "Knowledge", that there is no basis for believing anything in preference to anything else. "If we believe that fire warms or water refreshes, 'this only because it costs us too much pains to think otherwise." This led to an emotivist view of ethics which saw moral principles as no more than those social norms that hold a society together because and for as long as the members of that society feel them to be right, regard them as conducive to those things they approve of and thus agree and assent to them. This is also the central feature of modern emotivist theories of ethics, which believe that ultimately moral value is a matter of individual feeling. It is also the source of the existentialist's nausea, that feeling of hopelessness that comes from the awareness that one must make choices to assert both one's existence and essence as a moral agent combined with the simultaneous awareness that there are no rational grounds for believing one thing rather than another, for adopting one set of principles rather than another, for behaving in one way rather than another.

All of this would seem to suggest that there is no place for reason in morality, that one might as well plump for any set of principles, that, since anything goes, it is of as much value tossing a coin as going through elaborate cerebral convolutions to reach a moral conclusion. In the very ultimate, there may be a lot to such a view, as the existentialist believes.

However, it is only necessary to take this as evidence that reason has no place in moral discourse if we are determined to adhere to the idea that that place has to be in establishing the content of moral "knowledge" or producing moral "proofs". For although there can be no ultimate criteria to appeal to in resolving moral disputes, it is not necessary to assume as a result that rationality has no place in moral discourse. The role or roles of rationality in morals can best be discerned if we return to a distinction we have referred to before between the manner and the matter of moral discourse, between its form and its content, its language and its literature (Oakeshott 1962, Peters 1963). For although any attempt to establish the matter, the content or the literature of morality is fraught with the problems and beset by the dangers we have briefly listed, the same is not the case when we try to apply reason to the question of its manner, its form, its language. The content of morality is changing, as we keep saying, and people must be allowed to be autonomous moral beings, but in order to become such they must learn the language of morals and be shown what rationality can reveal about its form.

It is important, however, to be clear what we mean by form, manner and language, especially since we are claiming this distinction to be crucial for moral education. To achieve this clarity we must refer back to what we said in the first section of this chapter about rationality itself.

This is the distinction that is crucial, although it is often blurred. Richard Peters, for example, although, as we have seen,drawing our attention to its importance (1963), elsewhere (1970) loses sight of it and, in attempting to establish certain particular higher order principles, wanders back into the area of content, matter and literature, telling us "there are a limited number of principles which are fundamental but nonarbitrary in the sense that they are presuppositions of the form of discourse in which the question 'What are there reasons for doing?' is asked seriously. The principles which have this sort of status are those of impartiality, the consideration of interests, freedom, respect for persons, and probably truth-telling. Such principles are of a procedural sort in that they do not tell us precisely what rules there should be in a society but lay down general guidance about the ways we should go about deciding such matters and indicate general criteria of relevance" (Peters 1970, p.36).

However, these principles are not merely procedural; they are those higher order principles, those first premises from which rules of action in specific contexts can be deduced,which we saw just now it is both impossible to establish and wrong to seek after. In failing to adhere to this important distinction between form and content, Peters is thus following exactly in the footsteps of Immanuel Kant who in seeking for the roles or roles of rationality in morals also went too far in this way. For it is not irrational to be partial, to refuse to consider the interests of others, to deny freedom, to fail to show respect for persons and even, perhaps, not to tell the truth; and our concern is not with what is unpleasant or distasteful or even contrary to the views of the majority; it is solely with what is irrational. An appeal to rationality, therefore, cannot establish these as principles and that is why they are not procedural any why in arguing this sort of case Peters and others are not confining themselves to the form or the manner or the language of morality but essentially involving themselves in its content, its matter and its literature.

In order not to make this same mistake but to adhere very closely to the distinction we are claiming to be crucial, we must stick rigidly to a consideration of what an examination of rationality as such can tell us about moral discourse, what it means to claim that such learn from that. What procedural principles must we adhere to if our moral beliefs are to be regarded as rational? Or, conversely what would lay us open to a valid charge of irrationality?

To answer these questions we need do no more than refer back to the general points we made about the nature of rationality itself in the early part of this chapter. For we claimed there that for any body of knowledge or beliefs, any kind of discourse, to lay claim to being considered rational it must, in the first place, display coherence and it will be clear that this is as true of moral discourse as of any other. It is not enough, therefore, for us to plump for a set of beliefs; it is necessary also that that set of beliefs should display an inner coherence and consistency. For that, after all, is what rationality is. Thus, for example, it is not rational for me to believe that all other human beings must respect my interests if I do not at the same time accept that I must also respect theirs. On the other hand-and this is the important point to grasp-it would be equally coherent, and thus equally rational, for me to believe that no one need respect my interests just as I do not respect theirs. There are many people who live their lives out on this basis and, whatever else we may think of their values, we cannot dub them irrational. Again we see how an appeal to rationality can help us to discern the form of morality, but emphatically not its content. Whatever one's own moral code is, it must be coherent and consistent and one's behaviour must "chime" with that code in all respects-at least as far as one is able to ensure that it does; certainly one must accept that it should.

Secondly, we argued earlier that rationality is concerned with the generation of universals or general principles. This point is, as it were, a subvariant of our first, since it suggests another way in which the idea of coherence enters into morality -we must act according to setterled principles, whatever those principles may be. In short, I must not act on one principle today and another contrary one tomorrow-not at least without being prepared to produce valid reasons for my change of heart. The idea of a rational morality, then, requires that our behaviour evince an acceptance of universal moral principals, again without dictating what those universal principles must be.

Thirdly, we noted earlier the need to produce evidence in support of any claim that we wish to have considered as a rational claim. The question of what constitutes evidence in the field of morals is a vexed one. Certainly one must accept;t that it is more likely to be analogous to legal than to scientific evidence. It will also be extremely difficult to establish what shall count as good or bad reasons for a particular course of action, not least because this will depend very much on one's own point of view. Furthermore, it will be equally difficult to distinguish behaviour which is irrational from that which is merely unreasonable (Woods and Barrow 1975). I kick my dog every time West Ham Uited lose a football match (i.e, once or twice a week). This behaviour you may regard as unreasonable; but is it irrational? To resolve this kind of question in most serious contexts is very difficult. However, what we can say is that behaviour for which no reasons at all are or can be produced is irrational in the full sense and thus cannot be counted as moral. It is indisputable, therefore,that evidence that one regards oneseif as relevant and reasons one regards as good should be produced, again because this is part of what w mean by a rational claim to validity. We are concerned with respect for the idea of evidence as much here as in any field of scientific exploration.

Fourthly, we argued that whatever as felt to be appropriate evidence should be so regarded in the light of publicly accepted criteria, that to some extent what constitutes appropriate evidence or good reasons must be decided by the test of whether others see it as such or at least can understand our reasons for claiming it to be so. This is Dewey's answer to the problem of ever-evolving values. For he does not feel it necessary to accept that anything goes in morals any more than in the equally rapidly evolving field of scientific knowledge. On his view, rationality requires that we look for some public agreement. If we are totally idiosyncratic the whole point of rationality is lost, since, as we also saw, it is essentially connected with communication. Reason requires, therefore, that we produce reasons for our moral beliefs and behaviour of a kind that others can understand. We need not go all the way with Dewey and require that they themselves accept these reasons or the beliefs and behaviour they are adduced to support (for that is to get into content again), but they must be able to recognize that there is a connection between them that an overall coherence is being sought, even if it is not always attained.

One aspect of this is particularly important for moral education. We have already referred to the notion of rationalization and have contrasted this with rationality. Rationalization is at root the selective use of evidence to justify what we wish for other reasons to find justification for. In other fields this kind of selectivity is regarded as deporable. It is a matter for front page headlines even in the popular Sunday newspapers when it comes to light that some eminent academic may have fudged the evidence to support his thesis that the place of Knossos existed or that intelligence is innate. It is quite the worst crime that any academic can commit. Yet do we not all commit this crime in the moral sphere almost daily, when we "convince" ourselves that there are good reasons for doing what we want to do rather than what we ought to do? If the evidence we produce to support such decisions really will stand up to public tests of rationality then the danger is avoided. ONe of the major tasks facing the moral educator is to draw the attention of his pupils to this important distinction.

Lastly, we must note the role that reason must play in the calculation of the consequences of our actions and, indeed, in the mechanics and practicalities of carrying out our decisions. Whatever weight we give to these consequences, we cannot make any kind of decision that is at all positive or, indeed, rational, unless we have made some estimate of its effects. This, as we said earlier, is what rationality is all about it is about behaving thoughtfully and purposefully and it is for this reason that it is crucial to moral behaviour. We must being our reasoning powers to bear, therefore, on a good deal of knowledge and understanding that is not in itself "moral" but which is highly relevant to the moral decisions we make and the actions we perform.

We have argued, then, that although a consideration of rationality cannot provide us with any help on the issue of what moral principles we should adopt and act upon, it can tell us a good deal about the form, the manner, the language of our moral code, displaying the need for this to be coherent, consistent and subject to evidence and reasons of a public kind. This may seem somewhat disappointing to those who still want reason to tell them what to believe and how to behave. On the other hand, to ask this of rationality is in itself to be guilty of irrationality, since it is to ask that all real choice be removed and that moral answers be attained in much the way that answers to mathematical problems are reached, by the use of pure reason. To ask for that is to surrender one's autonomy and all claims to individuality. Not to be granted it is to retain autonomy and individuality and that must be a gain rather than a loss in real moral terms.

The distinction that we have been arguing for here is well brought out in what is perhaps the best summary of the place of reason in ethics, that given by Goldsworthy Lowes Dickinson in his dialogue, The Meaning of Good (1901, pp.86-87), and quoted by stephin Toulmin at the conclusion of his examination of The Place of Reason in Ethics (1950, p.225).

> It is the part of Reason, on my hypothesis, to tabulate and compare results. She does not dertermine directly what is good, but works, as in all the sciences, upon given data...noticing what kinds of activity satisfy, and to what degree, the expanding nature of this should that seek Good, and deducing therefrom, so far as may be, temporary rules of conduct...Temporary rules, I say, because, by the nature of the case, they can have in them nothing absolute and final, inasmuch as they are mere deductions from a process which is always developing and transforming itself. Systems of morals, maxims of conduct are so many landmarks left to show the route by which the soul is marching ; casts, as it were, of her features at various stages of her growth, but never the final record of her perfect countenance. And that is why the current morality, the positive institutions and laws...both have and have not the value (sometimes claimed for them). They are in truth invaluable records of experience, and he is rash who attacks them without understanding; and yet, in a sense, they are only to be understood in order to be superseded, because the experience they resume is not final, but partial and incomplete.

Stripped of its Victorian grandeur and related to the context of the developing morality of the individual, that quotation sums up very effectively the central point we have tried to make about the place of reason of morality.

Stripped of its Victorian grandeur and related to the context of the developing morality of the individual, that quotation sums up very effectively the central point we have tried to make about the place of reason in morality.

If we not turn to a consideration of the implication of all of this for moral education, the first thing we must note is that it reinforces a good deal of what we said about moral education in Chapter 1. For it reasserts the need to develop in pupils certain cognitive skills and to promote in them a recognition of the necessity for their moral thinking to satisfy those requirements we have listed it it is to claim acceptance as rational. IN short, we must recognize the need for moral educators to develop within the field of moral thinking and decision making those general features of rationality, such as respect for the need for coherence, consistence, public evidence and so on to which we keep referring.

This does, however, raise an important and difficult question for the moral educator, namely the degree to which these qualities can be developed by pupils of all abilities. If we may make reference once again to Plato's system of moral education (and we continue to do so because it illustrates better than any other single theory all of the issues that have subsequently come to be regarded as central to moral debate), there is no reluctance there to accept that a large proportion of the population of any state will lack the intellectual ability to attain a moral education in the full sense, to be able to do their own moral thinking. This is the real significance of his division of the populace into men of gold, silver and bronze, a myth which is deliberately created and fostered to ensure the acceptance by the men of silver and bronze of the right of those of gold to do their moral thinking for them. Only the latter, therefore, are regarded as being capable of being educated morally; the rest must be conditioned or indoctrinated into obedience and are thus offered an authoritarian from of moral training.

Nor must we see this as remote from our times and of merely antiquarian interest. We are only just ourselves emerging from a philosophy of differentiated curricula, of an "educational" provision for pupils of "average and below average abilities" that has been framed on different principles that have been attacked by some as centrally concerned to achieve a similar kind of control through largely unquestioning obedience as that advocated by Plato (White 1968,1973; Young 1971). From the advent of the idea of secondary education for all until very recent times, as a glance even at the title of the Newsom Report (1963),Half OUr Future, will reveal, the idea of one kind of education for the bright and another for the rest \has dominated our thinking, although-significantly enough-not always our practice, and there are still those who advocate this kind of approach and argue it strongly and quite vehemently (Bantock 1968,1971).

This has been given a strange twist in relation to specific projects in moral education. For these, like most of the projects sponsored by the Schools Council and other bodies, have been directed mainly at the "less able" pupil. For the most part this has been the result of mundane considerations such as the unwillingness of schools to experiment with the curriculum of pupils on traditional examination courses and, conversely, their need to find something "relevant" and "meaningful" to keep the other pupils occupied, especially after the raising of the statutory school leaving age. However, its effect has been to suggest that brighter pupils do not need moral education-a somewhat bizarre notion-or that they are bright enough to sort moral issues out for themselves and do not bend the help of the school in doing so, or else that the kind of moral "education" needed by the less able is precisely the kind that Plato advocated, a training in obedience.

In this context, it is worth noting that the Humanities Curriculum Project, as we shall see in Chapter 7, although its brief specifically directed its attentions towards pupils of average and below average ability, did start from the premise that such pupils are capable of the kind of abstract thinking we are suggesting a rational approach to morals requires, so that those responsible for the project did attempt, as we shall see, to develop materials that would demand this kind of fully autonomous moral thinking from all pupils.

Clearly, in the sphere of morality, as in all other spheres, intellectual ability will play its part. To reach moral conclusions of the kind we have tried to define one needs to be able to analyse situations,to recognize what knowledge is relevant, to apply that knowledge appropriately, to attempt some prediction of consequences and so on. All of these make demands on one's intellectual powers and here, as elsewhere, the ability of individuals to met these demands will vary. This is confirmed, as we shall see in Chapter 3, by Lawrence Kohlberg's cross-cultural studies which indicated that moral development do not emerge clearly in preliterate communities.

However, with the right kind of environmental stimulus, progress towards moral autonomy will be maintained,and ,if we are to say that some people will not be able to meet these demands at all and that as a result we must not try to educate them to the point where they can do so, we must recognize the seriousness of what we are claiming. For we are assuming not only that they cannot be morally educated but that ipso facto they cannot be educated at all. And we are further assuming that, if we were right to claim that it is the ability to think for oneself, to make choices and to act morally in the full sense of the term that constitutes what it means to be human, then those we regard as intellectually incapable of this are not fully human at all, an assumption which in turn could be held to justify differential and unequal treatment of them in many other contexts. UNless we are prepared to concede that point, therefore, we must make the attempt to bring all pupils to the level of autonomous moral functioning.

Finally, we must remind ourselves that intellectual qualities are not the only elements in moral choice and behaviour; other qualities, as we have seen and shall see, are equally important. INdeed, Plato recognized the need to look to more than intellectual ability in selecting the children of gold for moral education. Moral judgement and, in particular, moral behaviur are, as we shall see in Chapter 4, at least as much a matter of the emotional responses the individual is capable of making, so that this also would suggest that those who are highly endowed intellectually do not have the monopoly of moral judgement or moral behaviour. It is in any case unlikely that after observing the behaviour of some of the most intelligent members of our society we will still need convincing of this

If we set out to offer any pupils a form of moral upbringing that is different in kind from the one we are outlining here, that difference must consist in attempting to tell them what to think, in short in a concern with the content rather than the form of their morality, and thus in treating them as though they were not capable of achieving a fully human level of existence. This would be disturbing even if there were empirical evidence to support it. Since there is not, it is particularly reprehensible.

This discussion of the place of rationality in morals< therefore< highlights not only what we must attend to as moral education but also some of the pitfalls to be avoided. IN particular, it draws our attention to the fact that many problems can arise when we approach moral education through a concern with its content, with what children should be encouraged to believe rather than the manner in which their beliefs should be reached and held. For we then enter the realm of what many would wish to describe as indoctrination rather than moral education and, since the distinction between these two notions is both highly important to the whole enterprise of moral education and the subject of much debate and disagreement, we must now give some attention to the question of what indoctrination is, particularly in the sphere of morality, and whether and how it can be avoided in attending to the moral upbringing of children.

Moral education and indoctrination

Problems of indoctrination are not restricted to moral aspects of education or schooling but they do loom very large in that area since, as the etymology of the word suggests, it is centrally concerned with the teaching of doctrines or values of some kind. In every area, however, difficulties arise mainly from the degree of disagreement that exists over the meaning of the term and the resultant impossibility of achieving anything like an acceptable definition. Yet without such a definition it is impossible to derive any kind of practical guidance from a discussion of the issue.

Disagreement appears to centre on three main questions, whether the term applies to the teaching of doctrines only or to a wider range of teaching, whether it is used always pejoratively and by what criteria we can recognize examples of it in practice. A view on each of these questions will emerge as we discuss the whole problem of indoctrination, but a few preliminary comments may help to dispel some of the confusion in advance.

The term "teaching" is a purely neutral term in that the use of it does not imply that one has any particular views on the process one is describing or referring to. Thus we can speak of someone as teaching his pupils Latin and another as teaching them the term implying any attitude on our part to either of these pursuits. The term "education", however, since it encapsulates certain evaluative criteria, does imply much more than that. To speak of someone as educating his pupils is, first of all, to express one's approval of the process and, secondly, to suggest that it satisfies a number of criteria that we briefly discussed in Chapter 1, criteria such as respect for the autonomy of the pupil, the development of understanding, a recognition of the value of what is being learnt and so on.

The term"indoctrination" is evaluative in a similar way. In its normal current usage it is not neutral-not at least any longer, even if it once was (Gatchel 1972). For in the first place, it is normally used nowadays in a pejorative sense; we use it to condemn certain kinds of teaching which we disapprove of , and we never hear it used, except perhaps by certain educational theorists, in any other sense. If we wish merely to describe the teaching of anything in a manner which either ignores or even actively discourages the development of critical awareness and understanding in the pupil, we use the perfectly as adequate word "instruction"; only if we want at the same time to condemn the practice do we use the word "indoctrination"./ There are some, indeed, who see the term "indoctrination: as synonymous with miseducation, a term we use of a situation in which education has gone wrong in some way (Crittenden 1972). Certainly, it would seem that its use does imply some kind of contrast with the notion of education. The question then arises of whether it is to be taken as denoting any kind of miseducation or whether it picks out certain particular features that may be present in a situation in which teaching is taking place.

If the latter is the case, the problem then centres on what these particular features might be, what evaluative criteria are encapsulated in the meaning of the word, what characteristics must be Elated in the meaning of the word, what characteristics must be identified in an act of teaching if it is to be properly designated indoctrinatory. In offering answers to this question most theories have concentrated their attention on three aspects of the teaching process-methods, content and intention-so that it will be helpful if we consider all of these briefly in turn.

The idea that indoctrination is to be defined in terms of the methods of teaching being used is a popular one and, superficially at least, attractive. For the man in the street when asked about indoctrination would almost certainly be reminded of the teaching methods described in Orwell's 1984 Huxley's Brave New World or those said to be in current use in some countries, and would thus think first in terms of the methods used-subliminal suggestion, hypnotism, amplifiers hidden under bed pillows and so on (Wilson 1964). At a more sophisticated level it has been argued that the term has a purely descriptive meaning and does in fact describe those methods of teaching that are employed when an authoritarian form of teaching is adopted either from choice or necessity, such necessity arising either from the fact that the pupils lack in general the ability to think for themselves or-an important point we must take up later-are too young to have reached the age and stage of cognitive growth at which they can think for themselves (Moore 1972). Thus it is argued that when we speak of indoctrination we are referring to the use of certain kinds of teaching method. If this is the view one takes, then the term "indoctrination" is regarded as a neutral term used nonpejoratively to describe the teaching of doctrines by methods by methods that do not invite any response of a critical kind from the learner.

However, it is clear that in most contexts the term is used not merely descriptively but also to convey disapproval. Most people, for example, in using the term of the teaching methods employed in 1984 or Brave New World are condemning the kind of teaching Will is Moore describes would want to condemn it and would feel that by calling it indoctrination they would in fact be doing so.

If this is so, then on closer examination it quickly becomes apparent that the definition of indoctriantion in terms of the teaching methods used is inadequate. For, as John Wilson goes on to point out, we would not regard it as reprehensible if these same science fiction methods were used to teach pupils their multiplication tables or Latin grammar in a painless way nor would we use the term "indoctrination" of such processes. Nor is it the method we are concerned about in the kind of teaching that Will is Moore is describing. We must, therefore, look beyond method for the criterion we are seeking.

John Wilson himself suggests that the crucial difference lies in the content or subject matter of the teaching, that what we object to is not the use of these methods in themselves but the use of them to implant and ensure the uncritical acceptance of certain social roles or moral, religious or political beliefs. In short, he is arguing that, as etymology suggests, indoctrination is the teaching of doctrines and that we will recognize the truth of this if we consider the areas of subject matter of which it is normally used. For we usually use the term, he argues, of the teaching of politics, religion or morals, in other words, those areas which are concerned with doctrines, with sets of beliefs which are by definition uncertain rather than bodies of knowledge for which publicly accepted evidence can be produced (1964). Thus it is argued that the teaching of mathematics cannot be termed indoctrination, even if the methods used are of a subliminal kind, since indoctrination can only occur in those areas where doctrines, sets of values, are involved. Presumably, too, all teaching in these areas must by definition be indoctrination if this notion is to be defined entirely in terms of the subject matter of teaching.

There are two problems,however, with this approach. In the first place, it accepts that a clear-cut division can be drawn between those areas of the curriculum that involve doctrines or values and those that do not and that indoctrination is only possible in the former. But such a line would be very difficult to draw and, although in popular usage the term may be restricted to the religious, moral or political spheres, it would seem undesirable to deprive ourselves of the use of it to describe teaching that actively discourages criticism in any sphere, especially at a time when the status of all kinds of knowledge is seen as problematic.

Conversely, it suggests that all teaching in the areas of religion, morals or politics must by definition be called indoctrination and, since the term is accepted by John Wislon himself as pejorative, must therefore be condemned. However, it will be apparent that not all teaching in the realms of politics, religion or morals need or should be described as indoctrination. Indeed, we speak of political education, of religious education and of moral education, so that we must believe these expressions to be meaningful.

If would seem therefore, that a definition of indoctrination in terms of content or subject matter still does not get us to the heart of the issue. It is for this reason that several people have introduced the notion of intention (Kilpaatrick 1951, 1972;Hare 1964; White 1967,1972)suggesting that indoctrination is not so much a question of what we teach pupils nor of how we do it but of what kind of change we intend to bring about in them and that, if our intention is to persuade them to accept what we are teaching them uncritically and blindly, then the process we are engaged in is one of indoctrination. It was this aspect of Willis Moore's account of indoctrination as a method of teaching that was disturbing. For what he was describing was more than just a method; it was an approach to teaching whose intention was authoritarian, to bring about learning and acceptance without encouraging or even allowing any kind of critical appraisal or any resultant possibility of rejection. Clearly, in this kind of account, although we will most often be concerned with those areas of teaching which involve doctrines or beliefs, the notion of indoctrination could be applicable in any field of knowledge, since even in relatively straightforward areas of the curriculum, such as mathematics or science, a distinction can still be made between uncritical acceptance and understanding. It is being suggested, therefore, that unless the aim is to bring about understanding and critical awareness or, at least, if the aim is to prevent the development of these, then the process is one of indoctrination.

One major drawback of this point of view, however, is that it doe not allow for the possibility that some indoctrination might happen accidentally, and, since we will be arguing later that it is this feature of moral learning that is the most crucial for any discussion of moral education, we must look at some of its implications now. It will be clear that often, whether teachers or parents intend it or not, children do acquire quiet uncritical attitudes, prejudices in fact, in the fields of morals, religion, politics and even aesthetics, not to mention those things they "learn" in other fields without achieving any level of understanding or real critical awareness. If this happens they would seem to be as effectively indoctrinated as in any situation in which a deliberate attempt was made to achieve this kind of end-perhaps more so.

This consideration suggests, then a further criterion we should take account of in attempting a definition of indoctrination and leads us again to consider the importance of a notion about which we have already said a good deal in this chapter. That notion is that of the manner of learning that takes place as a result of our teaching, the way in which children or others come to learn and in which they hold whatever beliefs they come to hold (Green 1972) or, in the sphere of moral, the style rather than the content of moral decisions (Atkinson 1965,1972).

A consideration such as this illustrates very effectively the whole point of our argument in the last section., For there we were trying to establish that moral education is concerned not with what a pupil comes to believe but with how his beliefs are held. In particular we stressed that pupils should be helped to develop understanding, a respect for rationality, for truth and for relevant evidence. What we are now suggesting is that indoctrination involves the absence of these. It implies that knowledge or beliefs are held uncritically and without respect for rationality, truth or evidence. It suggests teaching that either by accident or by design precludes rationality, the central theme of this chapter. It implies the acceptance of a passive model of man. It encourages the development of minds that are closed to any consideration of evidence of a kind contrary to the beliefs that are held. It involves a violation of the criteria of inquiry appropriate to any given subject area (Crittenden 1972). That violation, that closing of minds, that precluding of rationality,that absence of respect for truth and evidence are vitally important whether they happen by deliberate intent or merely by accident or through inefficiency. It is likely, of course, that this will most often come about, especially in the field of morals, through that undue concern with the teaching of content that this chapter has endeavoured to show to be a misinterpretation of the notion of moral education.

But, however it comes about, the uncritical acceptance of any kind of knowledge or any set of beliefs is to be deplored and it is this that most people have in mid when they speak of indoctrination, even though for the most part they use the term to denote deliberate attempts to bring about this undesirable state.

It may well be that in taking this view we are really supporting those people who have argued for some kind of amalgam of all the criteria we have discussed (Flew 1972; Wilson 1972), that in seeking out examples of indoctrination we must look to methods, content, intentions and manner or to any combination of these. Certainly it is from all of these sources that indoctrination or miseducation in some form is most likely to arise. The important thing, however, is to recognize that the main use of the term is to define miseducation, however it comes about. The growing usage is to describe as indoctrination those acts of teaching which violate what we have several times referred to as the essential characteristics or criteria of education. If education is concerned with the promotion of autonomy, understanding, critical awareness, respect for truth, a love of knowledge and so on, then indoctrination is teaching that results, for whatever way, in the absence of these qualities.

Two final points must b made. The first of these is that we have accepted a definition that does not insist on intentionality but opens teachers to the charge of indoctrinating their pupils even if they do this accidentally or through inefficiency. A child is no less indoctrinated or miseducated if his teacher is inefficient than if he is a deliberate purveyor of his own beliefs, just as a patient is no less dead if his surgeon is inefficient than if he is a psychopathic killer. Teachers must, therefore, accept full responsibility for the education of their pupils and this implies accepting equal responsibility for any miseducation that occurs, although clearly we must acknowledge some difference between the deliberate and the accidental as much in this context as in any other.

The second point we must consider briefly in conclusion is the problem that this is said to create for the teacher of young children. We will be discussing in Chap;chapter 3 what developmental psychology has told us so far about the stages of children's intellectual growth and in particular the import of this for moral development. Two things are clear. ONe is that we do not know as much as we would like to know and need to know about this whole question. The second is that, while it may have particular implications for the work of teachers of young children in all areas, it has especial relevance for their concern with moral development.

For at any time before a child have the intellectual capacity, the cognitive skills, to cope with the tasks we are describing as endemic to education, to think for himself with all that this implies (and we must remember that some people never get to this stage), the question must arise as to whether everything a teacher does is indoctrination. For at this stage the child must have a "content" to his morality, a set of beliefs when he comes to school, since he will acquire his attitudes and his values from many sources, his parents, his peers, the media and so on. HOw can the teacher avoid indoctrination at this stage?

It was of course in order to solve this problem that some people suggested that the key criterion of indoctrination is intention (Hare 1964), arguing that, although one does have to tell young children what moral positions to adopt before they are capable of thinking critically about them, this is not indoctrination if one intends that critical about them, this is not indoctrination if one intends that critical appraisal should follow at some later stage. NOr is it indoctrination, it is claimed, if children ae taught to accept certain things before they can understand that reasons are relevant and appropriate and do not come to accept whatever they are told blindly. Thus they can be told not to steal, tell lies, hurt people and so on, so long as we give them reasons and intend that they should subsequently come to see the point of these precepts for themselves and, indeed, come to be able to relate them to particular contexts.

Clearly, this is a context in which intention is an important consideration, but it is naive to suggest it offers an adequate solution.

For, as we saw just now, it is not enough to exonerate a teacher if his intentions were good if his practice resulted in the closing of his pupil's minds in any area of knowledge. The road to hell, as we know, is paved with good intentions of this kind and, while this may be acceptable if it is the road to one's own hell, it cannot be when one is paving such a road for others. To say that intention is all is to discourage thinking on the part of teachers as to a more positive role they might be expected to play in this respect.

If we accept the notion of stages in the intellectual growth of children, we must recognize the need to work at getting every pupil from one stage to the next and through to the final stage of autonomous thinking in all spheres, but perhaps especially in morals. This is the point of Richard Peter's comments on the work of Piaget on the moral development of children; to tell us about the stages does not help us a lot as teachers with the task of getting our pupils through them or, conversely, avoiding their becoming fixated at any one of them (Peters 1960). In such a context to say that we intend to do it is not enough; we must work in a much more detailed and practical way at the mechanics of the process itself.

In the moral sphere,this raises an issue that we have already referred to and one which we must examine in detail in Chapter 5,the issue of how we can offer some kind of moral content to our pupils before they are capable of looking at it critically and, in particular, how we can set about moral education, as we are defining it, when we know that our pupils have already acquired and are constantly acquiring moral beliefs, attitudes and even prejudices from many other sources.

It will perhaps be sufficient, therefore, at this point, to say that this is a far more complex issue than many seem to have been prepared to recognize and, secondly, that it is dangerous to assume that it is a problem that only confronts the teacher of young children, although it may well have a particular relevance for that stage of education. We all know many adults whose moral development has stopped hurt long before the autonomous stage. Indeed, if we will but confess it, it is true of all of us in some aspects of our moral lives. Conversely, many of us have observed quoted young children displaying the beginnings of a critical approach to moral questions. As we suggested in Chapter 1, we may be see not to tie what is being said about the stage of moral development too closely to chronological age. We will do better, therefore, if, instead of relegating this issue to discussions of primary education, we recognize it as being central to the whole process of moral education at every stage, since that process must be viewed as developing the rationality of the individual stage by stage towards moral autonomy. Only if we approach our task in that spirit will we avoid indoctrination and focus our attention on moral education in the full sense.

Summary and Conclusions

We have tried in this chapter to gain some idea of the nature of rationality and of its place in morality. We have suggested than an examination of the relation of relation of reason to morality supports an approach to moral education whose main concern is with how pupils hold their moral beliefs and how they reach them rather than with what particular moral beliefs they hold, that the attention of the moral educator should be directed towards the manner rather than the matter of moral learning, and in particular that he should endeavour to promote understanding, critical awareness and an appreciation of the need for knowledge and skills of many kinds as a basis for the making of autonomous moral decisions that are sound and for thinking for oneself in the fullest possible way. Finally, we suggested that to fail to achieve this is to be engaged in a process of miseducation that is often called indoctrination, the result of which, whether intended or not, is the blind and uncritical acceptance of certain beliefs or values. IN short, the essence of indoctrination is the absence of rationality, just as the essence of education is its presence.

We referred finally to the particular problems that face the educator when his pupils may not yet have reached the stage of congnitive development at which they can look in a properly informed, critical and autonomous manner at beliefs and values and to the task that faces him in leading his pupils from each of these stages to the next. We also noted the particular complications that arise here for moral education from the fact that pupils will have acquired moral values and attitudes from many other sources and will thus have a content to their morality (as, indeed, they must in order to live) before they can be brought to this position of critical and autonomous appraisal.

These are the issues that we must turn to in subsequent chapters. First of all, we must consider the stages of cognitive development and their implications for moral education and, then, using that as a basis, we must face the question of how we can convert moral learning into moral education of the fullest kind.

the result satisfy moral consciousness? Is there any fitness or propriety between such a method and such an object? We shall be able to judge by the result.

3
Moral Development

If we wish to argue that one of the incresingly important tasks of education is to help children to develop the appropriate skills and judgement to cope with the variety of moral choices they have to face in today's complex world, then it follows that every teacher, regardless of his subject specialism, or the age range with which he is primarily concerned, must play a part in the moral education of his pupils. Morality is an area which permeates the whole life of the school. Moral issues may be dealt with formally as part of the curriculum, but they are just as pervasive in the informal or hidden aspects of the curriculum, in, for example, the organization of the school and in teacher-pupils relationships.

If we pursue the argument further, claiming that teachers should make a deliberate attempt to educate children morally, then questions are raised about children's levels of understanding, readiness for learning and modes of learning. Experience, as well as empirical research and developmental theory, have taught us that to base work for children on levels of thinking which are inappropriate to their developmental stage is educationally unsound, in almost every curriculum area. We should not hope to deal with the abstract concepts in mathematics or physics with five year olds any more than we should wish to limit our work with average sixteen year olds to purely fact finding or observational exercises or to the practice of simple skills. Such inappropriate choice of materials and methods leads on the one hand either to rote learning or complete incomprehension, resulting in a rejection of school work or feelings of failure, which have a detrimental effect on a child's self-image, motivation and involvement in school (Downey 1977). And on the other, where the level of material is to simple, boredom and frustration ensue, prompting the adolescent to regard school as a complete waste of time. To promote moral education, whether formally or informally, requires a similar understanding of the child's level of development and personality makeup.

With this in mind then, this chapter sets out to give some account of the main theories of moral development which will contribute to an understanding of the child's development, crucial to the planning of any kind of moral education programme.

Concepts of development

However, before we can consider some of the most useful theoretical approaches towards children's moral development,it will be illuminating to examine briefly what we mean by the term "development". The term itself suggests a progressive change towards some more complex level, a change usually of an irreversible nature. But whether it is possible to predict the end state of any developmental process depends on what it is that is developing. We can more or less predict with certainty that under appropriate conditions a caterpiller will develop through specific stages into a butterfly of a particular kind. The implication here is that there is some preexisting genetic structure which determines the end state, the culmination of the whole process, and also that there is a gradual unfolding which under normal circumstances is not arrested or reversed.

This model of development taken from plant or animal biology can be applied up to a point to aspects of man's biological development, but the same criteria cannot hold for man's social, intellectual or moral growth, precisely because of the very factors that distinguish him, as a human being, from other organisms.

Theories of the maturational or unfolding type, which presupposed a genetic structure that would gradually emerge as the child grew older, have been discredited, since evidence shows that man does not simply unfold without the help of outside influences. Children deprived of sensory stimulation, perceptual variation or adult contact (Bowlby 1975) are clearly hampered, since development depends upon accommodating to such influences, assimilating them and interpreting them. Social interaction and adult attention have been shown to be necessary factors in the developmental process.

Similarly, althrough it is possible to talk of an end state when referring to plant or animal life,few people now would want to claim any kind of end state in relation to human development. One reason for this that human life offers a vast variety of possibilities and since its quality varies so much from one culture to another it is impossible to predict how any individual might turn out. But more important,man is an active agent, capable of making choice and interpreting his experiences in his own unique fashion. He is not merely at the mercy of genetic influences on the one hand or cultural pressures on the other.

Thus, as Hirst and Peters (1971) make clear in their analysis, development is a necessarily evaluative concept, rather than a purely descriptive one, when applied to man. If we talk of a morally developed person, we are presupposing some idea of what it means to be morally mature. This in turn depends upon a view of morality that one can justify, and ultimately upon the view of man that one adopts. It is not an empirical issue to be decided on the basis of what we can observe about a person's moral conduct. What we have to decide, as we saw in the first chapter,is what it implies to be morally educated.

An examination of three main psychological approaches to

moral development-the psychoanalytical viewpoint, the learning theory approach and the cognitive developmental view-will show that,far from offering contradictory or incompatible explanations, as might be apparent at first sight, they are in fact complementary and offer insight into different aspects of a child's moral growth.

The psychoanalytical approach, an manifested in Freud's monumental work, sees morality as conforming to cultural standards through a process of internalization, Learning theories, as reflected for instance in the work of Sears, Bandura,Eysenck, assume that moral behaviour is the result of reinforcement, rewards or punishments, and that much moral conduct is a result of a child's modelling himself on an admired adult. Individual differences in moral behaviour are explained in terms of differences in condition, ability (Eysenck 1964). As with the psychoanalytical approach, morality or moral conduct is seen as conformity to some sort of cultural or social norm. Cognitive-developmental theorists, on the other hand (Piaget 1932, Kohlberg 1964), view moral development as an active, dynamic, constructive process leading to a state where the individual is able to act according to moral principles which he either accepts because he understands them and agrees with them or which he has worked out for himself.

These theoretical stances have different implications for moral learning and moral education and each will now be examined in further detail.

The psychoanalytical approach

It is to Freud that we owe out awareness of the effects of the unconscious on human behaviour. In the area of morality, Freud assumed an end state of rationality and the main impetus of his work in this area was to explain why some people deviate from rational behaviour and show an exaggerated or distorted mode of rule-following. The acquisition of morality was for Freud the development within the child's personality of the super-ego, the agency or mechanism which issues moral imperatives derived from standard of adults close to him which the child has internalized. These moral imperatives serve to control the impulses of the id (the unconscious), especially those relating to aggressiosn and to sex. The super-ego he sees as having two prime functions:it acts as the conscience and as what Freud calls the ego-ideal(Freud 1933).

The child's conscience is formed by means of identification with his parents and internalization of their moral standards in such a way that when the infant is frustrated or punished by his parents, his aggression towards them is arounsed. But rather than venting this aggression onto those he loves and thus fears losing, he unconsciously turns his anger inwards onto himself. The conscience henceforward operates when parents are not present to enforce moral standards by punishing the child or by preventing him from acting in a way that would infringe societal rules and norms. But what is difficult to explain is that the strength of a child's conscience does not appear to depend upon the severity or strictness of the actual standards or behaviour of his parents. Rather it seems to stem from the intensity of the child's aggresion towards his parents and thus,when it has been internalized, towards himself. A strict or even over-severe conscience is thus found in children who have a close attachment to their parents, who thus do not vent aggression on them overtly because of fear of losing the loved ones and who, unconsciously, take steps to avoid showing aggression by being over-punitive to themselves. On the other hand, there are those of course in whom the close attachment is lacking who do give open vent to their feelings or displace hostility onto others. According to Freud's theory such children develop a less severe conscience themselves.

The super-ego also acts as the ego-ideal which provides a positive standard against which the conscience measures the standards required by society. Like the conscience, it represents the voice of the parents and thus of society, giving some guidance on moral conduct (Freud 1914). The failure of the ego-ideal to reach its own standards results in feelings of guilt which are frequently far more severe than the person's actual behaviour warrants. Thus many of Freud's patients who consulted him as adults because of some severe nervous disturbance were found to be those who,even as children, had suffered from severe guilt feelings for minor transgressions or even for thinking of indulging in socially unacceptable behaviour, perhaps in the form of fantasy in the area of sexual activity. We are all familiar with those who suffer sever pangs of conscience for some trivial offence to others or even merely for thinking ill of others.

The value of Freud's theory of moral development lies in the fact that it draws attention to the importance of both aggression and attachments during the early years. As we have seen, his theory deals with the rather negative notion of taking the voice of prohibition into ourselves, but also the positive one of modelling our behaviour on that of an admired figure, albeit at an unconscious level. The theory thus deals with emotional aspects of moral development which later views, such as those of the learning theorists and of the cognitive developmentalists, tend to neglect.

Freud's concern was largely with those who exhibited such an exaggerated or distorted style of rule-following that the normal course of their lives was disrupted. To help such people, he sought to explain why they had not attained a rational level of rule following and suggested that their development was arrested through fixation at some critical stage of psycho-sexual development during the first five or six years of life. His explanatation was in terms of unconscious emotions rather than in terms of variations in social or environmental conditions.

However,although he offers no positive theory of moral development by suggesting conditions under which such growth might be promoted, apart from the general notion of the importance of a proper love relationship with parents in the early years, his work nevertheless prompts us to ask certain questions which are of fundamental importance to the moral educator. For he does suggest that some early experiences can inhibit or even prevent moral development in the full sense. Thus peters (1960), in comparing the contributions of Freud and piaget to moral devlopment, raises some important issues which recent research has attempted to shed light on. He asks whether certain child-rearing techniques lead to compulsive rule-following habits,blocks or breakdowns at some later stage, and whether a particular kind of training in early childhood tends to encourage blind conformity to rules, regardless of circumstances.

Learning theory approach

Since Freud did not concern himself with child-rearing techniques or social and cultural differences, but concentrated largely on the individual's inner states,we must now turn to the work of the learning theorists to see what light their work throws upon such issues.

Learning theorists with a behaviourist bent tend to argue that to postulate some kind of hypothetical construct like the conscience or super-ego to explain moral conduct is totally misguided since, after all, such a mechanism cannot be observed and must therefore remain hypothetical Assuming that moral behaviour is learnt they set out to explain its acquisition in terms of the laws and process of learning used to explain other kinds of behaviour such as retention, the aquisition of skills, the learning of habits. In their view then there is no need to call upon either hypothetical mental structures, such as the conscience, or cognitive structures and stages as suggested by development psychologists.

Moral behaviour can be explained in their view by three sorts of mechanism: reinforcement and rewards; punishment or the threat of it; and modelling or imitation. Following the Skinnerian pattern of operant conditioning, behaviour can be modified or shaped by the use of reinforcement techniques. The effect of rewards in this system is to increase the probability of a desired response or unit of behaviour. Such techniques are based upon animal learning under laboratory conditions and there is no dearth of evidence to demonstrate their success. Skinner successfully trained rats to operate levers and to learn mazes; he taught pigeons to turn in a circle and to play with a ping pong ball by administering food rewards at appropriate intervals, to reinforce the desired response. Children, he claims, can also be taught to adopt the kind of conduct their parents deem desirable or morally correct (such as telling the truth, helping others, being polite and considerate) as a result of parental praise and approval. Similar techniqaues are advocated by some psychologists for helping teachers to cope with deviant or disorderly behaviour in the classroom. Ward (1971) developed a training schedule for teachers, based on operant conditioning procedures and designed to help them eradicate disruptive behaviour of children in the infant and junior school. Teachers were taught to reward children's desired behaviour by praise, attention, smiles or approval and by ignoring unwanted behaviour.

Behaviour can similarly be shaped by punishment or negative reinforcement in the form of verbal rebuke, physical punishment, sarcasm, the withholding of privileges - in other words any treatment a child finds unpleasant or disagreeable. The desired effect of punishment is either to inhibit the undesired behaviour by operant conditioning techniques or, within the framework adopted by Eysenck, to arouse feelings associated with pain, fear or anxiety in the hope that, by association, the undesired behaviour will in future be refrained from.

Eysenck (1960, 1964) goes so far as to suggest that the learning of any moral values should be based on modern learning theory and attempts to explain the formation of a conscience in terms of conditioned responses. Conscience, in his view, is a set of conditioned responses built up during the formative years by the pairing of conditioned stimuli (arising from aggressive or prohibitive behaviour)with unconditioned stimuli (smacks, verbal admonitions) by a process of stimulus generalization; the two become associated so that in future when a child contemplates a forbidden act, conditioned feelings of anxiety prevent him from indulging in it. His "conscience", in other words, is acting as a moral rein on his behaviour. Individual differences in the force of this so-called conscience are explained in terms of inborn conditionability. Extroverts, Eysenck has demonstrated, are more difficult to conditioin than introverts. Experimental evidence to support such an explanation is drawn largely from animal studies. For example, the now classic work of Solomon and Wynne (1953) showed that puppies, punished for eating from a forbidden bowl of food, were in future inhibited from touching the forbidden bowl even though they were on the point of starvation and even in the absence of the experimenter who had administered the punishment. They had, it was suggested, developed something akin to what we call conscience in human beings.

Not only do children learn to adopt desired behaviour patterns as a result of rewards and punishments, but also by watching other people. Experiments have confirmed what we already know from everyday observation, namely that children readily copy or imitate what they see others doing, especially the actions of a parent or admired peer.

Bandura and Walters (1963) base their theories of social learning and personality development largely on the notion of imitation or modelling. Their claim that limitation plays an important role in the learning of deviant as well as conforming behaviour is well substantiated by cross cultural and laboratory studies. young children learn to adopt sex-linked occupational and domestic roles typical of their culture, by observing their elders' behaviour rather than through deliberate instruction of any kind. Cross cultural evidence (Nash 1958, Bronfenbrenner 1970) demonstrates the fact that children not only learn from what they are told to do by adults, but also from what they see the adults doing. And not only do they learn by watching real adult models-symbolic models on film, television or in books can also have a similar effect. In fact,the use of film sequences in the laboratory is the main technique chosen by Bandura and his co-workers (1963) to demonstrate the effects of observational learning on children's behaviour.

Such studies suggest that observing the behaviour of models may have several effects. Firstly, the child may acquire new responses which he has hitherto not shown spontaneously. This seems another case of confirming what we already know from everyday observation. We are all familiar, for instance, with young children who play at hospitals or schools, adopting the role of docter or teacher as they have seen it enacted. Bandura et al. (1961) carried out a study designed to test for delayed imitation of deviant models by young children. They exposed one group of nursery children to aggressive adult models and a second group of non-aggressive models and observed the children's spontaneous behaviour subsequently in a play situation. In a later experiment (1963) children's reactions to aggression displayed by real-life models, film models, cartoon-film models were compared. In all cases, children who had observed an aggressive model themselves displayed aggresive behaviour later on in a mildly frustrating situation, wheras such responses rarely occurred in control groups of children.

This kind of work does raise several important issues relating to moral learning. For instance, if part of what it means to act morally is to show consideration for others and not to vent aggression on them, what is the effect on children of being severely punished by an adult for their aggressive activity? An adult who loses his temper is perceived by the child as aggressive, so that, if the effects of modelling are as potent as Bandura would have us believe, this must serve to make a child even more aggressive and less considerate of other. Such work does imply too that much learning of social or moral conduct is likely to go on inevitably: children model themselves on adults they see around them, following the example they set. We shall consider some aspects of this in greater detail in Chapter 5.

However, not only do children learn new kinds of behaviour as a result of the observation of others. Bandura (1962) has demonstrated that children exposed to aggressive models subsequently display far more aggressive responses than they could possibly have seen during the course of the experiment. In other words, exposure to uninhibited aggressive behaviour may release responses which had hitherto been latent or forgotten. The model thus appears to have a disinhibitory or releasing effect. We are reminded here of the thorny question of the effects of violence seen on television on childrens behaviour. Several studies have attempted to examine these effects(Himmelweit 1958, Belson 1977) but naturally methodology is diffcuilt and so far results have been equivocal.

Studies of modelling or imitation go further in suggesting the vicarious effects of rewards and punishments on children's social or moral conduct. In yet another series of experiments (Bandura et al. 1963), four groups of nursery school children were observed under different conditions. One group watched a film model being punished for aggressive behaviour and a second group saw the model rewarded for the same kind of conduct. One control group was shown a highly active but non-aggressive model and a further control group saw no models at all. In subsequent observations of the children at play, those who had witnessed the aggressive model being rewarded indulged in significantly more hostile acts than children in any other group.

Learning theorists are divided in their views on the effects of punishment on moral conduct where this is seen partly as the conformity by children to norms and standards set by adults. Wheres Eysenck's conditioning theory assumes that children have to be punished before they learn to refrain from an "immoral act". Bandura's modelling studies suggest that children may equally well learn to inhibit undesired behaviour without committing a prohibited act and without themselves being punished. Watching a model being punished seems to suffice, at any rate in some cases.

In discussing the contribution of learning theories towards moral development, we have so far seen that the focus for them is on conduct or behaviour. Moral conduct is interpreted either as resistance to temptation involving the classical conditioning of emotional responses such as fear as in Eysenck's model, or learning to conform to certain standards as a result of rewards and punishments or through imitation learning. Since only conduct or behaviour is at stake. it could be argued that the explanation offered by learning theorists is applicable only to moral training rather than to any other aspects of morality. They omit to deal with moral feeling, reasoning or judgement. Their explanations fall into a mechanistic paradigm where children are regarded as passive learners, responding or reacting to the influence of others rather than acting and interpreting the world around them and progressively learning to form their own standards and apply their own moral principles according to the differing demands of prevailing circumstances. As we have already made clear, the growing dislike of a theory in which man is regarded only as passive makes the social learning approach untenable as a sufficient explanation of moral learning. It is therefore to the work of the developmental theorists that we must turn to seek an explanation for these more complex aspects of human moral developments.

Cognitive-developmental approach

Among the early investigations into moral development, the work of Arnold Gesell(1940, 1946) deserves mention. Gesell sees development mainly as a maturational, unfolding process, which advances more or less regardless of environmental influences. His evidence comes from wide-scale longitudinal studies of children from birth to adolescence so that he feels confident in talking of the typical child at any age level as the titles of his books show, for example, *The Child from Five to Ten* (1946).

Nevertheless, although his way of thinking still deals largely with moral conduct rather than with reasoning or judgement, his scheme does hint at a stage sequence of morality. His work seems to suggest three distinct stages in moral conduct: the first is typified by obedience to adult instructions and commands; the second reveals rigid adherence to rules even in the absence of an authority figure; and the third shows a personal morality where the individual acts apparently autonomously. Gesell suggests that parents and teachers should expect different kinds of moral conduct with different age groups and that in school we must accommodate our attempts at moral education to the developmental level of the children we are concerned with.

This kind of thinking is,as we shall see, similar to that of Piaget and Kohlberg in a sense, but Gesell does not go as far as exploring the nature of children's thought processes to explain why their moral conduct is as he finds it at these three stages. He tells us more about what children think rather than how they think. Piaget, who views moral development as one aspect of a child's overall intellectual and cognitive development, sets out to explore the child's processes of thinking.

The work of Piaget

Piaget's own thinking was influenced by the ideas of both Durkheim, in a socialogical context, and Kant, from a philosophical perspective. To Durkheim piaget was indebted for the emphasis he placed on the social context of morality. For Durkheim (1960) claimed that we are moral beings only in so far as we are social beings and was concerned with the individual's relationship with society through his attachment to it, with society's discipline on him and with the individual's eventual autonomy within a social structure. Piaget also drew upon the distinction Kant made between the heteronomy and autonomy of the will; piaget hoped to show that this distinction has practical application in the contrast he wished to make between conventional morality and a rational moral code.

In the former, children are at the stage of heteronomy where their conduct is dependent upon the wishes of others, while in the latter they have reached a stage of automony where they act according to their own moral choices for which they can give their own reasons.

Piaget's main aim was to explore the nature of children's moral judgements and, to do this, he worked in Geneva with individual children, talking to them and questioning them on three broad areas: their attitudes to rules; their judgements of rights and wrong; and their assessment of justice and fairness. He established that growth in moral judgement is a gradual developmental process, involving not the learning of rules by rewards, punishment or imitation, but rather a progress of cognitive restructuring.

In order to make clear how his conclusions were reached, we shall look briefly at his empirical work in each of thethree areas mentioned above.

In 1932 Piaget wrote that "all morality consists in a system of rules and the essence of all morality is to be sought for in the respect which the individual acquires for those rules." In view of this, then, one of the crucial questions for Piaget was how the young child's mind comes to understand and respect rules. He was concerned not only with the child's practice of rules (his moral conduct) but also with the way in which the child perceives rules as a restraint on his actions. For his investigations Piaget chose rules children follow in playing the game of marbles (universally popular among the child population of Geneva at that time), since this kind of rule is one seldom passed on by adults but learnt from other children during the game itself. He himself joined in their games adopting the position of one ignorant of the rules and conventions, and in conversation with children, discovered how their approach to rules changes as they mature.

The very youngest children play haphazardly with no regard for rules at all, but later, up to the age of about six, they become more and more aware of the rules of the game, now regarding them as immutable and following them rigidly. This reflects the child's heteronomy, obeying rules laid down for him externally which are not to be questioned. But later he gradually begins to realize that rules are not sacrosanct and have been formulated in order to regulate the game. Rather than being untouchable they can be modified by mutual agreement with the others players. It is during this stage that heteronomy begins to give way to autonomy and around the age of eleven or twelve children begin to show an interest in how and why rules are formulated. They are not now concerned with putting them rigidly into practice, but are ready to modify them by mutual agreement according to circumstance.

In Piaget's view, one of the main factors contributing towards this developing autonomy is the child's growing ability to cooperate with others. Where rules were seen, at an earlier stage, as emanating from some authority figure, respect for them was unilateral rather than mutual. It is only when children experience relationships with their peers, meeting together as equals, that the opportunity arises for mutual consent and cooperation and the scene is set for the growth of autonomy. But in order to move towards autonomy it seems essential for the child to be released from constraints imposed by authority figures where adults use their superior force. Cooperative activities and mutual understanding between peers are, in Piaget's view, necessary conditions for autonomy to develop.

If we now examine some of Piaget's work on children's judgements of right and wrong, we again find a gradual progression from a stage of heteronomy to one of autonomy. Actions are at first regarded by young children as right if an adult approves of them, wrong if he disapproves.Children at the heteronomous stage judge conduct accroding to its material consequences, rather than the intentions behind the act

.To explore children's judgements of rights and wrong Piaget used a story technique, presenting the children with pairs of incidents and asking them to comment on the behaviour of the characters portrayed. For example, children were asked whether a girl who accidentally cut a large hole in her dress when she was trying to help her mother with some dressmaking was naughtier than a child who deliberately played with scissors when she had been told not to and made a small snip in her dress. Younger children almost without exception judged the first case as more severe and more deserving of punishment: the act was judged as naughtier because the girl made a bigger hole. Piaget terms this stage in the formation of moral judgements "moral realism"; the child is forming his judgement on the basic of what he can observe happening around him in his reality, that is, on material consequences. Similarly, on hearing stories about a boy who stole a roll to give to a hungry friend and a girl who stole a piece of ribbon, judgements were made on the basis of the cost of he stolen article - that which was immediate and real to the child.

This tendency of young children to focus on external, observed consequences of actions and to ignore intentions can be explained by reference to the child's egocentricity. In Piaget's stage theory of cognitive growth, a child at the egocentric level is still limited in his ability to distinguish himself and his own feelings from those of others. He is capable of seeing things only from his own point of view, does not always distinguish fact from fantasy (dreams, to him, are real) and thus cannot conceive that other viewpoints are possible. He cannot internalize rules and apply them to actions in a flexible enough manner to take into account factors which might be variable; for example, other people's intentions or the different demands made by varying circumstances. It is only as he emerges from this state of egocentricity and begins to be able to focus on more than one aspect of a situation at a time, and, in particular, on unobservable, aspects, that his moral judgements become more flexible. Thus an older child, confronted with the anecdotes about stealing, might argue that whereas it is usually wrong to steal, it is not so bad if your friend in starving. Condsideration for others is now assuming an important part in a child's life, as a result, Piaget argues, of peer group cooperation and interaction.

To come now to the third field of investigation, we shall look at some of Piaget's work on children's sense of justice, the development of which, he claims, is also dependent upon mutual respect between peers. As he writes: "the sense of justice, though naturally capable of being reinforced by the precepts and example of the adult, is largely independent of these influences and requires nothing more for its development than the mutual respect and solidarity which holds among children themselves." Again, very young children interpret justice to mean that which adults tell them to do. Losing or breaking something deserves punishment, even if done by accident. Fairness involves being given equal shares, even if needs differ. A closer examination of Piaget's findings reveals the same progression here as in other areas, namely from an egocentric stage, where children's judgements stem from moral realism and where rules, duties and obligations are dependent upon adult constraints. They pass from this stage of heteronomy, which, as we have seen, indicates dependence upon others, to that of autonomy as a result of cooperation on an equal basis with their peers.

It is this development of mutual respect that enables a child to begin to see the world through other people's eyes. It is only when he can consider all possible circumstances and points of view before making a moral judgement, one that fits a particular set of circumstances, that he can truly be said to have reached a stage of autonomy or to practise a rational moral code instead of being tied to a conventional morality.

In summary, then, Piaget distinguishes between two kinds of morality. Conventional morality is reflected in an obedience to adult command and an uncritical adherence to rules. This is described as a stage of moral realism or heteronomy, characterized by unilateral respect for and dependence upon others for guidance in moral issues. Rational morality is reached where children are able to formulate their own moral rules by mutual agreement and to apply them according to circumstance rather than rigidly and immutable, Kay (1973) sees this kind of morality as creative, that is, applied flexibly according to the unique set of circumstances in operation at the time.

Children do not practise either conventional or rational morality to the exclusion of the other, but move from one to another by a process of maturation, development and cognitive restructuring. Thus Piaget assumes that a child's development in moral judgements is paralleled by his cognitive development in other spheres. A stage theory of development is thus postulated with the observation that children pass through stages in an invariant order even though not all at the same rate. Some do not ever attain the final stage of absolute autonomy, as we shall see later.

A stage theory of development is characterized by several unique features. Firstly the concept"stage" supercedes that of chronological or mental age and although it is possible to say, for example, that children do not begin to emerge from the stage of heteronomy until about the age of eleven or twelve, it must be remembered that age is only a very rough guide. Children do not all develop at the same rate, so some will progress more rapidly through the stages than others. Secondly, the sequence of stages has been demonstrated as being invariant: it is not possible either to miss out a stage or to pass through them in a different order, though exceptional children, as Williams and Williams (1969) have shown, will show flashes of insight characteristic of an advanced stage long before they are firmly established in that stage. Thirdly, progression from one stage to another does not involve simply an addition to what went before but, implies a reorganization or restructuring, enabling the child to see problems and thus to make moral judgements from a different and more complex perspective. Fourthly, as we suggested in Chapter 1, the concept of stages should not be taken in a literal or chronological sense. All adults will respond to some situations in a heteronomous manner.

The great value of Piaget's work on moral judgements lies both in the methods he used ot investigate children's thought processes and in the fact that he was the first to view moral thought as a developmental and restructuring process depending largely on a child's growth towards abstract thinking and interaction with his environment and with those with whom he comes into contact. Important questions, left unanswered by his own work, have stimulated further research. For example, although he demonstrates that children move from one stage to another in a fixed sequence, he does not examine the conditions which might facilitate or impede this progress, nor does he explain why some children are apparently arrested in growth before they reach the stage of autonomy. And although teachers and educators have drawn widely upon Piaget's work for guidance in planning work for children, Piaget himself never suggested ways in which parents or teachers might help children to develop further. Thus Piaget offers no deliberate guidance to teachers concerned with their responsibility for the moral education of their pupils. However, he did lay the foundations for later investigators to build upon.

Research stimulated by Piaget's theory

So vast is the wealth of research stimulated by Piaget's theory of moral development that only a few examples can be referred to here before we consider one of the major contributors. Lawrence Kohlberg. Many of the empirical studies set out to replicate Piaget's investigations and did in fact substantiate his findings (Morris 1958, Johnson 1962, Loughran '1967). Kohlberg (1968), in a twelve-year cross-cultural study of boys in the USA, Great Britain, Canada, Mexico and Turkey, found that although Piaget's stages emerged universally, children in rural societies showed slower progress. Hollingshead (1949), MacRae (1954), J. &E. Newsom (1963) amongst others all claimed to have established social class variations in moral development, where children from higher socio-economic groups were seen to progress more rapidly towards the stage of autonomy. Brennan (1961) showed that progress of E.S.N. children falls far behind those in normal schools and that few, if any, ever reach the final stage.

However, some doubts have also been cast on Piaget's findings, as a result of further investigation. Edwards (1959), for example, in an investigation of the moral judgements of adolescents, found that many of the older adolescent boys in his sample still formed their judgements on the basis of material consequences and paid no more attention to motives or intentions than younger children. Bandura and McDonald (1963) claimed that developmental stages could be readily altered by the provision of adult models who consistently adopted a moral orientation counter to that dispalyed by the child, even if this resulted in the apparent regression of the child to an earlier stage. Such a claim is in direct contrast to the work of Turiel (1969) who attempts to show that a child's moral thinking can only be changed when he is exposed to reasoning one stage above his own, but that he remains oblivious to arguments presented at a stage below that in which he is established. Furthermore, Rest *et al*, (1969) showed that children judged moral arguments one stage below their own as worse than their own in spite of the fact that they were being presented by an authority figure.

Other workers adopting a Piagetian framework for their research include Kay (1973, 1975) who pursues the stage theory further and suggests an attitudinal model of moral development, laying greater stress on social and environmental influences than Piaget did. Bull (1969) proposed a similar developmental continuum ranging from "anomy" at the very early stage where the infant is amoral, having no regard for others, and passing through stages where he is dependent firstly on authority figures, then upon the decisions of his peer group until he can finally make moral decisions for himself.

The work of Kohlberg

Besides Piaget's work, Kohlberg's can probably be said to have made the most important contribution to the psychology of moral development. Kohlberg, working in the USA, has in his empirical research both complemented and expanded Piaget's ideas. Like Piaget, he too concentrates largely on individuals moral judgement; that is, the reasoning behind the judgements they make, rather than their actual moral conduct. Kohlberg too (1966) adopts a cognitive theory of moral development and sets out to show that principles of moral judgement gradually develop as children grow older, but that this development is highly dependent on environmental and social conditions. His conviction that external influences can foster children's moral thinking and help them to move onto a further more complex stage leads him to offer a framework for practical moral education (1966) which will be discussed later.

Kohlberg's scheme of moral development takes the form of six main stages, each of which reveals a different kind of motivation for acting morally or for forming moral judgements. At stage one of the premoral level, we find that an individual's motives are oriented primarily towards obedience and punishment. A child at this stage will say that it is wrong to disobey his father because he will be found out and punished or that he must not, for instance, run across the road because his father has said so

At stage two, the actions which are regarded as morally right are those which satisfy the individual's needs. Stages three and four, at the level of what Kohlberg calls conventional role conformity, represent firstly, the "good boy" orientation where the child's actions and judgements are made in order to gain approval from others, while later (at stage four) this gives way to a respect for authority and the given social order. A child will, for example, conform to avoid censure from an authority figure. It is not until the individual reaches stages five and six at the level of self-accepted moral principles that he begins to apprach what Kohlberg considers to be moral maturity. At stage five the rights of others are considered and an effort is made to see that these rights are respected and safeguarded. It is rather more a contractual orientation than one involving any feeling for the position of others. At the final stage, probably not attained by the majority of the population, the morally mature person acts according to his own conscience or principles. He is now able to consider universal values inolving the rights and feelings of others and his own behaviour towards them.

As in any stage concept, the order of the stages is regarded as invariant; an individual can neither miss out a stage nor take them in a different order. And for Kohlberg, this invariance goes further ot include universality under different cultural conditions. This does not mean that in any culture movement through the stages proceeds at the same rate, but rather that the sequence is the same and that, regardless of the nature of the culture, all stages emerge, with the possible exception of the last. Kohlberg's own cross-cultural studies of moral development (1966) compared the moral judgements made by ten to sixteen year olds in Taiwan (urban population), in a Malaysian aboriginal tribal village, and in a Turkish village, with those made by an American sample. The findings suggest a similar sequence of development in all cultures, although stages five and six do not develop clearly in preliterate communities.

He also established (1966) that subcultural differences occur, not in basic moral values but in rate of progress through the stages. At all ages middle-class children tended to be somewhat in advance of their working-class peers. This he attributed to a difference in children's feelings of their participation in a prevailing social order and in their understanding of it. If working-class children find themselves in an authoritarian family set-up (though obviously not all working-class families are of this type) then their individual value as persons is accorded less importance than their position in the family. It would follow then that their moral orientations would lean further towards gaining the approval of others and avoiding censure (stages three and four) than towards a personal autonomous stance as in stages five and six.

Kohlberg's stage theory, like Piaget's implies a cognitive restructuring and reordering as the individual matures morally. Each stage of development allows a better and more complex cognitive grasp than the one before it; elements of earlier stages are taken account of but are transformed in the light of later understanding and more complex mental structures. Kohlberg attempts to explain how individuals pass from one stage to the next by drawing on the notion of cognitive conflict and introduces the "one stage above" principle, further developed on a practical level by Turiel (1969). His thesis is that when children are presented with arguments one stage above the level they have reached, the conflict or mismatch in the arguments will prompt them to attempt a resolution of the problem and thus help them towards the next stage of moral argument. It is this principle that both Kohlberg and Turiel hope will form a fundamental guideline for any programme of moral education in school

Although Kohlberg sets out a developmental sequence, showing how children's moral judgements develop and mature as they pass from a premoral level to one where they are capable of making mature moral judgements, his pattern does not only offer an explanation of the child's moral thinking. In addition it goes some way towards furnishing a theory of moral character, suggesting an explanation of individual differences in the moral nature of adults. As we have already mentioned, not everyone reaches the final stage of moral maturity and many of us do not even attain stage five. It is, however, possible to find adults who do not appear to have progressed at all from stage one, those who simply conform to certain standards set up by others because of fear of punishment. If punishment is unlikely, that is, if there is minimal risk of their being found out in their infringement of rules, they have no hesitation in doing just as they like - no inner moral principle appears to operate. Adults are then to be found at any stage, and from this we are able to talk of a character type, if a person's conduct and quality of moral judgement are consistent.

Although reserach in this area is still in its early stages, findings suggest that it might be possible to account for an individual's fixation at an early stage and therefore, up to a point, for his moral character, by exploring other aspects of his social and moral life. Haan *et al.* (1968), working with college students, found that relatively few came out at the level of self-accepted moral principles on Kohlberg's scale of moral judgements. Those who did were found to be highly independent of their parents, to play an active part in social and political organizations, and to rely very little on religious doctrines for moral guidance, a point which may provide additional support for what we said in Chapter 1 about the essential authoritarianism of a religious morality. Those who came out at the level of conventional morality tended to be generally conservative, to play little part in social or political activities, and to conform to conventional standards set by parents and other authority figures. More will be said about character typology in the next section, but the question to be raised here is whether it is possible to develop the quality of children's moral thinking, so that regardless of parental attitudes or child-rearing techniques, few children do get stuck at the early stages.

Turiel, working with Kohlberg, suggests two interesting and valuable principles derived from the stage theory and designed to form fundamental practical guidelines for those concerned with children's moral development. These are the notions of "one stage above", which we have already discussed, and of stage mixture. Turiel (1969) explains that a moral stage shows how judgements are made rather than whether they coincide with conventional standards or norms. The implication is then that moral stages are concerned firstly with processes of thought rather than with products, and secondly that they reveal qualitative rather than quantitative differences. And since differences are qualitative it would be very difficult to postulate a sudden cut-off point between one stage and the next.

Turiel sugggests therefore the notion of stage mixture which he shows to be consonant with the restructuring hypothesis. At any stage in development, children encounter a vast range of experiences, but at any one time they respond more to some aspects of the environment than to others. They respond to those aspects that they can readily understand or, in other words, those at their own developmental stage. But they also experience aspects they do not yet fully comprehend - those at a stage above their own. So although they do not respond directly to these more complex sitmuli, many different experiences are jostling in the child's awareness, and it is this variety that Turiel refers to as a stage mixture.

This, he argues, is a necessary part of development through successive structures. Moving from one stage to another is possible only if we admit a basic stage mixture, the practical implications of which are as follows. Slow progress from one stage to another implies little stage mixture - there is little to link one stage to the next; increased stage mixture is therefore conducive to change. Those who do not progress to a mature level of moral judgement show a levelling off of mixture, so there is little stage variability and little chance of progress and stabilization gradually sets in.

These hypotheses were confirmed by detailed analysis of data derived from experimental studies already carried out. It is particularly illuminating in explaining cross-cultural differences: moral development in isolated communities progresses more slowly than in technological societies, for the very reason that there is greater stability, less challenge by new and strange experiences, and altogether less intellectual, social and moral conflict. For anyone hoping to promote children's moral development, the main task then lies in increasing the disparate elements and thus increasing the level of stage mixture and the probability of a move forward. It is here that Turiel's second principle comes into operation.

Turiel and his co-workers found that it was possible to prompt cognitive restructuring of the kind that would help children onto the next stage by confronting them with a cognitive conflict which they were encouraged to resolve. They did this by presenting groups of children with moral arguments at stages other than their own. Arguments presented two stages above the child's own had little or no effect on his subsequent moral reasoning. The conflict was not apparent to children because the gap between the styles of argument was too great. Arguments presented a stage below the child's own similarly had no effect, in fact Rest *et al.* (1969) showed that children considered arguments below their own level to be worse than theirs and therefore rejected them outright. It was only when arguments were presented at one stage above the child's own that any progress was apparent in his subsequent moral judgements. Such children are able to perceive these arguments as contradictory to their own precisely because they function at more than one stage simultaneously. They thus experience cognitive conflict or disequilibrium and are challenged to think in a more complex manner. The practical educational implications of these theoretical notions and empirical findings will be discussed later.

Studies of character development

No account of research in the field of moral development would be complete without some discussion of two major studies of character development, the Character Education Enquiry under the direction of Hartshorne and May (1928-1930) and the *Psychology of Character Development* by Peck and Havighurst (1960). Discussion of these two important projects has been left until now, so that crtical reference can be made to the three major approaches to moral development where appropriate

Hartshorne and May set out to examine the conduct of children of secondary school age in the USA over a five-year period. Their sample consisted of over ten thousand school children whose resistance to temptation in the absence of an authority figure was measured over a whole series of situations allowing them to cheat, steal or tell lies.

The investigators found a very low and statistically non-significant correlation between the tests, suggesting that, for instance, a high score of cheating in one situation did not point to a tendency to cheat in all circumstances. Similarly, a child found to be honest in one context might easily tell lies in another. They found too that the tendency to cheat depended both upon the risk of detection and the effort they had to make in order to cheat. Non-cheaters were more cautious about being found out, it seemed , rather than being more honest. Honesty seemed to be dictated more by immediate situational factors, such as group norms and group approval, rather than by internal moral principles. Correlations between tests of moral knowledge and experimental tests of moral conduct were low; in other words, knowing the facts associated wth moral behaviour was not necessarily reflected in the individual's own moral conduct. Furthermore, direct moral guidance of the kind offered by Sunday school or Bible classes, scout or guide groups, did not appear to have a positive influence upon children's behaviour in relation to lying, stealing and so on. From these data Hartshorne and May concluded firstly that moral traits such as honesty are situation specific. Children do not show a consistent trait of honesty in their general behaviour, but their moral conduct varies according to the nature of the situation. Secondly, because didactic instruction seemed to have little or no effect, they suggested that moral character is a matter of deep emotional forces operating during the child's formative years - a factor reminiscent of Freud's concept of the development of the super-ego. If moral character is not a matter of consistent moral traits like honesty or generosity, but is rather a matter of emotional tendencies (fear, love, hate, guilt) which are basically affective, then any attempt to develop children's moral natures later on in school is doomed to failure, since the seeds of their moral character have been sown much earlier on.

However the work of Hartshorne and May was essentially an investigation into moral conduct; the nature of their study produced data indicating the products of children's moral thinking, that is, their actual responses or actual behaviour. What this study did not do was to look behind the conduct itself to probe children's reasons for behaving as they did.

Investigations of this sort, that examined the nature of children's thought processes rather than their thought products, were left until a later date, after the establishment of a structural stage theory of moral development worked out by Piaget and later by Kohlberg. A we saw earlier, Kohlberg's stage theory offers a kind of character typology but is based on very different arguments relating to a child's growing understanding of moral situations as he develops intellectually and passes from one stage to the next. Kohlberg attributes the failure of any conventional moral education programme to have a direct influence on moral character and moral conduct, not to the potency of earlier emotional bonds between parent and child but to a misconception of what form moral education might take in school. Hitherto, he argues, teachers have attempted to train children in "good" moral habits through example, rewards and punishments, rather than matching the level of moral argument they present to children with their stage of moral development. Again, therefore, this supports what we have said earlier about the need for an approach to moral education that is based on the promotion of the pupil's ability to think for himself rather than on any attempt to tell him what to think or how to behave.

There was to be a gap of about thirty years before the second major character development study was carried out, again in the USA,by Peck and Havighurst (1960). Peck and Havighurst themselves attributed the lack of significant research in the intervening years to the rather pessimistic interpretation of the findings in the Hartshorne and May study. These findings seemed to discourage further experimentation and objective study in the field of character education, partly because this area seemed too complex for psychological investigation and partly because the results suggested that even if a typology of moral character could be established there was nothing that could be done in the field of moral education to alter or modify traits so firmly laid down in early childhood. Havighurst and Taba (1949) had reopened research in this area of personality development, thus paving the way for the wide-scale survey published by Peck and Havighurst eleven years later.

These investigators focused not upon the specificity of moral conduct but rather upon its general persistence and the predictability that they detected in earlier research findings. Their basic orientation was a psycho-analytical one which drew upon Freud's view that personality development can be classified according to the orientation a child adopts during his early psycho-sexual development. Thus Freud's personality typology (1905), manifested in oral,anal,phallic and genital types, depending on the area of the body which most involves psycho-sexual and emotional satisfaction,is paralleled by a typology set up by Peck and Havighurst to indicate an individual's orientation towards other people,also in terms of the search to satisfy his own personal needs in a maximally pleasurable way.

They produced what is in effect a motivational theory of morality in psychosocial developmental terms. Five character types were hypothesized. The amoral type is entirely egocentric; he leads a life of self-gratification and pays little or no attention to other people's feelings. The expedient type is basically still egocentric, but acts in an apparently moral way even though he has no internalized moral principles and is still out to satisfy his own needs. The conformist fears disapproval and strives constantly to comply with the requirements of other people. His moral conduct is, as a result,fairly stable, since he always aims to avoid what society would disapprove of. He does not however act on the basis of his own moral principles. The irrational conscientious person begins to show signs of developing his own internal moral code. He has internalized standards of right and wrong but tends to be rather inflexible in his application of them, thus giving an impression of disregarding the feelings and wishes of others. The final type,showing a fully developed sense of moral maturity, is rational-altruistic; he considers the welfare of others and is ready to sacrifice himself to help others.

Peck and Havighurst worked out their scheme on the basis of findings from investigations using large numbers of adolescents between the ages of ten and seventeen, including those in the 1949 study. They suggest three main criteria for identifying moral maturity: firstly, the ability to attend to other people's feelings; secondly, to predict the consequences of one's own actions and the repercussions these might have on others; and thirdly, the ability and willingness to modify the application of one's moral principles according to the demands of a particular situation.

If we examine the typology suggested by Peck and Havighurst, two important points emerge. Firstly, as we have seen, the five main types of moral motivation they propose reflect ways in which individuals tend to behave in a consistent and predictable manner. Thus, if an individual at the age of ten tends to show behaviour that is mainly of the expedient kind, the model suggests that he will still adopt expedient techniques as an adult, even though the specific reasons he gives and moral situations he encounters are relative to his age group. Persistence and stability of behaviour are attributed to early parental influence, as we might expect from theorists adopting a Freduian perspective, Peck and Havighurst suggest, rather pessimistically, that each generation tends to perpetuate its strengths and weaknesses of character largely unchanged . Parents treat their children in a certain way and thus children tend to turn out very much like their parents. Such a conclusion does not offer much hope for a programme of moral education.

The second point of interest, especially in the light of our earlier analysis of development stages, is that each type seems to represent a definite stage in a developmental scheme. The amoral type is clearly far less mature morally than the expedient type for instance. However Peck and Havighurst did not themselves propose a developmental sequence showing how children can pass from one stage to another. They were, on the other hand, convinced that moral attitudes learnt in the early years were relatively unmodifiable.

Moral development and moral education

To end this chapter, some observations will be made on the implications of the various approaches discussed for teachers contemplating a programme of moral education and for those conscious of their own responsibility for the moral education of their pupils, even if not in a formal way. The psychoanalytical approach serves to draw our attention to the importance of the emotional aspects of morality. Many teachers, influenced possibly by their understanding of the work of Piaget, who pays little attention to emotional factors, seem to regard the formation of moral judgements and the taking of moral decisions as a largely intellectual matter. But as we shall argue in Chapter 4, morality and the emotions go hand in hand. The affective side of moral behaviour, that is, whether a person really cares about what he is doing and whether he has other people's interests sincerely at heart, is a matter not to be overlooked. Similarly his own emotional response to a situation as well as an understanding of and ability to cope with his own emotions, are important. Fellings of guilt such as Freud postulated in his notions of the conscience and the ego ideal serve to make the individual care about his own conduct to the point of concern even about his intentions, feelings or fantasies. Although Freudian thory cannot offer any positive guidelines to teachers that might help them to deal with the emotional dimension of morality, his case studies illustrate clearly that the effects of fixations at an early stage of development can result in anxiety and uncertainty. These are frequently manifested by a withdrawal from emotional involvement and a retreat into situations which are not emotionally thetening. And although most children do not suffer from the extreme neurotic disturbances such as those described in his case study of little Hans, who developed, amongst other things, a fear that once outside his own house, he would be crushed by stumbling horse or a falling building, there are nevertheless many children whose emotional responses are lamed, uncontrolled or misdirected.

Learning theorists concentrate mainly on one aspects of moral learning; that of moral training, if such a term is possible, or of moral habits. As we suggested in Chapter 2, some teachers will argue that because young children cannot understand moral reasoning there is no point in trying to reason with them over moral issues and all that can be done is to inculcate certain standard into them, thus helping them to form moral habits which will guide their behaviour. Others will challenge this view, claiming that any training or habit formation is entirely misplaced in the realm of morality, and make a case either for letting children simply formulate their own moral code, worked out by mutual agreement amongst peep groups, or leave them without adult guidance. Brennan, for example(1965), argues that all children should have the opportunity to live without direct adult supervision. A.S.Neill in his school at Summerhill embraced this basic philosophy. But these extreme viewpoints should surely not be mutually exclusive,as Peters argues when he talks of the paradox of moral education, referring to the need for habits to precede reason. Similarly Oakeshott (1962) argues that in order to cope with the complexities of life in a society such as ours, with its manifold choices and unpredictable moral dilemmas, we cannot always afford the time to stop and consider our moral principles before acting. Instead, where the moral choice is not a new or challenging one, we need habits to fall back on. It becomes a habit, or part of one's nature, for example, to show consideration for others; we do not need to stop to think whether to offer help to a blind man wanting to cross the road. Reflection on moral principles is clearly not necessary in this case. Part of our moral repertory must therefore lie in habits formed in the early years.

But the danger comes when an individual relies too heavily on habits or on what he has been taught by others. It is here that we see the limitations of a learning theory approach. Learning that relies solely on reward and punishment will stultify real moral thinking, simply because it is too inflexible. Such learning will be situation specific and is not easily modified or generalized to circumstances posing a different problem. Furthermore, once the supporting authority figure is withdrawn, the individual is bound to feel lost, since there is no one present to show approval of what he is doing. Adults in charge of young children may not always be aware of their influence as reinforcing agents in Skinner's sense, or of their potency as examples or models. Bandura's work points to the effects that modelling or imitation can have on children's behaviour and, although he does not offer deliberate guidance on moral education, awareness of his work does serve to draw our attention to some of the unintended outcomes of adult examples.

As we saw earlier in our discussion of indoctrination, it is particularly important for teachers of young children to ensure that they are not merely teaching their pupils a set of habits which they will continue to use unthinkingly. Offering children reasons and explanations appropriate to their level of understanding will go some way towards avoiding the risks of indoctrinating them in this way

Perhaps one of the most important things teachers can learn from the approaches discussed so far is that much moral learning has taken place before a child enters school. He has not only developed some kind of conscience and internalized some sort of moral standards in his early years, albeit ar an unconscious level,but has also acquired habits and learned conduct as a result of rewards and punishments meted out to him by those in authority. The nature of moral learning of this kind will be discussed more fully in a later chapter. The cognitive developmental theorists seem to offer guidelines suggesting what considerations teachers might take into account in formulating an approach to moral education once the child is in school. As we observed earlier, Piaget did not offer delinberate advice to teachers, but his stage theory nevertheless suggests what it is possible or impossible to achieve at any given level of developments. Turiel and Kohlberg go further in outlining deliberate techniques for moral education in schools, based on their own empirical findings. Some of the moral education programmes discussed in Chapter 7 would certainly benefit from the kind of psychological underpinning to be drawn from their work.

Summary and conclusions

This chapter has outlined three of the main psychological approaches to moral development and has attempted to show their relevance to educational practice. The psychoanalytical approach underlines the significance of earlier emotional experiences in the formation of the superego or conscience and draws attention to the unconscious nature of this process. The social learning approach stresses the effects of modelling, rewards and punishments on children's moral conduct, while the cognitive theorists examine ways in which children gradually learn to make moral judgements:

They all draw our attention to the fact that there is an important emotional dimension to morality and to moral development. It is to a consideration of this that we will now turn.

4
Moral Values

Significance of a value-oriented life

Amongst all the living, human life is the most evolved creation in the universe. The excellence or superiority of human life as compared to other living beings can be easily identified. I will mention only one and perhaps the most important one. A man's life has to posses some meaning beyond mere self-preservation or existence. In case of other creatures their life is manipulated by man in his own interest. Man is the only such unique creation in this universe who is under certain parameters free to make his own destiny. Now if man has to make his destiny, the question of values (life) comes up. He has, naturally, to think what are to be the guiding-stars of his life-process. Of course he would like to live along with his family comfortably. But here the end of his life cannot come to a stop. Man is a social being. As such for every man "understanding of our fellow-beings is important. But this understanding becomes fruitful only when it is sustained by sympathetic feeling in joy and sorrow." Therefore "a positive aspiration and effort for an ethical-moral configuration of our common life is of over-riding importance." "Without ethical culture' there is no solution for humanity." Here we would like to add that this ethical culture will be manifest in one's behaviour-pattern including one's thought, feeling and action.

Einstien says "A man's ethical behaviour should be based effectively on sympathy, education and social ties and needs; no religious basis is necessary."[4] He, however, also says, emphasising the great need for devotion and strength of emotion "without which pioneer work in theoretical science cannot be achieved", that "it is cosmic religious feeling that gives a man such strength." He further says that from science (which deals with what is') one cannot deduct "the goal of human aspirations"....."And it is hardly necessary to argue that our existence and our activity acquire meaning only by the setting up of such a goal and of corresponding values." Any clarifying the whole matter he further adds "mere thinking cannot give us a sense of the ultimate and fundamental ends. To make these fundamental ends and valuations and to set them fast in the emotional life of the individual, seems to me precisely the most important function which religion has to perform in the social life of man." By religion Einstien does not mean institutionalised religion but what he calls "cosmic religious feeling" or what I would call a spiritual approach to life.

It is clear therefore that the values (the guiding-stars) for man, which provide the prime motivating force behind his thought, emotion and action, have to be moral and spiritual if the socio-cultural and spiritual life of man has to be such as brings peace, progress and welfare of both, the individual and the society. And this is precisely the reason why the modern society especially the Third World (including India) is worried about what is called value-deterioration or value-crisis from which they are suffering.

Has man deteriorated as man?

Here an important question arises. Is the deterioration of human values indicative of deterioration of human species as such? My own reply to this will be a firm 'No'. If we look at the total span of human history, we will find that the central strand running through it, with of course occasional ups and downs, is one of progress and evolution. And the future of man will also, without doubt, take an upward course. Aurobindonian concept of 'super-manhood', a still higher stage in man's evolution, is an indication of this. This view is also supported if we compare the professed values of modern society with those of the past. Today we talk of scientific temper, egalitarianism, freedom, social justice and secularism. In the medieval and ancient past, superstition and dogmatism in religion, hierarchical ordering of society, adherence to custom, emphasis on inherited station in life and exclusive and blind-fold faith in one's own institutionalised religion were the values generally professed by public at large.

It is obvious that the former life values are superior to the latter. This fact is a definite indication that there has been not only no deterioration of life-values but a qualitative improvement in them so far as man as man is concerned. Here one point ought to be clearly understood, that the values we are talking of are socio-ethical values, which we may call horizontal values. There is, however, a different category of values which are related to personality-traits and which I will call vertical values. Values of Indian culture are such values. They help a person in his self-development, that is moral upliftment, and as such cannot fall in the line of socio-ethical or horizontal values of which we have talked above in the context of modern, medieval and ancient societies. These vertical values are eternal in nature and hence relevant even today and will remain relevant in future also. They do not disturb our view that values advocated by modern man are superior to those advocated in the medieval or ancient past and man as man has not suffered any deterioration of life-values.

When I speak of this distinction between values, I realise that this distinction between so-called horizontal and vertical values is not fundamental. Both values are not only mutually supportive, but progress in one results in progress in the other and still up to a certain level of development this distinction does exist

The Diagnosis

If our conclusion is that present deterioration of values (and I confine the word values to their socio-ethical context), which is more marked in developing countries like India than elsewhere, is not directly traceable to the deterioration of man as man, what are the other factors that can be held responsible for it. Any meaningful effort at remedying the present situation presumes a correct diagnosis of the problem.

As regards the factors that mould the values of man, we find that there are four such factors. Every man has some inborn qualities which are the traits of his personality and temperament, in brief, of his individuality. This is one factor affecting man's values. We may call it his '*samskaras*' which are inborn. How one's inborn traits of personality and temperament are formed, is a question that touches philosophy, psychology and biology. It is not for us to discuss it here. It is enough for us to start with the assumption that man at the time of his birth is not a clean slate on which anything can be written by the forces he meets in life. It is along with his '*samskaras*' that these forces mould his personality-system and life values. These forces are family, school and broad-society. Family is the cradle where a man develops in his early age. The character of parents and other members of the family and the whole family ethos produces great effects on the child and the values he begins cherishing.

Regarding the forces of education in value-formation, much clear thinking is required. In the task of value-formation of students there are two distinct steps that have to be taken by an educational institution. One is making available to the students appropriate reading material e.g. biographies and views of great men who had before them certain values and ideals of life and who practised them against all odds and making all sacrifices including in some cases even their very life. The other and the most important thing to make education, as far as possible, an effective agency of value-orientation is the institutional ethos and the personal examples provided by the teachers. The institutional ethos is built up primarily by the values that the organisers and the heads of the institutions actually practise while running the institution.

The teachers and other workers working in the institution will naturally be influenced by the values practised by the organisers and their heads who, by personal examples, would be able to do a lot in developing a right type of institutional ethos. The students would also have a role to play. It is a wrong concept of 'education' to treat the students only at the receiving end and the faculty at the giving end. Educational process involves an exchange of personality at both the ends, the students on the one and the teacher on the other.

But the most important factor in value-formation is the social ethos, It works not only directly but also indirectly through family and education which we have discussed above.

Social ethos has two central questions to answer. One, what are the present ills of our modern social ethos? Two, what determines the social ethos of society?

Before discussing the first, let us discuss the second question. To begin with, let us understand what decides the general character of a society so that we have an insight into what determines the social ethos. Broadly speaking there can be three approaches on which will depend a society's general character:

(i) It is the quality of individuals in general that determines the basic quality of a society and, therefore, the social ethos. It is argued that if by and large the individuals are good and are men of integrity and character the whole society will bear this stamp and social ethos also will be conducive to values required for human welfare and progress. The structure and functioning of the total social pattern and inter-relationships existing there in will also be moulded accordingly.

(ii) The second approach is the socio-political approach according to which it is the elite, especially the political elite, that determines the social ethos of a society. This approach is summarised in the dictum '*yatha raja tatha praja*'(as the ruler so the people). This is also, in a way, a subjective view where not only totality of individuals without particular emphasis on any section of society but a particular section of society and its values of life determine the general character of society. Both these approaches have their share of truth but their role in determining social ethos is not very important

(iii) The third approach, which I would designate historicoscientific, is, in my view, the primary approach. According to this view society in its general character follows a law of historical evolution. There are certain basic needs (hunger, sleep, fear, sex) that man feels. History is, in a sense, a story of man's efforts to use all others - animate and inanimate nature - for the satisfaction of these human needs. And thus the general character of society is laid down. Science, culture, polity, economy, religion and philosophy, art, literature, in fact all knowledge and skill have their origin in these human needs.

So far as the specific question as to what determines the social ethos of a society is concerned, my answer would be that it is the cultural and economic aspects arising from the society's general character which determine the social ethos of society.

Coming to the first question regarding the ills of the social ethos of modern society my view is that these ills usually originate from its over-emphasis on wealth and power. And it is these ills which make modern society much less helpful than the pre-modern society for the formulation of desired values. This may on the face of it appear strange but in my opinion it is true. I will explain a little in detail as to why I think like this. In a pre-modern society there was a natural limit within which man's basic desires for wealth and power could have their play. The primary reason was that means of production were not much developed, variety of goods produced was much less and pulls of power were much less subtle and also much less needed in this simpler society. Compared to this in a modern society with its much more advanced industrialisation and scientific technological base, we find that vast vistas have been opened for the fulfilment of human desires for wealth and power. In discreet multiplication of wants created by profit-and-power-motivated production of a variety of goods leading to a complicated and away-from-nature life of not only ease and comfort which may make life more efficient and meaningful but of wasteful luxury that saps away human vitality, initiative and freedom - is a dominant characteristic of modern life. This makes modern life extremely materialistic and encourages human greed, unhealthy competition, jealousy, and power-consciousness, resulting in power-centralisation on the one hand and at the same time multiplying centres of power as well as countervailing power on the other. All this has given rise to intense competitive struggle and power-politics thereby dehumanising the whole social life and making it bereft of all moral values. Therefore, looking at the problem of values from an objective point of view we come to the conclusion that modern society and its social ethos suffer from a number of ills which are responsible for deterioration of values we are talking about.

Suggested Solution

Having discussed and diagnosed the problem of present deterioration of values, we have to consider how this situation can be remedied. Our above discussion leads us to conclude that for checking the present deterioration of values we have to work both on the subjective as well as the objective levels.

Taking into consideration the subjective level we have to place before individuals such socio-moral-spiritual values of life which can be acceptable to a modern man who claims to be rational and scientific in approach though he may not always act accordingly. We have also to remember that while advocating such values the cultural heritage of a people - so far as such a heritage is worth preservation - should not be uprooted. In fact, for modernity to take firm root in a people it is absolutely necessary that on the one hand modernity instead of being imposed should be adapted to one's cultural roots and on the other the indigenous culture should also get adjusted to modernity. Looking from this point of view I am of the opinion that generally, and in case of India particularly, values of Indian culture and of modernity, both being complementary or, better still, values of modernity being natural projections of Indian values, should be combined into an integrated whole.

I will mention the two value-systems to make it clear that such an integration of modern and Indian cultural values is possible. The values of Indian culture are: (i) Depth (which ultimately leads to a spiritual approach to life and includes a socio-ethical approach as an earlier stage in man's development);(ii) Totality (which implies taking an all-comprehensive view of life rather than a partial view); (iii) Tolerance/generosity (tolerance being negative and generosity being a positive quality); (iv) Receptivity to learn (indicating absence of ego and dynamic nature required for growth);(v) Keeping a balance or avoiding extremes (this indicates maturity of thought and self-discipline). These values do indicate that Indian Thought has achieved a very wide horizon and a great and dynamic vision. I may be pointed out that the four stage (*brahmacharya, grihastha, vanprastha and sanyas*) and four *purusharthas (dharma, artha, kama, maksha*) indicate not only the depth and totality of view of Indian thought but also the qualities of behaviour, (iii), (iv), (v) above, advocated by Indian culture. When we juxtapose these values of Indian culture with the modern values (i. scientific temper, ii. egalitarianism, iii. economic justice, iv. freedom, v. secularism) we are at once struck with the fact that the two systems of values are not only not contradictory but are complementary. In fact, the modern values are merely adaptations and extensions of the old. Thus 'Depth' and 'Totality' implies scientific temper which aims at a constant search for truth. 'Tolerance or generosity' would lead to egalitarianism, economic justice, freedom and secularism. Receptivity to learn and keeping a balance/avoiding extremes are behavioral modes that should be followed by any society as eternal rules of wisdom.

It is through education, formal and non-formal, as well as other possible means, the above integrated value-system, its rationale and its dire need for the present society should be explained not only to the youth but also to the adults and thus an attempt should be made to strengthen their moral fibre and moral will to check the growing deterioration of values.

Coming to the objective or social level, we have notices that the over-all impact the modern, centralised, scientific society produces is materialistic for the simple reason that it encourages beyond limit the importance of wealth and power. Wealth and power are at the root of all kinds of problems humanity is faced with. The form of modern technology is an important factor that helps produce this impact on modern society. Therefore if we want to have a social system that produces a balanced personality and provides an honourable, fairly comfortable and satisfying life to all with freedom guided by discipline and more or less harmony in individual and social life we should think of a social system where all wealth and power is almost evenly distributed and man is free and has an opportunity to think and work for wider and higher goals in individual and social life.

For this such a structural transformation of the present society is called for where freedom goes with discipline, justice goes with merit, right goes with duty, moral and spiritual values go with material welfare and the whole or the collectivity respects the part or the unit. Such a society in my thinking has to be :)i) a society not to be far-away from nature where the machine does not kill man's creativity;(ii) a decentralised system which alone can give a proper balance of freedom, security and leisure to man for his self-development and urges for wealth and power have a limited scope; and (iii) a proper orientation of modern technology (and therefore science) is made so that giganticism is minimised and man continues to remain master of the machine. How all this is to be achieved cannot be discussed here. I can only say that it is a matter for the scientists, technologists, social scientists and social revolutionaries to ponder over and decide.

One point more! I have pleaded for solving the problem of values both at the individual and the social or collective plane. Regarding the individual plane, however, it is argued,and with some justification, that when the total social ethos is not favourable and odds are against him, what can be done at the individual level? My reply to those who suffer from this psyche of helplessness would be "where collectivity fails the individual should assert." After all man is at the centre of all creation. He is the building-block as well as the builder of society. He has to imbibe a spirit of conviction, subbornness and perseverance, and dedication to stand up and take the challenge that Time has thrown at him. And who will be more fortunate than those who show courage to meet this call of Time in all earnestness and faith?

When a child is born, he is just a mass of protoplasm thrown into the lap of society. He is capable of responding to the external stimuli without being conscious of his responses. It is after a few months that he becomes conscious of a particular name assigned to him. At this stage he begins to respond through that 'self', though rudimentary. We can say that the foundation stone of his personality is laid as soon as the development of his 'self' begins. Later this self comes in contact with the outer reality more and more, and gradually his inner self also expands.

The story of the development of human personality is the story of constant interaction between self (the inner reality) and environment (the outer reality). Upto adolescence the outer reality influences the inner reality more. The inner reality perceives the outer reality, interprets it and responds to it, enriching itself in return. By the time one attains psychological maturity, the inner reality begins to influence the outer reality is equal share, if not more. In fact, the psychological maturity which usually goes hand in hand with physical maturity can sometimes follow it and sometimes even precede it. The psychological maturity is a function of the assertion of the 'inner reality' over the 'outer reality'. Whether the assertion of the `inner reality', over the `outer realitv' is socially desirable or not is another question. It is, therefore, the adolescent period which is most crucial for the development of inner reality or insight, though this process goes on throughout life. But it has been noted that in a large majority of people, the pattern of inner reality that develops upto the early twenties remains more or less stable all through their life. One develops a style of life in which one begins to feel secure. He begins to justify that very style of life and defends it with all his might. That is why we see that in most cases it becomes very difficult to bring a change in one's style of life after it has been established. A shirker after a certain age remains a shirker, and a worker, a worker. However, there are a few dynamic personalities who do change the style of life through growth in their inner reality.

At this juncture a very pertinent question arises. What are the pillarson which the citadel of 'style of life' is built? The pillars are the 'values' which develop through an interaction of needs, perception, emotion, sentiments and attitudes. A value is well-defined as an endeavour which satisfies need system, psychological as well as physiological. Almost all human beings have the same physiological needs,, but they differ in their psychological needs; hence difference in their values and styles of life. It is here that through the practical strategy of 'catching young' the family and educational system play their crucial role to develop a set of values useful to the individual as well as to society. The clash between the individual and social aims of education is created by vested interests which worship individual even at the cost of society. For ensuring happiness and development, the two should not be at variance but should supplement one another.

Unfortunately what we find in our educational system today is not so much the clash between the two sets of values, but an utter neglect of value system - the polestar of education. The tributaries to education like sociology, psychology and history have their own clearcut standpoints on values. Psychology, being a science of human nature, is analytic in approach. It can lay out a schemata of development of a particular value and assess it. Which value preferably? This is not their job. For their development and measurement. Sociology and history have clearly evaded the problem and declared themselves as 'normlers' disciplines. Sociology aims at a dry and scientific analysis of the social processes and institutions. History aims at an impassioned enquiry into the past. Who shall give direction to education by charging it with values? Evidently he onus falls on the shoulders of philosophy. But of late, education has stopped to recognize the authority of philosophy as a galvanizing discipline. The result is the present chaos. For valuelessness in education is synonymous with lifelessness.

The influence of behaviourism, the most typical Western School of Psychology on education is very pernicious. The 'purpose' is no more 'purpose'. The 'aim' is no more 'aim'. They are now 'goals'. Reward and punishment are now 'reinforcements'. Character, sentiments and values are obsolete terms in the present day texts on education. They have all been simplified as Conditioned Response, S-R bond. It is strongly believed that man is only physiological man. There is no psychological man behind or inside the physicological man. The psychological man is a phantom, an illusion, a figment of imagination, a dummy construct and what not. Man is a very complex computer. Where is the place for values, sentiments and character in such a paradigm? The tragedy is that our educationists are innocently supporting such a model when the West, where it originated, is getting disillusioned with it. In spiritual India, one is disgusted to find a question in one M.Ed. paper in some university as:

> "All the learning and development of man can be explained through a mechanistic model without bringing in the irrel evant concept of self". Discuss this statement in the light of the contribution of Skinner and Hull.

It is well recognized that the models of learning based on behaviouristic thought are more suitable for teaching certain tricks to circus animals, for imparting information of for explaining phobias. They do not lead us to the development of noble sentiments like patriotism, self-respect and altruism or to values of Truth do not explain the development of insight and functions of creativity.

In my view, the valuelessness in education is due to the lack of a clear philosophy on the part of the Government of India. To take only one example, the age old value of Indian culture, *assimilation*, can be imparted without regimentaion. We have been believing: *aa no bhadra kratvo yantu vishvatah* (Let all good things from all sides converge) and also that there can be many different paths to the great Reality. All must be respected. But where is the fear in declaring them and weaving them into the web of education? In the name of secularism which in fact meant respect for all religions based on non-violence and non-exploitation and not irreligiousness or non-religiousness we have thrown the baby out with the bath water. Hinduism has the concept of unity of all religions, but in the absence of reciprocity, you cannot clap with one hand. The communal orgy of 1947 led our leaders to believe that religion is at the base of this bloodshed. May be so, but the remedy is not giving up religion altogether, but to check persons from politicising it. We do not touch certain things even though convinced of their utility, lest some one brands us as rank communal. The fear of truth speaking is at the root cause of valuelessness. It is not without reason that in the *Gita* (Chapter XVI) where the divine virtues are mentioned, the very first is fearlessness. What we see around us today is an all pervasive fear leading to a 'psychoric unconcern' on the part of our enlightened citizens. Even if we have 'passive' morality (I am content that at least I am honest) that becomes defunct in the absence of active morality. (I must not tolerate dishonesty around me). A vigilant observation of people in trains and buses and at other public places shall lend support to the above contention.

The values can be taught through lectures, text books, epics and several co-curricular activities and the young mind does catch them. But when he finds elders and leaders in the society going the other way, he suffers from moral conflicts. These conflicts may turn him into a morally debased person or a hypocrite who bears the facade of morality and does everything immoral. Still others may justify immorality vehemently moral values. They suffer, and in their suffering they are condemned as 'fools', 'maladjusted,' 'idealists' etc. On whom should this blame be laid? Evidently, the blame should be laid on the elders and leaders of society, for they do not provide good examples to the youngsters when they try to test the tenets of their moral values. At least here example is better than precept. If morality cannot be caught, it also cannot be taught.

Albert Camus once experimented with inculcation of moral values through teaching. He encouraged students to write down an essay on 'Truthfulness'. The best essay was written by the biggest liar of the class. He further said that if the purpose of education is merely to impart information and skills then thanks to the present day teaching technology, perhaps an idiot can teach another idiot calculus.

In the self-exploratory period of adolescence, the individual is in search of a hero from his immediate environment with whom he identifies and imbibes his values and character through the process of symbiosis. Formal teaching and discussions become relevant only when some good example is available to the youth.

'What is heard is audible. What is seen is visible. Therefore what is desired is desirable.'

See how trickily the phrase 'What ought to be desired is desirable' is distorted to support valuelessness.

Values not only help a man in self evaluation, but also in self-drive. An educated man without values has thoughts which never flow into action. "The thoughts of intellectuals are like arrows in a quiver which scratch the back but never fly." (Mao-Tse-Tung.) Bundestag (German Constituent Assembly) in 1933 declared that "Germans have been humiliated not because they are under-educated, but because they are over-educated, without values."

Values impart significance to life and meaning to death. WIthout values, life becomes a series of meaningless events, and death a shattering experience.

The question of human values has received great significance in the context of what justice Krishna Iyer has called "the world drought of human values caused by corrupt counter-culture and mafia in power(and) can be arrested only by sublime principles,"[1] He has stressed the need for developing a positive culture of mass action through non-violance and civil disobedience by blending revolutionary urge for change with Gandhian principles. Who can bring about the cultural revolution when the intelligentsia and the judicial-minded people themselves are jittery and uncertain and the "mugging mafia and the affluent lobby are vaccinated against law and the terrorism of the law and the lawless destroy the nation's integrity"? Such questions arise in the minds of all right-thinking people who feel utterly helpless in the prevailing situation.

However, we need not feel that desperately as there is always a silver lining in the dark clouds. Human values seem to be receiving the attention of those who may happen to be the saviours of tomorrow. This involves deeper understanding of human evolution and the limitations of human mind so that the 'sublime principles' underlying human values may have the lasting impact necessary for bringing about change in thought and conduct.

Limits of Understanding by Reason

Mass action motivated by enthusiasm is often misled as it is uninformed. Unquestioned eulogy of ideals often results in their being observed only through verbalism and lack of corresponding conviction deep rooted into the consciouness. Hence the need for rational understanding cannot be overemphasized. This brings us to our real predicament in understanding valves through reasoning since our mind-the only instrument we have for knowing-is inherently imperfect as it is capable of knowing only partially. What we understand of life through analysis and synthesis of the observed phenomena is only a part of the totality that it represents. In this process of knowing the 'gestalt'view becomes inoperative and the burden of reasoning becomes to define what is itself indefinable.

Therefore, in the quest of knowing all our knowledge remains but only tentative since the very nature of rational knowledge is 'contingent'. There can be no absoluteness of values at the plane of rationality as we can get only relative aspect thereof. "One man's meat is another's poison", so goes the saying. Emotions and intellections comprise our mental activity and hence the world is to us as it is to none else and, therefore, we have various philosophies of life. What we understand is dependent upon where we stand and which way we look at life. The organizing capacity of the mind unfolds to us meanings of stimuli that we receive through our senses. Bertrand Russel called it "Perception data" in ordering reality. Its correctness, however, will depend on the degree to which it corresponds to the facts of life. A philosophy which corresponds to all aspects of life and explains everything reasonably well will be perfectly correct. But a perfectly correct philosophy of life is just not available and this sets a serious limitation on our rational way of knowing. Yet the redeeming feature of rationality is that it can prepare the way for unfolding understanding of life at higher planes of reality.

II

Evolution of Consciousness As the Spiritual Way of Knowing

The phenomena of life, subtle aspects of knowing open to us heightening our capacity to know and act according to our knowledge to acquired. Scientific discoveries may be said to be the result of this level of knowing, which the eminent psychologist. Bruner has designated as intuitive leaps in thinking' facilitating inventive knowledge possessed by the genius. Yet there is another level of knowing that goes well beyond the intuitive level and we prefer to call it the 'spiritual way of knowing' possessed by the super genius or the mystic, which may be witnessed once in a millennium or perhaps more. In his recent studies Prof. Bruner examines the nature of man as a species and the forces that have shaped and continue to shape his humanity. He poses three questions and seeks their answers from the evolutionary standpoint in epistemology. His enquiry remains non-committal as to the question of genesis but his quest for evolution can be termed as generic. The three questions posed by him are as follows:

1. What is human about human beings?
2. How did they get that way?
3. How can they be made more so?"

Prof. Bruner arrives at the conclusion that man has the distinctive capability as discernible continuity in his evolution and calls it his adaptability which is achieved by the vehicle of culture. He holds man's urge to explain his world as the distinctiveness and potentiality for further evolution. Obviously, the nature of man's world view, whether formulated in religion or science, depends upon and is constrained by the nature of his own evolution.

In the scientific field we find its expression in the lead for technological acceleration and control of the forces of cosmos; and in the field of religion and spirituality it refers to man's ascendance and control over his own nature and opening up new vistas of knowledge unexplorable by science. A man's consciousness may be said to be independent of any institutionalized religion from the standpoint of spiritual evolution.

Spiritualiy, on the other hand, has the intended role of providing values that give the technological civilization its moral character and moral intellect, which is today left far behind. What is at the root of contemporary horror is not nuclear capabililties wrought by science and technology, but rather the moral intellect and moral character of society to make use thereof for its own good. Unless individuals develop their own system of values to live by and die by, if necessary, there is no possibility of developing the kind of culture which can act as an antidote to the prevailing counter-culture and mafia when gross injustice and grievous negation of values is witnessed and the nation becomes submissive; when the leaders of the day become unmindful of the masses and the classes chase pleasure, position, and shameless wealth; and the intelligentsia is plunged into deep depression and inaction.

In the process of his evolution man has developed certain values as there are always forms of legitimacy and sanction that define the limits of possible behaviour; but there has always been the need to redefine these values in order that the middleman and the political peddlars in religion no longer remain the traffickers. These values are the bounds set by society, and do not depend upon the individual's choice. For example, one cannot commit theft legally, one cannot ignore friends with impunity although the law has nothing to do with it. A society has a world view, a way of defining what is 'real' and what is 'good' and what is 'possible' which creates questions of values without which it is highly unlikely that human society would have been what it is like today.

What Prof. Bruner has concluded can be said to be the innovative urge of man which has given him an accelerator to control his environment and go beyond the immediate need for adaptation in the process of his evolution. This view explains far more and we gain understanding by applying it to further levels of human evolution, which do not stop short with man. Why should it?

Our view explains human evolution in terms of spiritual unfoldment where it no longer remains a blind force of nature, but becomes a purposeful activity. It gives us a better understanding even of biological evolution and we know better why way of knowing' since it is the evolution of consciousness which unfolds an understanding of the phenomena of life and also its values from the standpoint of the world view it presents.

The presence and pressure of 'conscious energy' trying to manifest itself is the urge for biological evolution. As the evolution proceeds, we find gradual emergence of mind from almost non-existence to an ever increasing complexity and dominance. It is the emergence of active will (conation) and the growth of his far-reaching capabilites that constitue the distinguishing discernibility of man from the preceeding levels of evolution; and that make him not only the controller of his environment but also the master of his human destiny which truly would make man human rather than the technological acceleration.

The scientific advances man has made and the control that he exercises on the cosmos is the result of his 'conscious energy' unfolding the realms of understanding environment and controlling it to his benefit when it is focused externally in the explorations of science. When the same 'conscious energy' is directed inwardly, focused on the 'central point' of human existence, there is the emergence of spiritual evolution. Consideration of human values then receives the ascendance that it deserves. This view bestows a meaning upon human life and gives value to all human values that explain what is human about human beings and how they can rise still to further level of evolution that awaits them, namely their spiritual evolution.

Conscious mind is but a rung in the ladder of this process which proceeds on the consciousness of the 'Ultimate Reality'. The proof for this viewpoint is in the lives of many saints and sages (the scientists of spiritual evolution) in all countries and climes cutting across all religions and cultures and contributing to the spiritual heritage of man through the ages.

This evolution does not divide the world into less evolved or more evolved beings as does the "technological acceleration causing misery and socio-political oppression. This view holds the possibility of unification of human experiences and helps in the attainment of acceleration of our spiritual evolution and enter into consciousness which is Divine.

and developed the philosophy and science of evolution of consciousness from which anyone can profit. We are launched on unfamiliar ground if we want to have a higher view of life; and are required to outgrow our present consciousness and shall have to depend on the understanding of those who have already outgrown their mental consciousness and reached the supramental level. We can use reason here, but not misuse it as understanding of higher values of life comes by living them and not by merely debating about them.

III

The Ultimate Reality and expansion of consciousness

To understand the value of human values on a spiritual plane we have to understand the ultimate reality of life in its various aspects. The human mind is staggered when it thinks of Infinity. The bounds of our consciousness are capable of vast expansion when we come to know 'Becoming' more fully and reach a level of consciousness where there is no longer any transformation. It is a state of pure 'Being'. It is a positive state of existence, though different from the phenomenal one. This aspect of reality is called 'Being' and we can experience it when we grow into a higher state of consciousness. It is called *Sachidananda* - the absolute *Brahman* - by Ramakrishna Pramahansa who declared that one can reach it: and we quote: "But can one not see God as formless reality? Of course, one can. But not, if one has the slightest trace of worldliness. The sages of the olden times renounced everything and then contemplated on *sachidananda*, the Indivisible *Brahman*."

Again he said: "When the Godhead is thought of as creating, preserving, and destroying it is known as the personal God, *Saguna Brahman*, or the Primal Energy, *Adya Shakti*. Again, when it is thought of as beyond three *gunas*, then it is called the Attributeless. Reality, *Nirguna Brahman*, beyond speech and thought, this is the Supreme *Brahman, Paratahman*". (*The Gospel of Sri Ramakrishna* by Swami Nikhilananda, Sri Ramakrishna Math, Madras, 1974.) We thus launch our march in human values from a state of 'Becoming' or the changing aspect of consciousness to a state of 'Being or the changeless one and in the process transcend the three *gunas*. For one can not attain the *Brahman* unless one transcends the three *gunas.* In the *Srimadbhagvadgita* the former is called "*Kshra Purusha*" and the latter "*Akshara Purusha*", and we quote:

Dvavimau purusha loke ksharakshar eva cha
Ksharah sarvani bhutani kutestha-akshar uchyate. (Ch. 15/16)

(In this changing and changeless world there are two aspects of *Purusha.* Of them all beings are destrucible, but the one Being is beyond destruction).

Some might see a contradiction in the two levels, and 'Becoming' may be seen as unreal on the analogy of the dream world; while others might see no necessity of the second pestulate 'Being' - in the unfoldment of consciousness. However, such a contradiction is a mere appearance since Being is the necessary basis of Becoming and Becoming is impossible without the support of Being (Sri Aurobindo: *The Synthesis of Yoga*). The phenomenal reality is not possible without changeless stay. The Ultimate Reality must be transcendental with Being and Becoming as its two aspects capable of maintaning them yet something beyond and above the two aspects which is callled by Ramakrishna as *Parambrahman.* The transcendental Ultimate Reality is the Supreme - the Love Divine - and the world of ours and the numerious universes and the various states of mind and energy are all its manifestations. All have sprung from it; and all are subsumed in it as the *Upansihad* proclaims:

Ishavasyamidam sarva Yarkichita jagatyam jagat. Isha.
Sarva Khalvidam brahman. —Chand. 14/2

(All this manifested world is permeated by God; and there is nothing besides Him. All this world is verily God).

When one has reached this state in one's spiritual evolution, all knowing ceases; and one is filled with the experience beyond description and calls out, 'Eureka....Eureka..." The value of human values lies in fortifying an aspirant in his onward march to this transcendental state of Being. This we know from the spiritual experience of saints and devotees as enshrined in the scriptures; and that can not be dismissed lightly. They testify to different types of experiences which only prove that the divine is Infinite and is capable of manifesting itself variously.The supreme Divine as the basic unit of evolution is called "conscious energy"representing both the aspects of being and becoming. What is that which evolves? What is that which remains there throughout, and which assumes various forms? God-consciousness- Supreme Divine- must be there as a potentiality in the basic unit of evolution, or how else could it be manifested? It is testifed in the *Ishavasyopanishad* as follows;

Aum purnamadah purnamidam purnatpurnamudachyate
purnasya purnmadaya purnamevavashishyate

(The Supreme divine is full *Sachidananda*, omniscient and indivisible. This manifested world is also taken to be likewise as it is from the full and complete entity that the like entity emerges).

Ramakrishna too testified this in these words: "All is the manifestation of God's power. No one can do anything without this power. God exists in all Beings as the all pervasive power; but the manifestations of his power are different in different beings" . Again he said; "As long as a man has not realized God, he thinks he is free. It is God himself who keeps this error in man. Otherwise sin would have multiplied. Man would not have been afraid of sin, and there would have been no punishment for it. But the attitude of one who has realized God is- I am the machine and thou art the Operator. I am the house and thou art the in In-dweller. I am the engine and thou art the Engineer. O Lord, I do as thou doest through me. I speak as thou speakest through me."

The involuted Supreme is the basic unit of evolutionary process and the 'conscious energy' represents the mind-matter paradigm. They are the two inseparable aspects of the same reality. The conscious energy is gradually mounting up, as evolution proceeds, and nearing its perfect unfoldment-the attainment of the Divine Consciousness-the *Sat, Chit, Ananda. 'Sat'* means the power to act, to transform and to resist. As the soul evolves it becomes more and more powerful. *'Chit'* means knowledge. The capacity of the soul to know enhances in evolution. *Ananda* is bliss, lasting peace. The higher a soul in evolution, the higher the joy which it can experience.

IV

Enlightened Socio-Political Structure and Transformation of Values

This brings us to a consideration of the implications of spiritual evolution of society in terms of human values. Social environment is indispensable for human evolution. A larger field for the evolution of human consciousness than the individual and the family comes into focus. It helps the growth of human emotions and the spirit of self sacrifice and a sense of responsibility comes into play that enhances social security.

The individual learns to identify himself with the larger humanity and outgrows his lower nature. There develops in the course of evolution a natural consciouness like the group-soul, although every individual remains unique as far as his own evolution goes. While evolving, the group soul modifies the national consciousness to an appreciable degree until the dawn of wisdom consciousness and the higher nature of man becomes powerful.

Man is best with baffling problems on account of the dominance of his lower nature. He exploits the social and political institutions in harnessing his selfish designs and thereby causes a great deal of misery to other. And so do the nations. Perfection in social and political structure is an imposssibility with imperfect individuals constituting them and they reflect increasingly various forms of suppression of human values. Every 'ism' and 'cracy' suffers from its drawbacks and the political structure that man has assiduously developed stands disintegrated. The very survival of humanity is increasingly at stake. Nations make pious declarations of human rights but frequent deadlocks are witnessed in what is called 'negotations for maintaining world peace and security'.

The present day level of humanity is wrought by the magnification of the lower nature of man and there was never such a time and never such intense man-made suffering, although evil had been witnessed in all ages and had to be subdued. Today man is going down to even below the beastly level in his own self-degradation. The beast kills other animals for the satisfaction of his hunger-the need for survival. But man indulges in it for the pride of his power or the possession of pelf and for his avarice. Evil in man is getting vehemently and deliberatively effective. However, there is a certain strength as well in this all pervasive madness for mundane indulgence and we can not condemn the present humanity and its helplessness outright as we stand at the threshold of the dawn of wisdom consciousness. It is common knowledge that the sun glows brighter moments before it sets and the rising sun comes on the horizon only with the twilight.

The final day, however, is yet far off for the present humanity to arise where this higher stage of evolution will demand a more refined and impartial social and political structure as also will transform human nature and values in a complete metamorphosis. Then we will have an awakened humanity, an age of innocence inspired by *satya, dharma, shanti, prema, and ahimsa.* Until then we must wait patiently and work silently for the hastening of this process.

Wisdom is the consciousness of a distinctly different order rather than what is conveyed in the worldly sense of the term. It is the knowledge of Being and Becoming. The reasoning mind has to undergo a laboured process of induction or deduction in order to know, whereas wisdom enables one to identify oneself with everthing and every setting in an intimate knowledge without any possibility of error. The earliest manifestions of wisdom consciousness are the flawless flashes of intuition. This instuition is in centrast with its counterpart wrought through reasoning and is of a higher order emanating from the consciousness beyond time and space, where man is released from both good and evil. At the dawn of this wisdom consciousness there is no need and use for appropriation or self-aggrandizement; and all turmoil begins to settle down. The principle of desire, a characteristic of the preceding level of evolution, is replaced by an aspiration for the higher values which make a man Super-man. Order returns to life with lust, anger, avarice, hatred, envy, and pride and all other baser attributes of human nature being outgrown; and one proclaims: "*Manush deh dhare ko dharma ka bhai. Jo hari na mile to ka bhayo paye prabhutani.*" (What of donning human body! What of pride of power and pelf if Godhold is not attained!)

The reasoning mind, not understanding the nature of this higher consciousnees, even doubts whether such a state of existence would ever be possible. But when wisdom comes, reason gives in recognizing it to be superior to it. The various levels of consciousness are cleansed,as it were, with the dawn of wisdom consciousness, setting up new notes of vibrations and clearing away all that cannot vibrate in accord with it-*Prana* is cleansed of zest for pleasure and desire principle of pride and egoism all disappear, and a general refinement and vivification comes about in the whole'being'. Man stands as a *deva* (god), may even greater than *deva*,blessed with Wisdom-the final level of evolution.

V

Divine love and the pledge to redeem mankind

Evolution is meaningless if it brings us no nearer the truth as explained above. So long as we believe we are approaching the Truth we are reconciled to the activities of the world for the realization of this end; and the world is not taken as complete in itself but rather as a 'gap between two miseries' as Nanak exclaimed - "*Nanak dukhia sub sansar*"; and as Patanjali reiterated: "*Klaishmulam jagatah.*" The unfoldment of wisdom sets the stage of the final consummation of human evolution the Love Divine. The transcendental Supreme - the Father and Mother, the Eternal Beloved is envisioned. His Grace has descended and the silence of the Ocean of Infinite peace has drowned in all pervading rhythm of Divine Bliss. The man of God-consciousness becomes the Bliss Himself. The principle which is responsible for this consummation is Love which gradually grows to fullness, "God is Love, Love is God." Without Love the Divine can not be realised. It was for the love of man that God gave. His only begotten son who suffered at the cross for the sins of man.

As one needs eyes to see, ears to hear, one must have Love to see and realize the Divine. Wisdom can bestow miraculous powers, as it does and Patanjali has described them in the Vibhuti Pad of his *Yoga-sutra* at length, but not the vision of the transcendental Godhood. Love is absolutely indispensable.

What is love......? Ramakrishna lamented the people who ignore this question and answered it in the same vein when he said:"The spiritual wisdom of the worldly people is seen only on rare occasions. It is like the flame of a candle. No, it is rather like a single ray of the sun passing through a chink in a wall. Worldly people changt the name of God, but there is no real zeal behind it. It is like the children swearing by God, having learnt the word from the quarrels of their aunts." And again he said:"worldly people have no grit. If they succeed in an undertaking, it is all right' but if they do not, it scarcely bothers them at all. When they need water they begin to dig a well. But as soon as they strike a stone, they give up the digging and begin at another place. Perhaps they come to a bed of sand. Finding nothing, they give up that place too. How can they succeed in getting water unless they continue to dig persistently where they started?" (*The Gospel of Sri Ramakrishna*).

Human love is a vibration of the emotional body, a limited reaction of the mind. It has the aspect of self-giving as well as infatuation, and even madness; and therefore, binds down man to worldly attachments, however painful they might be. Human love is only a reflection, at its best, of the Divine Love on the emotional level. Love Divine manifests only when the control of the wisdom consciousness is fully established in the entire being of a person. It keeps reason steady and straight and helps in the transcendence of 'ego'. Divine Love is a joy in Itself. It seeks no fulfilment. The Lord, Love, and the Lover become a triune unity the three-in-one. Love-*sadhana* is really a tremendous force. Like a fresh conflagration, it burns away the dross, awakening wisdom and speeding up remarkably the entire process of evolution. In the Love-*sadhana*, the aspirant is accepted without any pre-conditions and Divine love is kindled in him, and it flourishes according to the intensity of his aspiration and yearning. *Tapas, Tyaga* and such other qualifications of the *Gyana-marga* are the results that are attained during the process and indicate the progress of the aspirant.

Love is the '*chit*' aspect of the evolving conscious energy. When the spark enters the flame, it becomes identical with it.

A man of Love has no consciousness apart from God-consciousness. God is omniscient, and so are those who are God-conscious. The man of Love lives in the Divine and the Divine lives in him. He is filled with compassion, and is a friend of all.

VI

Human Values and attainment of *'Sthitpragya'* (Equanimity)

Satya, dharma, shanti, prema, and *ahimsa* are the constituent postulates of one Absolute. Truth on the human plane which are sought to transform the human nature from a state of its declension and degradation of its *dharmic* existence. It is not the dharma that declines, but the practice of *dharma*: and therefore, through a revival of human values it is sought to be re-instated into its pristine glory, and declared by Tulsidasa:

Jab jab hohi dharma kee hani
Barahi adharma dhara akulani
Tab tab dhari manuj sharira
Harahu bhar bhav bhaya pira.

(Assurance to Mother earth and other Gods by *Vishnu Bhagwan.*) In the *Srimadbhagvadgita* the same principle is reiterated thus:

Yada yada hi dharmasya glanirbhavati bhararta
Abhyutthanamdharmasya tadatamanum srajamyaham. 4.7

Paritranaya sadhunam vinashay cha dushkritum
Dharmasansthapanarthaya sambhavami yuge yuge. 4.8

(As and when there is declension of the *dharmic* living, O Arjuna? I incarnate for the re-establishment of *dharma.* For the removal of sufferings of the righteous and the elimination of the unrighteousness, I reincarnate from age to age.)

There is accordingly a constant influx of redeming energy manifested into the world by the Love Divine or the Divine Will. This redeeming energy constitutes the activities of the pure souls as witnessed in their careers. Their life is their message and a continuous mission. There is an eternal reincarnation of God, so to say, directly intervening into the affairs of this would whenever it goes wrong or deviates from ethical and moral values.

Most of the people agree on things that are right or wrong and both the educated and not so educated learn most of their ethics from living. But there is more to ethics as Dr. Albert Schweritzer holds about it when he says:"In a general sense, ethics is the name we give to our concern for good behaviour. We feel an obligation to consider not only our own personal well being, but also that of others and of human society as a whole."

Honesty is the beginning point of all ethical behaviour - one can not be ethical without being honest. When we leave honesty out of ethics we get hypocrisy, an insidious and pervasive form of dishonesty. Young people can not learn human values when the actions of their parents and leaders in society contradict their practice. Hypocrisy thrives when being ethical is equated with being nice. One often gains advantages by agreeing with all sides and tabling one's own convictions about values. The only antidote is to have courage and the ability to take the alternative course following the two continuing obligations: i.e., to benefit others, and to do no harm to others. Good begets good, no matter what the reason for doing it. It is the law of the universe; each thing creates its kind. A continuing erosion that attacks the full range of human values in a society can not withstand for long the courage of honest people however few in number.

How one can get this courage and honesty of one's convictions is a matter of living life itself in a manner far too different than it is generally held by people. History stands testimony of the life and events of Living Saviours in the world who provided such examples and taught men ways of righteous living. *Satya, dharma, shanti, prema*, and *ahimsa* are such value guidelines that transcend all culturally held notions. Having goodness is not nearly so easy nor so culturally acceptable as having religion; and therefore value standards, although common to all major religions, need not be necessarily contingent upon a belief in any of them as traditionally held. Ethical values precede and lead to law. The ethics that is embodied into the law is usually based on the morality of the majority. When the morality of the majority operates at a lower level than the law, it requires great courage for someone to set the trend in the right direction.

The human values not only provide for postulates along which spiritual evolution is facilitated, but they help us in ushering a new era transforming the entire socio-political system for the material well being of the society as a whole by broadening our concerns. It is in the practice of human values that a society can lay secure in peace without causing social disintegration and disharmony. In this context it is denied that social conflicts and tensions are basic to human nature, but reaffirmed that they arise only due to the baser elements in human nature and the corresponding drawbacks in the social system. Hence the need to rectify at the two levels - elevation of human nature, and perfection of socio-political system.

Truth is the basis of *dharma*, and *dharma* is indestructible. So truth and *dharma* are unchangeable by human connivance or convenience. The true interpretation of *dharma* is to ask for the well-being of the entire human community, where there is no place for selfishness, pride of power and pelf, and envy; where wars may be waged but only for the protection of rights of others and not for self-aggrandizement. Wars can not be avoided in the reality of human situations, and the power of battle has to be recognized in the true interpretation of *ahimsa;* for it is not the militarily weak who can practise *ahimsa* but the strong and the powerful who can commend its practice for others as well while themselves establishing an example. This interpretation is, however, to be distinguished from the contemporary declarations of peace at the world forums today, since they are characterized by their hollowness as can be seen from preparations for further deadlier nuclear arsenal, and the human distress caused on account of them in the world economy.

When the fire of unrighteous living spreads so much, as it does today, the righteous living contained in the dignity of labour and of human personhood as seen in what Tagore acclaimed 'work is worship" has to triumph; and we must constantly be engaged in a crusade against what brings about a state of inequalilty and disorder on account thereof in the society. "Hate the sin, and not the sinner" is the greatest revolutionary fervour endangered by the principle of *ahimsa* than any progressive revolutionary ideology can generate among the masses for civil and political action to rejuvenate society along human values that are needed to sustain it.

Dharma is related to *dharana* which means wearing, like clothes. Everthing in the universe has its *dharma*, so also every human being, which is the very core of existence. For example, water is to flow, fire to burn and consume, the magnet to attract and to draw unto itself. So has man his own *dharma*. This *dharma* is said to be the *swadharma* in the *Gita* and is eulogised thus:

Shreyansvadharma vigunoh pardharmatsvanushthitat
Svadharme nidhanam shreyah pardharmo bhayavah. (3.35.)

(To try to live in the manner of the others' '*dharma*' is worse than even to be ill-adapted to one's own. It is better ot suffer ignominy in one's own *dharma* than donning others' *dharma* as it is fraught with dangers.)

This explains that *dharma* is something akin to every person's way of life and that there is no superior or inferior aspect involved in it: and hence it is the progressive evolution that characterizes the onward march of man in the scale of human values. Man is said to be a rational being having as his distinguishing features from the other levels of evolution described as follows:

Ahar-nidrabhaya-maithumam cha
Samanyametatpashubhinaranam
Dharmohi teshamdhiko vishesho
Dharmena hinah pashubhih samanah.

-Neetishatak Ch. 17 / 17.

(Eating, drinking and having sex relations are common behaviours among man and animals, but *dharma* is the distinguishing feature of man. Without *dharma* as the additional quality, man is no different from animals.)

And again:

Yesham na vidya na tapo na danam
Gyanam na shilam na guno na dharmam
Te martyuloke bhuvi bharbhutah
Manushyarupena mragashchrantri. (Bhartri, *Neeti*, 13).

(Those, who do not have any of the qualities mentioned as *vidya, tapas*, charity, wisdom, humility, *guna* (good attributes) *dharma* , are the people as burden on this earth and therefore are no better than animals.)

A steady adherence to *dharma* leads to truth in all its aspects, thirteen of which are described as follow:

Satyam cha samta chaiv damashchaiv na sanshayah
Amatsaryam kshama chaiv hreestitiksha anusuyata
Tyago dhvanmatharyatyam dhritisheh satatam daya
Ahims chaiv rajendra satyakarastrayodashan.
(*M.Bha.Shan.* 162/8-9).

(Truth has these thirteen aspects, O king!Impartiality, selfcontrol, lack of envy, tolerance, forbearance, humulity, lack of fault-finding, charity, contemplation, righteousness, *dharma*, graciousness, *ahimsa*.)

The Vedas are the root of all dharma - "*Vedokhilo dharma mulam*" - and they belong to those who desire to practise it. Vedas have laid down the principles whereby one can distinguish between right and wrong. These principles belong to all mankind: and all ideas, laws, customs and codes are to be judged on the twin points of intention and consequence,which are embodied even in modern jurisprudence. *Dharma* is enshrined in that which is pure, borne out of *prema*, is based on truth. For example, the haste to secure an immediate advantage has to be curbed so that later advantage may be more lasting: the benefits to the individual have to be given up in favour of the community, country, or mankind. That which does not inflict harm to others is right and is *dharma*, as Tulsidasa proclaimed:

Parhit saris dharma nahi bhai
Parpira sama nahi adhamai.

Dharma is to make the thought, word and deed march in harmony,. What we do depends on what we are; and what we are depends upon what we do as the two aspects are interdependent.

Doing right makes things easier. And habits grow into consciousness. Society, then, becomes for us the veritable field for *sadhana*, the place for our *seva* and worship as the Lod inheres in it. It is in this context that Ravindranath Tagore remarked:"Work is worship."The *dharmic* way of life is to do as we speak, and speak as we feel; and we must not play false to our own conscience. *Dharma* trains us to be secure in equanimity and one becomes a *sthitpragya* established in one's own Reality. A *sthitpragya* is no different from the Divine Himself as it is said : "*atmavid atmaiv bhavati*", and "*Brahmavid brahmaiv bhavti*": since there is no difference between *atmabhav* and *aksharbrahman* as we have discussed earlier. One becomes a *sthitpragya* after having outgrown the duality of human existence

Arjuna enquired as to who is a *sthitpragya* and the Lord replied in the *Gita* as follows:

Prajnati yada kamansarvanpartha manogatan
Atmanyevatmana tushtah sthitpragyastdochyate. Ch. 2/55

Duhkheshvnudvignamanah sukheshu vigatsprha
Vitraghbhayakrodhah sthitdhirmuniruchyate. Ch. 2/56

yah sarvatranbhishnehstatprapya shubha shubham
Nabhinandanti na dveshti tasya praina prati hita. 57

Yada sanharate chayam kurmo anganiva sarvsah
Indiyanindriyarthebhyastsya pragya pratisthita 58

(When one gives up all desires and is contented within one's own *atmic*. Reality, such a one is called *sthitpragya*. When one is not distressed by miseries and misfortunes and is not envious of the pleasures of life; when one is free from the shackles of fear and anger, such a sage is *sthitpragva*. When one is detached from every thing and experience - good or bad - one who is neither attrated by the desirable and the benignant, nor is repulsed by the undesireable and the malignant, such a person is a *sthitpragya*. As the tortoise withdraws its limbs from all directions, similarly when one withdraws from the objects and attractions of the senses, then one's *pragya* is established in the Supreme.)

"*Pragya*" is said to be discerning faculty and is drawn from its closeness to the *atmic* experience rather than the intellectual process of descrimination and discretion which indeed get their nourishment from it and are called the higher levels of intellectual judgement. It would, therefore, be seen that the spiritual consciousness is *dharma* as the sensous pursuits lead to *adharma.* It is in this context that the four types of `*purusarthas*' namely, *dharma, artha, kama, moksha* - are preceded by *dharma* and their ultimate goal is said to be the attainment of liberation; *moksha,* and verily *kama* and *artha,* are not intended to be the summum bonum of life; but only the means to the other two goals of life. "Earn by means of *dharma* and enjoy the pleasures of life in the manner so as to reach *moksha*" - is what is enjoined upon in these for `*purushartha'* for all right minded men. If the first `purushartha goes wrong, the others can not be said to be right; and therefore one finds topmost priority being given to it by the life and message of those who have attained `*pragya*',

The common definition of *dharma* is adherence to the rule: "Do upto others what you wish them to do unto you: do not do upto others what you do not wish them to do unto you. We should not have a double standard, and treat all as our ownselves. The treatment we wish others to render to us is itself the measure of our duty to them. We must respect ourselves and respect others if we wish to be respected by them. *Dharma confers shanti* and fosters an attitude of *ahimsa.Ahimsa* is not merely not to harm others or inflict any injury - by word or deed, what to say to physical injury - but not to think ill of others even inadvertently.

"Ahimsa parmodhramah" is dot a mere rhetoric; it is in fact an active principle of higher living. Questions are often raised as to the use of force in society, and how far it could be said to be a *dharmic* act, or legitimised. It is often said that waging war is *adharma,* since it violates the principle of *ahimsa.* However, a lilttle consideration would dispel such a confusion. *Himsahimsa* both are essential for the protection of social order. That *himsa* (use of force)

which is used to curb unrighteousness and anti-social activities is perfectly in accordance with *dharma.*

The *Mahabharata* was not a war waged for self-aggrandizement; but for the protection of the rights of the weak and for securing justice against the tyranny of the autocratic wicked rulers of the day when all peaceful avenues had been exhausted. Sri Krishna was not a war-monger, but surely a 'prince of Peace.' The idealist tradition of the justification fo state authority supports this view even today. T.H. Green upheld such action in the modern times in his well-known doctrine, "Will, not force, is the basis of state," and has considered use of force justified when peaceful avenues of settling disputes have been exhausted, and frustrated by the might of the powers that be.

VII
Human Values and the path of justice and goodwill

Human values lead us to get rid of our *tamoguna* (sloth and anger) so that we can understand the spiritual nature of our being; and *rajoguna* (temper and excitement) so that we can take interest in our spiritual aspects of living. *Sattva* helps us in outgrown the *tamo* and *rajo-gunas,* and has finally to be outgrown in order that we may establish ourselves in our *atomic* Reality. In the practice of human values, how can this be brought about is the moot question. Can the *shastras* help us in this matter? No, lamented Kabir, when he exclaimed:

Pothi parhi parhi jug muya pundit bhaya na koy
Dhai askshar prem ka parhe so pandit hoy.

Shastras show us the paths, and we can choose the one suitable for us, but the success is led by the *prema* principle as nothing succeeds as much. We find one such path demonstrated in the *Gita,* which is called "voluntary *karma-sanyas yoga"* (giving up *karmas'* fruits):

Karmanyevadhikaraste ma phaleshu kadachan
Ma karmuphatheturbhurma te sangoastvakramani

Ch. 2/47.

Yogasthah kuru Karmani sangam tyaktva dhaunanjaya
Sidhiasidhyoh samo bhutva samatvam yoga uchyate.
Ch.2/48

Durch hyavaram karma budhiryogadhnanjaya
Budhau sharanamnvichh kripanah phalhetavah.
Ch. 2/49

Budhiyukto jahatih ubhe sukritduskrite
Tasmadyogaya yujyasava yogah karmashu
kaushlam. *Ch. 2/50*
Karmajam budhiyukta hi phalam tyaktva manishinah
Janmaban hvinirmuktah padam gachatyanamyam
Ch.2/51

This is not to suggest that such a path befits only those who have given up their home and hearth, but every house-holder, nay, even kings are recommended this path. There is none who can remain without *karma*, so to say. Everyone must do his allotted duty. Arjuna was taught this path right in the midst of the battlefield, nay prodded into it; yet Sri Krishna called it the highest yoga. Why?we must consider this aspect. *Karma* is nobler than *akarma*; and even for the accomplishment of one's selfish goal one has to undergo the process of sacrifice; or how else can one proceed in the ladder of one's higher evolution?The Lord told Arjuna:"*niyatam kuru karmatvam*"Surely, you do your allotted *karma*.3/8

Why giving up the fruit of the *karma* is enjoined upon can be seen from the subsequent *shlokas*. It is the *karma sanyasa* that connects the aspirant with the Lord, since attachment to karma is the cause of his bondage and *karma-sanyasa* releases from it and restores a proper balance in human nature, bringing about harmony, peace and co-operation in society. The state of mind thus attained is described further in the *Gita* as follows:

vihaya kamanyah sarvanpumamscharati nihsprihah
Nirmamo nirhankara sa shantimadhigaehhti Ch 2.7

Esha brahmi sthitih partha nainam prapya vimuhyati
sthitvasyamant kale api brahmanirvanmrichhti. Ch 2.72

The one who (having given up all desires and attachments and the ego of self-doing and being without aspiration for doing on his own lives his life on the principle "Thy will be done", has verify reached supreme Bliss. O Arjuna, this is the state of having attained Godhood, and one who has reached this is never attached to the duality of life and finally merges in the Ultimate Bliss (*Brahmananda).*

The history of our culture, as of other societies, is replete with the examples of kings and common men who attained such a state of mind and their lives were shining examples of human values. It is indeed our great misfortune that both the rulers and the common men today are afflicted with the baser elements of their nature and the society has no respite from their evil propensities. We still remain in spiritual darkness and degradation although our heritage is adored as the heart of spirituality by the entire world. Who will show the example to us when the human values, which sprang forth from our sacred culture and sustained it throughout the centuries in its essence, are being forgotten by the learned and the high and mightly in society, and no attempt is being made through our secular education to promote the wisdom contained in our culture?This can not be done by passing resolutions or by sermons addressed on the eve of sacred occasions, but these values have to be lived through our lives here and now.

The value of human values lies in the fact that the render the lives and hearts of people pure and sacred who will not allow the kind of anarchy and disorder as is rampant in society. Dedicated and duty-bound citizens, who no longer remain weak and wavering, would lead the way in the manner as Arjuna initially presented the picture of being the learned but cowardice. They would be rather moulded into Arjuna of the later stage, the greatest *karma-yogi.* It is to such people that the path of justice and goodwill opens itself,who are eulogised by *Bhartrihari* thus:

Nindantu niti nipuna va stuvantu;
Lakshmih samavishtu gachhatu va yatheshtham;
Adyaiv va maranamastu yugantare va,
Nyayatpatham pravichlanti padam na dhirah.

- *Neeti,* 74

Such *karmayogis* are inspired by no other person than the Lord Himself *establishing* them in the *sadhana* of *lokasangraha* for the preservation and protection of *human values.* The Lord called upon Arjuna:"By relinquishing all your aspirations and attachments with your considered judgement be engaged in your duty.

"Those who thus follow my advice and are fortified with an unflinching faith in Me and free from fault-finding shall be released of their bondage. I shall light the lamp of their *gyana (*wisdom consciousness) by My grace":

Mayi sarvani karmani sanyasyodhyatma chetasa
Nirasi nirmamo bhitva yudhyasva vigatjvarah. Ch. 3/30.

Ye me matamidam nityamnutishthanti manvah
Shraddhvanto anusuyanto muchyante pi karmahbhih.
Ch.3/31

Tesamevanukampartha mahmgyanam tamah
Nashyamyatmabhavastho gyandipen bhasvatah.
Ch. 10/11

Having been born as human beings and endowed with the rare gift of reasoning and spiritual awakening we have to sanctify our lives and put *satya, dharma, shanti, prema,* and *ahimsa* into practice. How this can be achieved needs a bit of *explaining.* Man has got the quality of human nature and an animal has the quality of a brute. When the inner vision or the basic human nature disappears we can not call him a man. Similarly when the external vision or the brute nature disappears we can not call it an animal. To have an inner vision is the natural quality of a human being. One may in appearance be a human being but if one has only external vision and is unable to see within oneself he can not be called a human being.

Individuals by focussing their attention to something higher and nobler as the 'central point' of their lives can earn promotion to a higher level of evoluton and thereby contribute to the society by making it a little more civilized. By seeking the company of elevated beings we can get an opportunity to elevate ourselves. The practice of human values fosters such an attitude. It can be based on stages which proceed higher and higher from a selfish to a 'selfish-selfless', and to a *'purely selfless'*and finally to the '*atmic* level' of our existence.

When we wish good for others, we will get good too and if we wish ill for others we will get only ill for ourselves. Such an attitude of mind can be brought about through *atma-budhhi* and not by mere intellectual reasoning. *Such budhhi* is inspired by Truth which is the basis of everything and there is no greater *dharma* than the Truth - *"Satyam nasti paro dharmah."*

But if we take a backward step in regard to finding out and getting the truth regarding ourselves how can we take the path of truth in society? Values like *satya, dharma, shanti, prema and ahimsa* would sound hollow in our daily lives when we do not have a living faith in them. Our life depends on our words, our thoughts, and our deeds. And it is only when there is harmony among then that we can contribute to our sacred existence and go up higher in our spiritual evolution. But if we pur them along the wrong path we go deep downwards.

To purify our thoughts, words, and deeds and bring about harmony among them we must enquire into our nature and see whether these values are present there. Understanding the real value of our nature,we shall rise higher in the scale of human values and ennoble the community life as well. As the seeds grow into big trees, we must also try to grow and become Madhava, for which our qualities have the basic potential and responsibility. Promotion of human values in society depends on promotion of good qualities among individuals. We must,therefore, put the necessary efforts to make our thoughts sacred by practising these value and generate them among others.

"Arise; awake, and stop not till the goal is reached" must be our watchword. If we make our thoughts, words, and deeds sacred there can be no better way of coming out of evil, ill will, and despondency. We must be prepared to put into practice the values that we want to proclaim to others.

All talk about human values can be put under four categories: the first is when we take the faults of others and our own on the same footing and talk on that basis. The second is when we speak about the good that is in us and the faults that are in others. The third is when we speak about the good in us as well as the good in others. The fourth is to claim the good that is not in us and speak about the faults that are not in others. The last is the worst aspect of the whole lot, and the best way to promote human values is to make a resolute effort to root out this fourth tendency in us. If we take care of the first step,the subsequent steps will be taken care of. We can best conclude by once again quoting Ramakrishna Paramahansa:

"People don't trust a man when he speaks about God. Even if a great soul affirms that he has seen God, still the average person will not accept his words. He says to himself,`If this man has really seen God, then let him show Him to me?' But can a man learn to feel a person's pulse in one day; He must go about with a physician for many days; only then can he distinguish the different pulses. He must be in the company of those with whom the examination of the pulse has become a regular profession. Can anyone and everyone pick out a yarn of a particular count? If you are in that trade you can distinguish in a moment a forty count thread from a forty-one".

May this note of optimism thrill our hearts and enliven our quest of human values!
Sah navavatu,sah nau bhunaktu
Sah veerya karvavahau. Tejasvi navdhitmastu
Ma vidvishavahai. Aum Shantih! Santih! Shantih!

(Let the Lord protect us both. Make good use of us both. Let Him strengthen our efforts. Let our vidya be magnificent, we may never envy each other. Let there be Peace, Peace and Peace!)

Asato ma sadgamaya. Tamaso ma jyotirgamaya
Mtyorma amrititam gamaya.

(O Lord, lead me to righteousness from unrighteousness;from darkness to light; and from mortality to immortality)

Sarve bhavantu sukhinah sarve santu niramayah
Sarve bhadrani pashyatu ma kashchiddukhamapnuyat

(Let all be happy and all be healthy. Let all see the good in all and let none be afflicted with suffering and pain.)

MORAL EDUCATION AND THE EMOTIONS

The reality of moral experience would suggest that the emotions may well be the most important factor in the moral behaviour of most people. Certainly, it would be difficult to imagine a moral dilemma or an occasion requiring a moral choice in which the emotions were not involved in some way and it was for this reason that we stressed in Chapter I the importance of including this dimension of human behaviour in any worthwhile discussion of moral education.

Furthermore, as we saw in the preceding chapter , there is some evidence to suggest that moral character is much more a result of deep emotional forces operating during the child's formative years than of any attempts that are made at offering him rational guidance, and the work of psychologists in general on moral behaviour and moral thinking reveals quite clearly the importance of feeling in this area of human experience. Tyere can be no productive discussion , then, of moral educations that does not take full account of the part played by the emotions in moral behaviour.

In spite of this, however, the tendency has been for this aspect of human life and experience to be largely ignored by both philosophers and educationists, some because they have felt it to be not in any way their concern, other because they have deplored the very existence of man's emotional life and have regarded it as an obstacle to be overcome rather than as a feature to be given full weight in its own right in any consideration of moral behaviour.

More direct attention has been given to this aspect of human existence in literature, from the time of the Greek tragedians, and even of Homer himself before them, up to the present day. We have already referred to the fact that this conflict between reason and feeling was a major feature of Sophocles' depiction of the dilemma of Antigone. More recently, we have Herman Hesse's account of Joseph Knecht's attempts to resign as Master of the Glass Bead Game because "I have been standing at the frontier where my work as Magister Ludi has become eternal recurrance, an empty exercise and formula. I have been doing it without enthusiasm, sometimes even without faith. It was time to stop. " For the most part,however, again, reason and felling have been regarded as in conflict with each other, as incompatible, the major difference between this approach and that of the philosophers being that when this battle is fought in the arenas of philosophical disquisition it is reason which usually ends the victor, while when it occurs in the pages of literature this results is more often reversed.

Thus, since the beginning of organized thought-certainly in the Western world-there has existed this tension between the intellectual and the emotional dimensions of man's life, the head and the heart,reason and feeling. It is a tension that has never been satisfactorily resolved and it is one that from the beginning has had serious consequences for all aspects of education, as well as having particular import for moral education.

No discussion of moral education could be complete, then, without an attempt to consider what is the proper role of the emotions in moral behaviour or at least the direction in which an answer to this question might be sought. It is the main intention of this chapter,therefore, to suggest some of the areas that need to be explored if we are to begin to look for a solution to this difficulty.

First of all, however, we must familiarize ourselves with the nature of the problem in rather more detail by examining briefly the view of the emotions taken by philosophers and the resultant attitudes that has been adopted to education in general and to moral education in particular. For only when we have seen where the thinking has gone wrong can we hope to discern what form a proper approach might take.

Moral philosophy and the emotions

We have already commented on the remarkable influence Plato has exercised on the thinking of the Western world. That influence can be discerned in so many of our present-day attitudes and practices and this is especially true in the sphere of education. Nowhere has there been a better example of Platonism in practice than in the implementation of his recommendations for the differentiated treatment of children of gold, silver and bronze in the organization of the English system of secondary education for so many years on tripartite lines. Furthermore, this is one aspect of a more general feature of his thinking that has pervaded the thinking and the practice of the Western world in a much more insidious manner, namely the preeminence that he gave to intellectual development in all that he said about education and,indeed, about all other aspects of social living.

He described the soul of man as having three aspects-reason, "spirit" and the appetites. In analogy he likens these respectively to a man, a lion and a beast with many heads. Reason, then, is for him the element which is fully human, even godlike, so that this is the element that he regards as the central concern of education whose task it is to enable us to overcome as effectively as possible the animal life of the passions within us. The appetites, the beast with many heads, must be tamed; "spirit", the lion, must be trained to be the ally of reason; only reason itself, the intellect, the godlike aspect of man's nature, can be educated in the proper sense.

Moral education is central to Plato's scheme. The main goal of his educational system, as we saw in Chapter 1, is the production of moral beings, but this is seen as a purely intellectual matter. The state of being a moral agent is one in which the individual has come to *know* what is right and this knowledge is the culmination, the keystone, the apex of the vast edifice of human knowledge, so that it is only to be attained after a long process of intellectual development. Socrates, Plato's predecessor, had declared that virtue is knowledge of the good. This assertion Plato interpreted in a completely literal manner and he also made the illicit process to its coverse, that knowledge is virtue. For not only did he believe that virtue or morality was to be attained purely by intellectual effort (and was thus accessible only to those of high intellectual calibre):he also believed, as perhaps he had to, that once one had this knowledge, one could not avoid being virtuous. For who could know what was good and right, yet do something else? For Plato this would be analogous to knowing that a straight line is the shortest distance between two points and then setting out on an unnecessarily circuitous route to one's destination. Plato's model for all knowledge was mathematical knowledge and this view of human behaviour followed from that.

This kind of rationalist approach to the problem of human knowledge, then, from the outset created a dichotomy between reason and the passions that has remained with us ever since. Reason is regarded as the supreme factor in moral behaviour; the passions are unfortunate additional features of human life and are to be controlled, subdued, tamed.

Aristotle takes the same basic stance, although, perhaps because his model for human knowledge is biological rather than mathematical, he is more realistic in his view of the strength of the passions, For him, God is "self-thinking thought", pure thought. This, then, is the highest form of existence and man's true happiness consists in sharing this perfect life of God by engaging in this kind of intellectual activity for as long and at as high a level as possible. This activity he calls *oewpia* (theoria), the godlike, intellectual activity of contemplation.

This is the only truly moral life but it represents a strange view of morality, since of necessity it is a purely private existance that it recommends. It also seems to advise us that this kind of activity is to be chosen always in preference to spending time performing deeds that might be to the advantage of our fellow men. The question must arise, therefore, as to whether in Aristotle's view it would be right to break off from one's contemplation to save a drowning child, for example, a question that many teachers of philosophy have worried their students with. It would seem that Aristotle himself would have to answer that question with a negative, but he does recognize that there has to be another kind of morality and he offers us another, second-order theory of morality, one that focuses on relations between human beings. It is here that he introduces that rather more realistic approach to the passions we mentioned above.

As we saw in Chapter 1, Aristotle, like Socrates and plato, sees morality as a matter of knowledge, of knowing, in the full sense, what is right, what he calls "the right rule". If one knows the right rule, one will know in every circumstance what the right and moral course of action is. However, unlike Socrates and Plato, he does not believe that acting in the right way will follow automatically from such knowledge. He is well aware of the strength of what he called "pleasure" and of the conflict that arises between what we know to be right and what we recognize as pleasurable. In short, as we also suggested in Chapter 1, he is fully congnisant of the condition that St. Paul was later to refer to when he said, "The evil that I would not that I do and the good I would I do not." "This phenomenon Aristotle called (*akrasia*) incontinence, lack of self-control or self-discipline.

This can only be overcome, he believes, by the right kind of upbringing. Thus he advocates that, although young children cannot be expected to have the intellectual power to understand and recognize the "right rule" for themselves (for the sorts of reasons we discussed in the last chapter), they must be told how to behave and made to act according to it. Only in this way will they develop the right habits and correct patterns of behaviour, the "settled disposition" that will provide them with the self-discipline they will need when as adults they come to see what is right for themselves if they are to act according to it and not be seduced from the right course by the temptations of pleasure. As Richard Peters expressed it more recently, they "must enter the palace of Reason through the courtyard of Habit and Tradition"(1963, p.55).

Again, therefore, we see the appetites, the passions, the emotions being treated as in conflict with reason, as a serious problem to the would-be moral person and,as a result, as a feature of human character to be deplored, wrestled with and overcome, or at least tamed, in the interests of moral education and moral behaviour.

The Judaeic tradition, as is apparent from the words of St. Paul that we have just quoted, is not dissimilar, nor is the Christian ethic that derived from it. There is little in that tradition that is seriously at odds with Greek philosophy, so that the Christian theology that was developed from a fusion of the Greek and the Judaeic traditions by such men as St. Augustine and St. Thomas Aquinas and which has changed very little in its fundamentals since that time, manifests the same attitude towards the passions. Man's appetites are the domain of Satan, whose machinations with the assistance of Eve led to man's fall from grace in the person of Adam and resulted in all men entering the world carrying from birth the burden of original sin. Thus there has resulted a doctrine and, especially, a view of education which has dominated the thinking of the Western world. At the heart of that doctrine is the notion that original sin is to be overcome by whatever means are necessary,the passions are to be suppressed and man is to be given control over his emotional life, so that he can develop to the full and in an untrammelled manner his capacity for reason, his intellectual potential and especially his ability to attain what Aquinas called"the intellectual love of God".

This dualaism, this dichotomy of reason and the passions has dominated Western philosophy ever since. When philosophy reemerged at the time of the Renaissance and freed itself from theology for the first time since the Greek era, it emerged with the same kind of strongly rationalist base, which again led to a view of morality that stressed its intellectual components, usually to the exclusion of all others. Thus, as we mentained in Chapter 2, Spinoza sets out his *Ethics* in Euclidean form, offering us definitions, hypotheses to be proved, proofs of those hypotheses and conclusions clearly marked QED. Morality continues to be regarded as analogous to mathematics and moral reasoning is seen as the them same kind of unemotional deductive process.

Even the advanced form of rationalism that Immanuel Kant developed in response to the challenges offered to the traditional view by the new wave of empiricists such as John Locke and David Hume made no allowance for man's emotional life. In fact, Kant is at some pains to stress that his system of morality is for rational beings rather than for human beings, a distinction whose importance lies in the fact that it reveals a view of human brings as hindered in their search for a rational morality by the unfortunate condition of being lumbered with feelings and emotions. Again, therefore,these are to be overcome so that the individual can behave in that way which is shown to be right by the application of reason. To discover the right course of action is a rational and intellectual activity. One's natural inclinations merely serve to deflect one from putting such right conclusions into practice.

What never seems to be appreciated is that nothing that could be called a moral life would be possible without these same inclinations for the moral will to overcome. Thus there exists a fundamental contradiction in Kant's system. "It has to be allowed that morality is committed both to the destruction of the natural passions and to their preservation: to the former because, in any conflict between reasons and the inclinatons, it is axiomatic that reason ought to triumph, to the latter because moral reason needs the natural passions both as its antithesis and its instrument." (Walsh 1969, p.30)

Again, therefore, there is the same tension, the same conflict between reason and the emotions, and man's problem is seen as that of achieving control over his natural inclinations, so that he can repress them and attain the self-discipline necessary if he is to be able to live a rational moral life.

Thus rationalism, as we suggested in Chapter 2, offers a moral system more suited to Daleks then to human beings. Certainly it is a system that recommends that in order to achieve morality we should try to become like Daleks and reject those emotions that in a very real sence contribute towards making us human.It is for this reason that rationalism in general has been regarded by many as unsatisfactory and unacceptable. Kant's view of morality in particular has been criticized on these grounds. "The kantian doctrine which makes practical reason in effect the godlike element in man and writes down the passions as belonging to his animal nature amounts to a form of dualism as objectionable as any to be found in Descartes.The unity of the human being is entirely lost in this account" (Walsh 1969, p.32). Indeed, one might go even further and argue that this dualism is the direct descendant and result of that dualism that Descartes imposed on modern philosophy, the dualism of mind and body, subject and object,consciousness and experienced reality. Again,"The voice of reason in kant was as remote from the living being as was Jehovah from the ancient Jews" (Walsh 1969, p.38). This was a point made by Hegel, Kant's immediate successor, who recognized this problem and the need to bridge the gap with what he called "a morality of love". His attempts to achieve this, however, perhaps reveal the inevitable limitations of rationalism in this respect. For it was this feature not only of rationalism in general but of Hegelianism in particular that invited the reaction that has followed.

That reaction has taken two main forms, but fundamentally both have accepted the significance of man's emotional responses to the world only by rejecting the possibility of achieving a rational basis to morality. Thus, although rejecting the rationalist solution, they have nevertheless seemed to accept the dichotomy we have described as part of it and have seen reason and the emotions as in conflict.

The empiricist reaction against rationalism is based on the view that knowledge of any aspect of the world and of human experience cannot be attained by the use of reason or the intellect alone but must begin from some kind of empirical observation of how things are. The approach to morals associated with this view does seem initially to have been prompted by an awareness of the need for moral behaviour to involve some kind of caring attitude on the part of the moral agent (early theories, for example, stressed notions such as that of benevolence) and this is one reason why they looked at the role of the emotions in moral behaviour.

However, such an empiricist epistemology led to the conviction that we can only find answers to moral questions by observing how people do in fact behave, what they believe and what they do in moral situations, and that , as a result, no moral position can in any way be "proved". Thus, as we saw in Chapter 2, they produced in various forms an emotivist theory of morals, which, as its name suggests, recognizes the importance of the emotions in moral behaviour but does this by claiming that moral beliefs and behaviour are explicable only in terms of the emotions people have or the way they feel. They suggest, therefore, that moral behaviour is to be assessed in terms of social utility, of what people feel to be right, of maximizing pleasure and minimizing pain, or that all statements of approval or disapproval are to be regarded as mere expressions of the feelings of the individual who utters them, subject in no way to the application of the reason. The role of reason here, therefore, is a subordinate one to that of the passions; as Hume said, "reason is,and ought to be, the slave of the passions." Thus the roles are reversed but the dichotomy and much of the tension and conflict remain.

Existentialist philosophy too began as a revolt against rationalism or, at least, the extreme rationalism of Hegel and the German idealist philosophers generally. A central concern here has been with the loss of individualism that must follow from this kind of rationalist view with its emphasis on the general, on universals, that preoccupation with rational beings rather than human beings that we referred to above. Existentialist theories have also been concerned to offer views of existence that will be more than academic, intellectual exercises and will lead to changes in the way the individual organizes his own life. Thus Jean-Paul Sartre tells us, "Existentialism must be lived to be really sincere. To live as an existentialist means to be ready to pay for this view and not merely to lay it down in books ."

Again, however, this approach has led to a rejection of reason so that these philosophies are sometimes described as irrationalist. Their claim is that the individual must make his own choices, assert his own unique existence without reference to any universal rules or standards, since adherence to such rules or standards must involve a loss of individuality. They have also come to realize, however, that this creates an insoluble problem for the individual since he cannot refer to any kind of helpful criteria or norms in making these choices so that he experiences what Sartre has called "nausea". It is for this reason that sartre himself has attempted to develop a more positive theory of the emotions, one that would effect some kind of reconciliation between reason and feeling (1962).

Thus the Western philosophical tradition, having created a dichotomy between man's intellect and his emotions, has for the most part failed to offer any kind of a solution to the problem it has thus presented to us, except to suggest that we reject one or the other. The emotions have either been regarded as unfortunate aspects of humanity which stand in the way of the proper exercise of reason and should be repressed, or they have been seen as the clue to all interpersonal relationships in such a way that those relationships have been regarded as beyond the influence of reasoning of any kind. The same stance has been adopted by those who, as we mentioned earlier, have explored such issues through literature throughout the ages, and its practical expression can be seen still in the celibacy of the Roman Catholic priesthood.

Implications for education

Throughout this time it has been the rationalist tradition that has been predominant in educational theory and practice, perhaps because of the strong influence of the Christian church on the development of education in the Western world. Its effects have been considerable and widespread. In general, it has led to an emphasis on the intellectual development of children at the expense of other aspects of their development, a process whose dangers and potentially disastrous consequences are well portrayed in Herman Hesse's account of the effects of this kind of education on one particular pupil in *The Prodigy*. It has several particular facets that we must note here.

The first of these has a relevance that goes beyond education itself. It is the effects of this view on art itself. For it has led to an intellectualizing of art and to its being given a reduced role in human life and development. Again it was Plato who set things off on this track. For in Plato's society the function of art of all kinds was to assist in the process of holding the society together by promoting those values that were the fabric of the society. It was not to bring to the attention of any citizen the existence of anything evil nor to provide him with examples of bad behaviour. Its role in education and in society as a whole was to promote those qualities of character that were necessary for the stability of society and expressly not to challenge nor do anything that might undermine the norms of society. To this end it was to be subject to the strictest censorship. It is significant and supportive to the view we are arguing here that within the present century this conception of the role of the arts in society has been described as giving to art an important and responsible, even a noble, social role (Nettleship 1935).

As a result of this kind of attitude, a good deal of art over the ages has been the handmaiden of the church or of society, illustrating and decorating, being used to further particular ends but not able to make any significant comment in its own right.

This is one significant feature of that critique of Western art that is offered by the German philosopher, Friedrich Nietzsche and in particular the distinction he draws between what he calls the Apollonian and the Dionysian cultures. The former is based on a form of art that sees it as its task to gloss over the harsh realities of human existence, to beautify them and thus render them acceptable. The Dionysian culture, on the other hand, is based on a form of art that endeavours to face existence as it really is and to reveal reality to man in its stark and true form. Both of these forms can be seen in Western European culture from the earliest times, says Nietzsche, but it is the former that has been emphasized because the latter involves too open an acceptance of the passionate side of man's nature.

One effect, then, of this divorce of reason and feeling that we are discussing has been this kind of reduction of scope for art in all its forms both in education and in society. And many developments in art in the present century can be seen as the beginning of a movement away from that kind of attempt to intellectualize it or to give it this limited social role towards an acceptance of it on its own terms and as able to offer valuable perspectives on human nature and the human condition.

A second effect of this divorce of feeling and intellect has been the devaluing within education of any activity that has not appeared to have a fully intellectual content and, conversely, an emphasis on those areas of the curriculum that stress the development of the intellect to the almost total exclusion of all else. Thus, again, to an extent that would certainly bring the colour back to Plato's cheeks, the degree to which a subject has found a ready acceptance on the school curriculum has had a very direct relationship to its cognitive content and an inverse relationship to its emotional appeal. Mathematics and science are currently the most well-entrenched subjects on the curriculum, and classics, even without such utilitatian advantages, dominated the curriculum of the public and grammer schools for many years, while art and "handicraft" are still often taught in a shed at the other side of the playground and usually only to those pupils who appear to lack the intellectual capacity for anything apparently more demanding.

However, there are signs that the value of aesthetic and creative activities in education is being increasingly recognized. There is a growing conviction that an education that is concerned with only one dimension of human experience is no education at all. There is still too little appreciation, however, of the implication of this for the intellectual activities, the traditional schools subjects, themselves. We are more aware now of the educational value of those activities that have a strong aesthetic or emotional bias, but we have yet to appreciate the existence of this kind of dimension to all educational activities.

For a further result of this emphasis on the intellect in education has been the loss of something of great importance to the intellectual activities themselves, namely a proper concern with the place that feeling must have here too. A lot has been heard in recent educational discussion about the cognitive and the affective dimensions of education. Benjamin Bloom, for example, in his taxonomy of educational objectives, discusses objectives in three separate domains, the main two of which are the cognitive and the affective (1956). One of the most serious criticisms of this approach, however, derives from the impossibility of distinguishing these two element in practice. It is not possible to set up any educational programme that does not take full account of both of these dimensions. For this reason it is important not only to recognize the value of those areas of the curriculum whose main value lies in their contribution to the education of feeling itself; we must also take full account of and give full weighting to the affective aspects of those subject which too often have been regarded as purely intellectual. Feeling is an integral part of education.

There are at least two aspects of this. Firstly, it would be difficult to argue that there is any area of human knowledge and experience that does not have its aesthetic dimension. This is true even of a subject like mathematics, which for Plato was the body of knowledge that came closest to being a completely abstract and thus purely intellectual activity. Mathematicians will often speak of the beauty of mathematics and, indeed, they are right to do so. However, because of the emphasis on the intellect that we are discussing, this aesthetic dimension has often been ignored. The same of true even of a subject like music in which the aesthetic dimension is easier to recognize and where, in fact, it might be said to comprise its main, or only, *raison d'etre.* For, although this is an art form that in one mode or another is appreciated aesthetically and emotionaly by more people than any other, the teaching of it in our schools has often stressed its intellectual content almost to the exclusion of everything else. As a result, there are many people whose instrumental skill is of a very high order and whose understanding of the "mathematics" of notation is supreme but who evine little feeling for the music they are producing. (The converse of this is equally true, of course, since there have been many musicians whose work reveals great"soul", but who lack any kind of intellectual understanding of music.) The same has been too often true of the teaching of literature-classical, foreign and even, unforgiveably, English. Education in any subject area must include an attempt to reveal its beauty and to encourage a recognition and an appreciation of it.

This brings us to the second aspect of the role of feeling in those suhjects that have often been regarded as purely cognitive. We referred in Chapter 1 to some of the characteristics that distinguish education from other activities that involve teaching. One of those characteristics is that the educated person must have come to value and appreciate that in which he has been educated. In any truly educational context, therefore, it will be impossible to distinguish the learning of a subject in the intellectual or cognitive sense from being brought to enjoy it, appreciate it, recognize its worth and so on. This remains true even of a subject like mathematics, which for Plato was the subject that came closest to being a completely abstract and thus purely intellectul activity. Furthermore, mathematicians often speak of the beauty of mathematics and,indeed, they are right to do so. Again, however, this implies that any attempt to offer an education in mathematics must be at the same time an attempt to reveal this beauty and encourage a recognition and appreciation of it. Thus there is an affective component even to this most intellectual of activities, which cannot be ignored if we are serious in our efforts to educate people in this area.

The samc is truc in all arcas of knowledge. For it is not possible to conceive of an intelligible concept of education that ignores this dimension. It is not possible even in theory to conceive of claiming that one has educated someone without bringing about in him an attitude of appreciation of what has been the substance of that education. It would be a logical absurdity to say of someone that he is an educated man but that he loves nothing, is interested in nothing, is enthused by nothing. To be educated is to have been brought to care about certain things, whatever those things are. Even in the most abstract of subjects, therefore, we must be constantly aware of this affective dimension, of the "feeling" that is involved in the study of it and of the need to attend to this in all aspects of our teaching. We must promote the enjoyment of education in all its element. For this is required of us by the notion of education itself.

To ignore this in attempting to educate children is to take a purely rationalist approach, to deny that our pupils have feelings, to deny them their individuality, and to attempt what is fortunately an impossible task, that of turning them into computers, automata, Daleks. This, then, is a further effect of the divorce of feeling and reason in education that we are discussing.

We must finally turn to what is, at least in the context of this book, the most crucial of the implications of this divorce of intellect and feeling for education-its effect on our approach to moral education(or the moral aspects of all education, since, as we saw in Chapter 1, all education is essentially moral education). Whatever view one takes of the role of feeling in activities such as mathematics and science, there can be no denying that it is central to morality. A moral education, therefore, which directs its attention solely towards the cognitive or intellectual aspects of moral behaviour must be a caricature, distorting by the exaggeration of one, not necessarily salient, element.

Worse however is the attempt to recognize the importance of the emotions by recommending devices for their suppression. Yet there is no doubt that until recently this has been the only view of the role of feeling in moral education that has been offered in theory or revealed in practice. The influence of Plato has been total and we have sought for the most effective ways of "taming" the passions, of bringing them under control. Suppression has been the only device that has been discovered and certainly it has been the main result of this kind of practice. Thus the problems of advancing puberty have been tackled in most boys' schools by the simple application of "rugby and cold showers" and the general attitude that has been engendered by this kind of approach is that the feelings one is experiencing at this stage are nasty and people who have been properly brought up don't show them any longer. Any intelligent pupil can, of course, be expected to wonder where he came from if this is really true.

The essence of this process is the denial of one major aspect of man's humanity. It is also an approach that makes it impossible for us to find a proper set of criteria by which we can distinguish between feeling themselves and thus promote and encourage those that most people would agree should be developed. It also makes it impossible to work out a theory of how any of the emotions can be developed. Thus we have often put ourselves into the inconsistent position in which at the same time we have urged pupils to show love and compassion towards their fellow man, but have not been able to help them to distinguish the different contexts in which such feelings might be aroused and the different ways in which they might be displayed.

The most serious aspect of this kind of approach, however, has been revealed to us by those who have explored the dangers and the far-reaching after-effects and side-effects of repression. In broad terms repression is the result of the introjection of the taboos of others, mostly those adults who have access to us, particularly, because of the importance of the early years, our parents, often reinforced by the unpleasant experiences of punishment. It may also result, of course, from unpleasant and frightening experiences that are not deliberately engineered by personal agencies. Thus a child who steals and eats all of his mother's recently baked cakes may have his desire for delicacies as effectively inhibited by the unpleasant experience of vomiting as from any punishment his mother may subsequently mete out to him. As we saw in Chapter 3, this is, of course, part of the development of conscience, of what Freud called the superego or ego-ideal, and of the growth of a self-image. It is no longer realistic to regard conscience as the still, small voice of God, a kind of universal Tannoy system with which we are kitted out prenatally. This is supported not least by the evident fact that, unlike most public address systems, conscience does not offer everyone the same message and advice. We must view it rather, then, as the internalization of the admonishments we receive and the experiences we have, especially in early childhood.

In particular, it is important to realize, again as we pointed out in Chapter 3, that this development is the result of the child's perception of the attitudes of others, especially his parents, towards him and the image of himself he develops as a consequences of this (Williams 1967). In some cases, therefore, it may be based on a misconception of those attitudes, if the adult is not especially careful about the words in which and the behaviour by which those attitudes are communicated.

The other aspect of this that it is important to be clear about is that to a large extent this is an unconscious process. What is internalized affects our attitudes and our behaviour in ways we are not fully conscious of; and the emotions and feelings that are repressed in this process continue to affect our attitudes and behaviour in unconscious and unrecognized ways. This is why in later life we often find ourselves behaving unthinkingly in ways that reveal attitudes the basis of which we are unaware of and quite incapable of explaining to others or even to ourselves. A refusal to imbibe any kind of alcoholic drink under any circumstances, even where the medicinal value is obvious, for example, can often not be explained by the individual concerned and is only explicable through some exploration of early childhood experiences, such as being beaten for getting at the cooking sherry or, worse and unfortunately more likely, witnessing the ill-treatment of one parent by the other when "in drink".

We must be aware, of course, of appearing to assert that this process is totally to be deplored. Some kind of conscience, some kind of ego-ideal, some kind of self-image must be developed by everyone. How else could one make any kind of choice or decision? In some cases, therefore, this process will lead to a proper control of one's emotions and thus of one's behaviour. The dangers of a wrong approach here, however, must be stressed, as must the fact that such a wrong approach is most likely to result from adopting the view that the process is merely one of repression, of subjugation, of " taming the emotions".

At one end of the scale it can be seen to result in an odd, unreasonable, distorted sense of the relative importance of different values and different kinds of behaviour. The example we just offered of the totally unreasoned and unreasonable rejection of alcohol in all its forms is one example of this kind of distortion. For on occasion it will lead to a willingness to die or to see a child or other relative die rather than to break that taboo. Another example is the celebrated case of those young children who, when asked to list in order of seriousness the worst crimes one could commit, placed killing people first and running in the corridors second (Kellmerpringle and Edwards 1964). These are prime examples of the effects of the development of an overstrong superego conscience.

Another aspect of this is that this kind of strong early childhood experience can lead to an overdeveloped conscience even in areas where some reasonable dictates of conscience are to be expected. The strength of the prohibitions placed on some people by their conscience can be such as to make it impossible for them to take a balanced rational view of a particular situation, so that they are led into actions that not only may be disadvantageous to their own lives but may also be detrimental to those whose interests their conscience may bid them to place before their own.Thus a person may attempt to save his marriage in the interests of his children because of the strength of the dictates of his own parents, internalized and thus mediated through his own conscience, and in doing so ill-serve the interests of those very children whose welfare he has most at heart.

At the other extreme, this kind of early experience, as we know only too well, not least from the many films that have been made on this theme, can lead to psychopathic conditions in later life. It would seem that if the early experiences we have been dicussing are too unpleasant or unbearable,then they become in a sense counter productive; they result not in the development of a strong conscience, ego-ideal of self-image, but in the development of the none of these at all. The same also seems to be the result of being deprived of the love of a mother or mother-susbstitute in the very early years (Bowlby 1973), or, as we saw in Chapter 3, of lacking the kind of close attachment to parents that inhibits the expression of feelings of aggression or hostility. For, without involving ourselves in the technical aspects of psychopathology, we can recognize that what characterizes psychopathic behaviour above all else is the lack of any conscience. The behaviour of the psychopath is not so much immoral and antisocial as moral and asocial; he reveals a complete indifference to the effects of his behaviour on other people or on society. He is often described as the "affectionless character". "He appears to be without any sense of guilt. Every action is assessed in terms of personal advantage, and the world is seen as a place where jungle law operates. As one might expect from this description, the psychopath may be frequently observed in prisons, for he is often a habitual offender, who seems to be untouched by punishment. In short, he appears to be the very antithesis of the morally developed person" (Williams 1967, p.272).

This deficiency of moral development that is revealed by the behaviour of the psychopath illustrates dramatically the importance of achieving a view of moral development which takes a proper account of the role of the emotions within it. What we have said in general about this process by which conscience is developed also highlights the need for such a view. For the central feature of this process, as we have seen, is that it is unconscious. As such, it leads to a loss of control over behaviour. In the last analysis, this is the major criticism that we must offer of any attempt to approach the moral development of children that stresses the repression of feelings or of certain kinds of feeling. For such an unconscious process cannot be regarded as in any sense educational, since by definition it is not open to conscious appraisal. This is the central message of Freduian psychology, which attempts to offer us advice on how to make these processes conscious, precisely in order that we may begin to exercise control over them.

This is also a further and very important criticism of those traditional attempts to attend to moral upbringing by means of religious training. For the emphasis there has often been on the repression of feelings, usually reinforced by fear of eternal punishment, and thus, as we suggested in Chapter 1, represents a quite deliberate attempt to develop a form of morality that is completely authoritarian and does not invite the conscious thought of the individual.

This is why this kind of approach is unacceptable as a form of moral education. To be brought up to act on the dictates of others, especially when these are internalized in this unconscious form, is not to be morally educated at all. As we saw in Chapter 2, it is a kind of moral conditioning or indoctrination, since it denies the individual his right as a human being to think for himself. It is not only, therefore, an unsophisticated version of moral education. It is no version at all. We cannot begin to plan moral education as we have defined it on the basis of establishing unconscious motivation for behaviour. It is for this reason that we need to begin the search for a more positive theory of the role of the emotions in moral behaviour and thus in moral education, not only in the interests of moral education itself but also in the interests of mental health.

The emotions in moral education

We have suggested in what has gone before that morality has been seen too much as a matter for rational beings and that we need to consider it in the context of the behaviour of human beings. We argued in chapter 2 that behaving morally is not the completely rational process that people such as Plato and Kant seemed to think; we have been arguing further in this current chapter that it is not even enough to note and recognize the tension that exists between feeling and reason, whether this leads us to try to suppress the former or to abandon the latter. What is needed is a positive examination of the role the emotions play in moral behaviour, of the links between feeling and reason."A satisfactory moral philosophy must give an altogether different account from that found in Kant of the relationship of moral reason and the inclinations"(Walsh 1969, p.32). Furthermore, in the context of this book, we need to explore some of the ways in which moral education might be approached in order to take full account of the need for such a philosophy. We must develop a more constructive theory of the affective aspect of moral education. It is to this issue that we must now turn.

The first step towards such a theory must be to recognize that the distinction between reason and feeling is itself a false distinction and encourages a wrong view of the relation of the emotions to the intellect. For it suggests that they are usually in conflict, each one tugging us in a different direction, that we must choose whether to act according to the one or the other, that in practice what each will lead to can be separated out, and that, while the one offers us a rational solution, the other is always and by definition irrational. Each of these features of this view of the emotions we must look at in turn..

A moment's reflection will reveal that our inclinations do not always push us towards behaviour that is at odds with rationality. Sometimes our inclinations and reason are in agreement. Kant himself recognized the truth of this and it seemed to worry him that in such situations one would enjoy doing one's duty, a fact that seemed to him somehow to make it less than fully moral. For example, it is our duty at certain times of the week to meet groups of students who have gathered together for educational purposes and to use such skills as we possess to the best of our ability to forward those purposes. Only occasionally do our inclinations favour spending such times differently. Quite often, therefore, reason and feeling are in harmony. There is no inevitable conflict.

Secondly, seldom if ever in practice are we faced by two quite discrete courses of possible action, one dictated by reason, the other offered enticingly by the passions. Moral behaviour is not as simple as that, nor are moral choices. Even if the rational course of action is clear enough, what the passions offer is always a confused and confusing jumble of conscience, desire, pleasure, concern for the feelings of others and many other emotions clamouring for our attention. Just as it is impossible in any practical educational context to separate cognitive from affective goals, so it is impossible to distinguish these two aspects of any practical moral issue.

Lastly, and perhaps most importantly, it is not the case that the passions are irrational and can thus be held in this kind of contrast with reason. The etymology of the word "passion" may suggest that w are concerned here with things we suffer (Peters 1973b) and that they are not as a result susceptible to reason, but other words such as "emotion" do not have this kind of connotation and it is clear on reflection that there are such things as rational passions and that "although manifestly these terms relate in some way to our feelings, they are also intimately connected with cognition, that is, with our ways of understanding situations"(Peters 1973b, p.81).

Some emotions, for example, are the result of the way in which we view certain situations; they result from what reason tells us about the world. A feeling of fear is often prompted by a rational appraisal of a situation in which one is faced, say, by a man-eating tiger. The small child who lacks such reasoning powers and the knowledge and experience on which they must be based might not feel fear in such circumstances. Conversely, our emotions sometimes affect the way in which we perceive situations. This is the essence of the phenomenological viewpoint which asserts that every man's perceptions are unique and individual since they are intimatley interwined with his emotions and his personality. It is not necessary to go that far, however, in order to recognize the influence of emotion on perception. We all see different things in a painting, a photograph, a poster since we all respond emotionally in different ways to the content. It is also a well-known feature of the condition known clinically as paranoia that the paranoid perceives a good deal of his world as threatening and hostile, sees persecution in relatively trivial and innocent acts of others, experiences unreasonable sexual jealousy and in general has a view of the world which has been considerably influenced by his emotions.

Furthermore, not only may reason influence the kinds of feeling we have; it often also affects the way in which we give expression to those feelings. It may reveal, for example, that we have two or more feelings that are incompatible with one another and suggest ways in which such conflict can be resolved in our actions. It may also indicate that a particular feeling, say, to punch one's boss on the nose, may best be dealt with by some method other than the actual behaviour it is urging, by violently abusing him from a safe and private place, by hammering a ball around a squash court, or even by thinking through his problems and trying to see things from his point of view. Again, however, the converse is also true. For it is not just a matter of reason guiding the emotions.It will itself in turn be influenced by them and take full account of their presence and their strength. Thus, if we are lucky, it may on occasion recommend that the only solution to our problem is to punch the boss on the nose. The desire and the need may have gone beyond the point where sublimation is possible.

The relation of feeling and reason in human experience, then, is one of reciprocity rather than conflict. The conflict model is unsatisfactory. The fact/value distinction is difficult, if not impossible to maintain at any level. The interaction is of a much more subtle kind.

It is the presence of this element of cognition in the emotions that has encouraged some people to accept that the emotions can be educated rather than merely tamed. From what we have said so far it would appear that, at least in respect of their cognitive element, this ought to be the case. We must also, however, explore the question of whether the education of the emotions has to be limited to their cognitive aspects. Certainly, it would seem that an exploration of the role of the emotions in moral education might be forwarded by a consideration of the kind of education the emotions the emotions in general might be susceptible to.

The first thing we must note is the role of education in relation to that element of cognition in the emotions that we have already drawn attention to. If we are to understand and deal adequately with our emotions a lot of knowledge is required, some of it of a largely "factual" kind. The feeling of fear, for example, can only be dealt with by learning more about the object of our fear. When we do this we either find we have dispelled the fear or we have a clearer idea of precisely what there is to be reasonably afraid of and thus of whatever necessary action should be taken to protect ourselves. It is not true that fear is always the result of ignorance, but often it is. We need, therefore, to know both what we should be afraid of and what we need not be afraid of. Feelings of jealousy and envy, and even desires and wishes, can be dispelled or brought into clearer focus in the same way. In short, we need to be able to make a realistic appraisal of situations and to understand them in order to be able to act appropriately. To do this involves learning of a clearly cognitive kind. It is information about the world we need in order to make such appraisals. It is plain, then, that in this respect at least the emotions are susceptible to the influence of education (Peters 1973b).

This is why we must avoid the divorce of reason and feeling the we referred to earlier in all aspects of education. The only way in which we can attend to the education of the emotions even in relation to their cognitive element is by taking full account, in all of our teaching, of their impact. As we said above, it is impossible to separate the cognitive and the affective dimensions of any educational experience.

Furthermore, if we do not take full account of the emotional aspects of all our teaching, it may be detrimental even to the purely cognitive learning we are seeking to ensure. Children have feelings, whether we acknowledge them or not, and they do react emotively to what is offered them. Children's emotions and fantasies can also obstruct their learning, but this happens only when those emotions and fantasies are uncontrolled (Jones 1968). If we do not help pupils to control these emotions, then the learning we are seeking to promote may well be impaired. On the other hand, it can only be enhanced if we recognize the existence of these emotions and endeavour to harness them to our educational purposes. Again it is not a matter of creating conditions of control in order to repress or of offering cathartic opportunities for letting off steam and thus getting their emotions out of the way. Emotion and fantasy are substantive elements in most kinds of learning.

This is one of the most interesting points to emerge from the experiences of those who have been concerned with that major curriculum project. Man - A Course of Study (MACOS). For the early experiments with this project revealed not only the need to recognize the emotions that were aroused in children by the project materials but also some of the ways in which they could be used to further their education on both the cognitive and the affective fronts. Thus Richard M. Jones, in describing and analysing the early experience of the project tells us, "The first claim on our attention should be that many teachers....will jump at a chance to make these films part of their routine stock of teaching tools and will get out of them only a portion of the teaching power that is in them" (1972, p.26). He goes on to say, "The crux of this issue is not obscure. Only in the vicinities of schoolrooms do we make it so. Normally, the human mind and the human heart go together. If not normally, may we say optimally? We are witnessing a revolution in pedagogy which is commited to honest dealings with the minds of children. It follows, therefore, that we may also enjoy more honest dealings with the hearts of children. Not that this *necessarily* follows, nor that it should always be made to follow. Admittedly, there are times for dispassion in schoolrooms, but teachers need no reminding of this. They do, however, need reminding that there are also times for passion in schoolrooms"(*ibid*).

Nowhere is this more important than in moral education. For here the education of feeling and reason in harness is crucial since it is intimately concerned with the life, the values and the behaviour of the individual. In fact, this serves merely to highlight a point we have made several times, namely that there is a moral dimension to all education and that moral education is the concern of every teacher. Certainly, it is by this kind of approach to most of what we offer pupils in schools that we stand our best chance of providing them with the kind of education of their emotions we are claiming is crucial to a proper moral education.

This attempt to take full account of the emotions in education has several further aspects that we must briefly pick out as being of special relevance to moral education. In the first place, we have said a good deal in this chapter about the control of the emotions. We must not let it appear that we are saying here that this is to be avoided. We have tried to argue that it is dangerous to regard this as the only way of approaching emotional development, so that we are accepting by implication that it is one aspect of the problem. Certainly, children need to learn to control their emotions. They need discipline. They need to be able to avoid that problem of (*akrasia*) that Aristotle drew our attention to. They need, therefore, to develop whit John Wilson has called KRAT (1967), the ability to translate moral principles into action. It may well be true also that the best way in which we can help children, especially younger children, to develop this ability is, as Aristotle advised, to help them to develop certain habits of "good" behaviour when they are young. It is for this reason, as we saw in Chapter 2, that some people have claimed that the moral education of young children must always be indoctrination.

However, there are different kinds of control and discipline and the only kind of discipline that can be accepted as part of the educational process is self-discipline and, whatever devices we use, the goal must be to produce a person who is in control of his own emotions and can thus prevent them from getting in the way of his executing his own moral decisions. Thus, while control is important, we must work to ensure the is is truly self-control and that it is not the kind of unconscious repression of the emotions we discussed earlier. It is, then, a matter of giving pupils, or helping them to attain, control of their feelings rather than controlling them for them or establishing unconscious control mechanisms within them. This, as we saw earlier, is the process that Freud was concerned to assist us with, the bringing to the level of consciousness of those unconscious urges that result from repression. Education, then must help us to understand our emotions in order to give us this kind of conscious control of them.

However, control of the emotions is only half of the story. It is also necessary to help children to understand their feelings in order to accept them. This is a major feature of the value of those areas of the curriculum such as dance and drama which allow and encourage pupils to express their feelings in socially acceptable ways and thus enable them to come to terms with them. Again, we must beware of seeing their function as merely cathartic,a letting off of steam. To take that view is to do scant justice to the valuable work that many sensitive teachers are doing in these fields. It is far more a matter of enabling pupils - especially those who lack the facility to use other more formal media such as the written or even the spoken word - to face their emotions, recognize them for what they are and thus come to terms with them, developing understanding and acceptance as well as control.

This kind of experience will provide them with an understanding of the feelings of others too. This is another important aspect of the work that is done in these areas of the curriculum. The role-play that is part of some work in drama and dance clearly has as one of its central concerns the development of the ability to see things from someone else's point of view, to put oneself "in their shoes". This kind of insight into the feelings of others is a central feature of the teaching of literature too. What we must not fail to recognize is that again its main point and purpose is moral and that this is another element in a proper and comprehensive moral education. For this reason, it is another of the components of moral education that John Wilson has identified. "EMP refers to awareness or insight into one's own and other people's feelings, i.e. the ability to know what those feelings are and describe them correctly. A distincion might be drawn between self-awareness (AUTEMP) and awareness of others (ALLEMP)" (1967, pp.192-193).

Again, however, we must beware of assigning this task to teachers in certain subject areas and assuming it is not a legitimate concern of those of us who are involved in teaching other subjects. The experience of those associated with MACOS is relevant here too. -Fot it is precisely this kind of understanding of one's feeling and those of others - especially through considering the feelings, attitudes, values and so on of human beings living in a totally different environment - that they have suggested can and should be developed by adopting a new approach to teaching, certainly in the areas of the social studies and the Humanities and possibly everywhere. By studying the life-style of the Netsilik Eskimoes, for example, not merely at a descriptive level but by means of filmed material specially designed to highlight the starkness of some aspects of their existence, the harsh decisions they have to take - like infanticide and the abandonment of older folk - the moral problems they face, the solutions they come up with and so on, it is hoped that children will "deepen their comprehension of their species, of what makes all humans human "(Jones 1972, p.22). They should also in this way gain a deeper understanding of their own feelings of a kind that will give them more than a mere control of them.

What is important here, of course, is not only the content of our teaching but its approach, its manner and its method; and there is no doubt, as the MACOS team also discovered , that the crucial element as always, is the quality of the teacher.

There is a final point we must note that some people would want to make about the education of the emotions that is especially relevant to moral education. Some would want to claim that there are some emotions that we need not to control, nor even merely to understand but rather to welcome, embrace and promote. Some feelings are not generally regarded as bad, are not seen as inclinations or impulses to be controlled or repressed but are felt to be the motivating force for behaviour that would be acclaimed as good and positively encouraged. We mentioned earlier Kant's doubts about the moral value of an action that is done for the sake of duty but at the same time in accordance with one's inclinations. Many people have been as worried about the converse of this, those actions that are performed because they accord with duty but are done in a mechanical, loveless and almost grudging manner. It would seem that to be fully moral an action should not only conform to certain standards of rationality, it should also be performed with certain kinds of motivation. It is not for nothing that the basic tenet of Christianity bids us to love our neighbour. Kant's completely rationalist approach makes no allowance for this and perhaps to that extent may be felt to be more realistic. Certainly one will find it easier when dealing with a filthy tramp to recognize and even to fulfil any duty one may have to feed or clothe him than one will to embrace and love him in any sense of those terms. Yet there would seem to be something beyond this cold performance of duty in most people's concept of moral behaviour and the Christian doctrine of universal love lays emphasis on this. As we saw in Chapter 1, Kant stressed the centrality of the will to truly moral behaviour and Aristotle too suggested that it is not enough for an action to be performed "not unwillingy", but that to be moral it must be done, in the full sense, "willingly". However, it is perhaps also not enough to regard this as a purely intellectual or cognitive matter. Questions of motivation, again as etymology would suggest, cannot ignore the emotional state of the individual whose action is under discussion. There are two ways in which one can "go through the motions" of behaving morally. One can do what seems to be expected without oneself understanding or accepting the reason for such behaviour or intending it in the full sense. But one can also do it for the right reasons but with the wrong emotions, or worse, with no emotions at all.

Thus there are those who would claim that moral education should also concern itself with the promotion of certain kinds of feeling in pupils. John Wilson, for example, offers us a further component of moral education. "PHIL refers to the degree to which one can identify with other people, in the sense of being such that other people's feelings and interests actually count or weigh with one, or are accepted as of equal validity to one's own"(1967, p, 192).

However, he speaks of these components, both EMP and PHIL, in a manner that suggests that he sees them largely as kinds of cognition, recognizing the feelings of others and understanding them rather than feeling for them and with them. Thus he also says of PHIL, "Like the other components, this is a matter of whether, in principle, one accepts others as equals; not a matter of how far one loves them, feels for them, etc."(1967,p.192). Many would want to go beyond this and argue that the moral educator must be concerned to develop in his pupils the ability not only to recognize the importance of other people's feelings or to understand them, important as these abilities are, but to sympathize with them, to feel for them, to have empathy with them, even to love them. This represents a more positive development of, or education of, certain of the feelings and the emotions of our pupils, an attempt to enable them to become people who not only know and recognize what is right at the intellectual level, who not only can make reasoned moral choices in an autonomous manner, but can also recognize the importance of so doing not merely because it fits some rational scheme that may appeal to their minds but because it also involves a response to their fellow man that comes from their hearts. It is not merely a matter of controlling those feelings that are at odds with our reasoned moral decisions, however we set about that; it is also a matter of promoting those that will support and enhance them.

Thus there are a number of levels at which the emotional life of our pupils may be seen as of legitimate concern to the moral educator. Children will need help with the task of developing control of their feeligs. Furthermore, such control is better based on understanding and self-discipline than on authoritarianism and suppression. It may also be argued that they need an understanding of the feelings of other people. Lastly, however, it might be claimed that such understanding is of limited value in its contribution to the moral life if it is not accompanied by appropriate feelings in the individual himself.

Finally, we must note that this kind of feeling for others can best be developed by certain kinds of curriculum subjects or educational experience. Here again dance and drama have a major part to play. Here too the kind of outdoor pursuits and "outward bound" activiites that many teachers of physical education and others now engage their pupils in has a lot to offer. For there is probably no better way of developing this kind of feeling for others than by learning to live with them, to work with them and even to face and share hazards with them, This again must be one of the goals of those community service projects that have come to be a feature of the work of some schools with older adolescent pupils. Again, however, we must stress that, while certain areas of the curriculum may have more to contribute to this process than others, opportunities for pupils to work together exist in every subject. Conversely, every teacher can allow the opposite kinds of feeling to develop by encouraging too much competition between children and perhaps also a resultant intolerance of the slow worker. Thus again we note that moral education runs right across the curriculum and no teacher can evade his share of responsibiliy for it.

Summary and conclusions

We have tried in this chapter to outline briefly the divorce of reason and feeling that has characterized most of our thinking in the Western would since the time of the ancient Greeks. We have also tried to identify some of the implications of this for education in general and for moral education in particular. We then went on to suggest some of the directions in which we might begin to search for a more positive theory of the role of the emotions in moral a more positive theory of the role of the emotions in moral education. In doing so, we acknowledged the need to assist children to develop control over their emotions but stressed the advantages of the kind of control that comes from an understanding of them; we suggested too that an understanding of the feelings of other people is important; and, finally, we considered the suggestion that certain kinds of emotion, such as respect, and even love, for others might need to be positively promoted and encouraged. In considering these issues, we discovered again that it is difficult to divorce moral education from education itself and impossible, as a result, not be acknowledge that every teacher must accept his share of the responsibility for moral education.

However, it is not only teachers who contribute to the moral development of children. The teacher's responsibility derives not only from the content of his teaching but also from the fact that every act of teaching involves interaction between him and his pupils and every act of human interaction is an act of moral interaction. For this reason all adults play a part in the moral development of the young - parents, other relatives, neighbours, passing strangers and especially those who interact with children via the media, television, radio magazines, comics and so on.

It is this that makes for one of the peculiar difficulties of moral education. For, unlike the teaching of French or Latin or even, for the most part, science and mathematics, history, geography and so on, moral education has to be directed at pupils who come to school with a good deal of moral learning already behind them and further moral learning goes on continuously, out of school as much as, if not more than, within it. Thus teachers cannot regard themselves as offering moral education from scratch or developing it in the isolation of the school. Their contribution is only one of many contribution and often not even the most important. What is important, however, is for every teacher to ensure that what he is offering is moral education in the full sense rather than furhter moral learning of an uncritical kind, that he is in fact helping to transform that moral learning that goes on elsewhere into something truly educational in the sense we have defined.

It is to the problems of that task that we must turn in our next chapter.

5

Moral Education and Moral Learning

In the earlier chapters of this book we have attempted to consider some of the major dimensions of both moral behaviour and moral education, looking in particular at the part that both rationality and felling must play in both. We have examined some of the psychological and developmental factors that we must bear in mind as we plan the moral education of the young. And we have stressed the inevitable responsibility of all teachers for the moral development of their pupils. In the final chapters we shall explore some of the ways in which teachers can and do attempt to meet this responsibility through the curriculum in general and special provision for moral education in particular.

Before we turn to that, however, we must give some attention to a feature of moral education that makes it a particularly difficult area of responsibility for the teacher, the fact that children do not wait until they come to school to begin their moral development nor is their moral learning restricted to what they are offered in school.

They bring a good deal of moral learning with them and they continue to acquire moral attitudes, to adopt moral beliefs and to develop patterns of moral behaviour as much, or even more, as a result of their experiences outside the school as from any deliberate provision that may be made for them within it. Furthermore, throughout their time at school, they need to make moral decisions and thus need a code of values to base these on. The teacher of French can assume that most of his pupils will know no French when they first come to him; he can also advise them not to chance a visit to France until they have reached a reasonable level of proficiency. But the moral educator faces pupils who have already done a good deal of moral learning and he cannot advise them not to make moral decisions until they have had the benefit of all he has to offer. In this respect, moral development is again like language development. For not only is it the concern of every teacher; it is also the product of many different kinds of interaction between pupils and many "significant others" both inside and outside the school, and moral decisions have to be made while moral learning is still going on. No provision that we make for the moral education of pupils, therefore, will be or can be adequate unless it takes full account of this feature of moral development and it is to a consideration of both the major characteristics of this phenomenon and its implications for the teacher's task that we must now turn.

As we approach these questions, it is worth noting that this is a place where the distinction between education and other kinds of teaching and learning is again of crucial significance. For the problem we have identified really boils down to a question of converting moral learning into moral education, of accepting that our pupils will already have acquired many moral attitudes, beliefs and habits, and exploring how we can convert that learning into moral education of the kind we have defined.

There would seem to be three main aspects of this problem and we must look at all of them in turn. In the first place pupils acquire and go on acquiring moral attitudes, beliefs and habits from many sources other than their teachers. Secondly, we must note that the school itself is also a source of this kind of incidental moral learning and, as we have noted before, such learning is as much a result of the way in which the school is organized as of the behaviour of the teachers in it. Thirdly, as we try to convert this kind of moral learning into moral education in the full sense, we must not deplore the presence of previously learned moral attitudes in pupils; we must acknowledge and accept this. For we must recognize the need for pupils from the beginning to have a system of values to guide their behaviour, a content to their morality, and the resultant obligation on teachers to see the development of such a content as an important part of what it means to offer them a moral education.

At all stages, therefore, we must accept that pupils will have moral attitudes and beliefs, held with different degrees of both consciousness and intensity and at all stages we must recognize that it is the task of the moral educator to guide pupils in the acquisition of such values as well as to help them to become more reflective, more thoughtful and overtly conscious both of the values they hold and their reasons for holding them.

In order to gain a clearer view of the factors to be borne in mind as we set about this task, we must first of all look in a little more detail at the sources of such moral learning outside the school, then at some of its hidden sources within the school and finally at the problem of how we can use this learning to provide a content for a moral education of the form we have earlier defined.

Sources of moral learning outside the school

One of the major factors in the recent questioning of the assumption that there is any one absolute system of valves has undoubtedly been the growing awareness of the many variations in moral beliefs that are to be observed in different societies. The recent rapid development of communications of all kinds has brought with it a greater familiarity with the customs and habits of other societies and other cultures, as has the cultural mix that has occurred in many societies in recent times. We cannot now fail to be aware that in some societies polygamy is accepted, that some societies practice euthanasia, that others permit abortion, that some even accept infanticide, while others regard all or some of these practices as immoral and in some cases even render them illegal.

Furthermore, it is no longer possible for anyone who claims to be rational and reasonable objective in looking at such issues too readily to assume that those societies that do things differently from his own are necessarily primitive or misguided or evil. The range of value positions that can be observed in any one advanced society make it clear that many different viewpoints can be taken, in a perfectly reasoned and sincere manner, on any of these issues.

This has important implications for the status of judgments of moral value and for moral education, some of which we have examined elsewhere. Its particular relevance for this discussion, however, derives from the fact that it highlights the central role that society plays in the development of moral attitudes and values. If a person believes in monogamy, it is as likely that belief will be explicable in terms of his having grown up in a monogamous society as that he has come to the view through a rational and objective appraisal of its advantages and disadvantages. Different societies will be both the result of and productive of different social norms and a large share of the work of sociologists has been directed over the years towards questions of the relationships between the economic and political aspects of societies and the social norms that characterize those societies or, perhaps more importantly, between economic, political and technological change and changes in value structures. This indicates, then, that society has to be seen as a prime source of that moral learning that we are suggesting here is the foundation on which moral education has to be built or the raw material with which it has to work. Moral values are the very fabric of any society and it is from society, in the broadest connotation of the word, that children absorb most of their values, attitudes and beliefs.

In considering some of the agencies that contribute to this process, we must begin by distinguishing those deliberate attempts to manipulate people's attitudes and beliefs from those that happen in a "hidden", implicit, incidental manner. For children are subjected to quite explicit efforts from many quarters outside the school to promote in them certain attitudes and standards of behaviour as well as imbibing such values unconsciously from the infra-structure, as it were, of experiences not overtly or specifically designed to have that kind of effect. In practice, of course, but it is important to be aware of and to distinguish the explicit and the implicit sources of moral learning.

The most obvious source of explicit attempts to affect children's values is, of course, the parents. There are those parents who think that they can leave this to the school, but most parents recognize that they have a responsibility to bring their children up "proper" and none in any case can escape the moral training that is endemic to the necessity to exercise some sort of control over their children's behaviour from the earliest age.

There are several points arising from this that are of importance for the teacher. In the first place, the practice of parents will vary enormously both in the degree and the kind of attention they give to this aspect of their role. Their approaches will reflect all shades of the spectrum from the authoritarian through the democratic to the laissez-faire. Child-rearing practices will vary from the immediate gratification of the quick slap or the silencing dummy or sweet to the long drawn-out attempt at reasoned debate and persuasion. The range here can be quickly appreciated by a half-hour's observation of the different methods of control used by parents on a trip around any supermarket on a saturday morning.

Evidence shows that there are in fact social class differences in child-rearing practices that affect children's moral development. Studies by Sears et al. (1957), Kohn (1958), Kohlberg (1966), Kay (1968) and Bull (1969), to mention but a few, all suggest that children from families of higher social status show greater maturity in moral judgement than those from lower social class backgrounds.

There are several possible reasons for these differences. Firstly, it has been suggested that children from higher status families tend to be future-oriented. Parents offer them guidance in advance so that they are encouraged to consider the consequences of their actions. Conversely, parents of lower social status tend to punish after a misdemeanour, so that their children are more likely to be concerned with the immediate present. Linked with this is the practices in higher status families of defering gratification; children are thus further helped to consider long-term consequences and, it is claimed, are less likely to break promises, tell lies or steal out of pure expediency and a consideration only of present circumstances. Furthermore, as Henderson and Bernstein (1969) demostrate, middle class parents spend more time answering children's questions, giving them reasons why they are expected to behave in certain ways and explaining why they consider some behaviour morally unacceptable. Children from such families are thus more likely to understand reasons offered them and to formulate their own at an early age than those from lower status families where "because I say so" takes the place of a reasoned explanation.

William Kay (1975) also stresses the importance of personalism in child-rearing practices. Parents who treat their children as persons worthy of consideration and respect rather than merely as occupants of an inferior status are more likely to help them to learn to respect others and show consideration for them

Rigidity and flexibility in thinking are also reflected in children's moral conduct. Those accustomed to an authoritarian background are used to being told what to do and feel insecure outside such a framework. They seem to prefer authority to autonomy and are reluctant to make their own moral choices because of the degree of uncertainty involved. They are more concerned with particular instances than children who have learnt to be flexible in their moral thinking and to look for a general principle underlying particular rules and regulations.

Studies by Sears *et al.*(1957), Kohlberg (1966) and Sugarman (1967) all offer similar explanations for these differences. Middle class children usually have more say in family decision making from an early age, are encouraged to consider the movies and intentions of others and to develop some sort of inner self-control.

Kay(1975) stresses the importance of moral flexibility, the ability to consider particular circumstances and special consideration surrounding a moral action or choice rather than applying blindly a rule that one has been taught. He suggest that it is only by being morally flexible that children can develop what he calls moral dynamism or creativity-something akin to what we have referred to earlier as moral autonomy.

We noted in Chapter 3 how strongly attitudes and values are affected by early social experiences of this kind, so that we can appreciate how this degree of difference will lead to a similarly wide variety of levels of moral learning in pupils when they come to school. Some will be used to attempts to reason with them and will thus perhaps be some way on the road to moral education and to moral autonomy; others will be used only to the quick authoritarian reaction and will thus be still very firmly at the heteronomous stage. Indeed, one might even borrow the terminology of the language experts and speak of "restricted" and "elaborated" codes of morality. This is just as likely to be a function of social class too. This wide variety of experience will create as great difficulties for the teacher as a moral educator as the equally wide range of language experiences creates for him or her in other aspects of their work.

Secondly, there will be a similar variety in the content of the moral learning that has taken place. Not all parents will, either through their overt attempts at moral training or the incidental effects of their own behaviour, offer the same kind of moral guidance. For example, reactions of parents when their child has been physically attacked by another range from "Never mind, dear. I expect he was upset at something" through "What had you done to him first?" to "Next time he does it you make sure you hit him back harder". Other problems arise too from those differences of belief and practice that derive from the cultural differences to be found in a multi-ethnic school or classroom, such as the unwillingness of Pakistani girls to discard clothing in public for P.E or games lessons. It is not for teachers to involve themselves in conflict with parents over the content of their pupils'moral beliefs, since as we have suggested elsewhere, such conflict must be non-productive. It is important, however, for teacher to recognize that the variety of attitudes to be found amongst any group of pupils again creates very real difficulties for the conversion of such moral learning into moral education.

Further, we must note that a good deal will have been learnt unconsciously from parents-perhaps more than is learnt from their deliberate efforts at moral upbringing, since children are more likely to learn to do as their parents do than as their parents say, to pay more attention to what they practice than to what they preach. This means that they will have acquired, probably uncritically, most of the attitudes of their parents. The unthinking racial prejudice of some young children would seem certainly to derive from this source.

It also means that in those situations where their parents' practices and precepts are divergent,the children's moral attitudes are likely to be highly confused. This is a major source of those double standards of moral behaviour that are to be observed throughout society, the inconsistency of "one rule for myself and another for the rest of the world" that we suggested in Chapter 2 was incompatible with the notion of a rational morality. Young people are likely to be highly confused by parents who steal quite unashamedly from their places of employment but punish their children for behaving in what appears to them to be the same way, by parents whose attitude to sexual matters generally is liberal but who try to insist on firm sexual discipline in their own children, just as they will be bewildered by a society which condones and even encourages acquisitiveness but condemns greed or by a church which proclaims "Thou shalt not kill!" and blesses the troops before battle.

All of these factors create problem for the moral educator. Nor is it only parents who are a source of moral learning of this kind. Siblings, other immediate family members and many other adults will play their part too, from the archetypal grannie of Giles cartoon fame who expresses stern disapproval of almost all childish behaviour to the equally archetypal jovial Uncle Fred who encourages every kind of horseplay and seems to regard it as his mission in life to undermine all the restrictive practice of the most dutiful parents. Other adults too, either by accident or design, will influenced children and young people morally through any kind of contact they have with them, so-called "charismatic"personalities being particular influential. For the most part, attitudes will be caught from such sources rather than taught buy them and we noted in Chapter 3 some of the evidence for the importance in moral development of imitation and modelling.

The peer group too is a particularly fruitful source of values, especially at adolescence, and will play a major part in determining the value positions young people adopt and the behaviour pattern they come to feel they ought to conform to,a point which a visit to any first-class Association Football ground on any winter's Saturday afternoon will quickly and deafeningly confirm. This source of learning will give rise again to conflicts of values which are particularly difficult for the young person to resolve without the sensitive help of the teacher or another adult. Nor should we assume that, because the peer group is particular influential at adolescence, it is not important at other ages and stages; at the "gang"stage of the seven and eight year old it is perhaps equally important. We noted too in Chapter 3 Piaget's claims that not only does moral learning derive from this sources but that also operative activities and mutual understanding between peers are necessary conditions for the development of autonomy. On the other hand,we should not forget, as Kohlberg points out, that isolates can be as morally developed as other children.

It is also worth noting that in some societies the influence of the peer group is far greater than it is in others. Bronfenbrenner's comparative study(1970) of child-rearing practices in the USA and USSR demonstrates some of these differences clearly. Because of the nature of Soviet society, children are brought up in a collective atmosphere from the time they enter nursery school. Rather than being encouraged to act as individuals, they have stressed to them the importance of the group, so that they grow up learning to act in the interests of the group, to conform to its standards and norms and to accept responsibility for the behaviour of group members. Using observational and experimental methods, Bronfenbrenner found that Soviet children were less willing to engage in antisocial behaviour than their peers in the USA, England and Germany, mainly because they are held in check by other group members-not by adults. However, such practices tend to produce children who are obedient and conformist and who perhaps remain at Kohlberg's stage 3 or 4 in terms of their moral development. But, as Bronfenbrenner points out, Soviet society is slowly changing and patterns of upbringing are showing signs of greater flexibility, with a shift away from features which foster dependency and conformity to those conducive to individuality and independence.

Similarly, children brought up in Kibbutzim, the Israeli collective setting, were found to display values which were more peer group oriented than those brought up in ordinary families (Luria et al. 1963). Spiro (1958), however, had shown that adults who had lived in a Kibbutz as children nevertheless reached a stage of moral responsibility similar to that of those brought up in their own homes.

Another major source of moral learning is the many forms of mass media to which children are exposed-radio, newspapers, comics and, especially, television. We noted in Chapter 3 in discussing the importance of imitation and modelling for moral development the influence of symbolic models observed on film and television or in books.

Again some of the learning here is the result of deliberate attempts to foster particular moral attitudes, while some is the result of the same kind of unconscious absorption that we have just spoken of. Those television programmes and novels, for example, that are produced or written expressly for children usually offer a positive moral message. The triumph of "good"over "evil" is the theme of a good deal of children's literature, a point particularly well illustrated by C.S. Lewis's tales of Narnia, and it is clear that the community of Camberwick Green displays what Durkheim would have called a mechanical solidarity, a social cohesion that is based on the thoughtfulness and altruism of every one of its inhabitants.

Other values, however, of a kind that one might not regard with so ready an acceptance or with equanimity are implicit in programmes and other offerings that do not make any explicit attempt to promote them. This is true even of those that are specifically devised for children. Whatever toys Andy Pandy and Teddy choose to play with and whatever mess they make in playing with them. they can enjoy in an untrammelled manner and in the full knowledge that faithful and subservient Looby Loo will come along later and tidy everything up. This kind of programme is a major source of that learning of sex roles that must infuriate any liberated woman. Nor are the values implicit in the comments of those who present some of the magazine programmes directed at children always of a kind that one could believe the presenters themselves would accept if they were fully conscious of them. Items that are not specifically designed for children, of course, are likely to present even more serious problems of this kind. The violence of many of the most popular of television programmes, the attitude to sexual relationships evinced by such programmes, by some of the offerings of the popular press and by many other publications are but the more obvious examples of this. Less obvious, but perhaps of equal importance, are the effects of those many quiz programmes whose appeal is based on the monetary or material rewards they offer their contestants and over which an acquisitive audience drools.

Advertisements too, which scream at us from television, radio, newspapers, magazines and, sometimes it seems, every available blank space in the environment, contribute to the same process. The fundamental values of advertising itself are such that many people would want to question, based as they are for the most part on a morality of acquisitiveness, materialism and sometimes downright greed. Some advertisements that are directed specifically at children, however, are particularly questionable, such as that which in promoting the sale of a certain kind of confectionery based its appeal to children on the philosophy of "Wot a lot I got", or that which drew children's attention to the fact that the lucky child was the one that had two bars of a certain brand of chocolate rather than one.

Other agencies too, such as organized religion in its various forms, which will attempt in a quite overt, explicit and deliberate way to influence children and young people morally, will contribute both by accident and design to this process of moral learning and each child's system of values will be the product of these many forces acting upon him with varying degrees of strength and impact.

The relative influence or each of these agencies and sources of moral learning will vary also according to the kind of society in which they are experienced. In some societies, for example, the influence of the family is greater than in others. The same can be true of different groups of communities in the same society. In our own society, for instance, the family unit plays a more dominant role in the moral upbringing of Jewish children than it does in that of other children, a fact that has been appealed to as an explanation of the lower level of juvenile delinquency among Jewish adolescents. The relative influence will also vary according to be age of the children. Parental influence is usually very great in the case of young children, while as we have noted several times, the peer group comes into the ascendant at adolescence. All combine, however, in varying degrees of strength and influence to create the moral content of each child's value system upon which the moral educator ,must work. They present him with three major problems. For, firstly, they lead to a great variety of learning, attitudes, beliefs and values. Secondly, there is a similar variety in the manner in which pupils will have come to hold these beliefs. And thirdly, in all cases, much of this learning and many of these attitudes, beliefs and values are unconscious or, at least, are held uncritically. For either they are the result of unconscious influence and absorption that will entail uncritical acceptance or, as in the case of an authoritarian approach by, say, organized religion or parents of particularly strong and dogmatic convictions, they are the result of deliberate attempts to secure uncritical acceptance. Because of this they are often in conflict with each other and lead to double standards of behaviour of a kind that we suggested in Chapter 2 cannot be accepted as rational nor, therefore, as constituting a moral education. Thus, the unreflective and uncritical nature of this learning makes the moral educator's task an especially difficult one, since he must help his pupils to become conscious of them before he can encourage them to reflect critically on them and to make a reasoned appraisal of them.

The school as a source of moral learning

It would be mistake to assume from what we have said so far that all the moral learning that goes on outside the school in unreflective are uncritical while all of that which goes on inside it is always educational in the full sense. Clearly, a lot of the experience and direct tutelage that children have outside the school will be of such a kind as to encourage them to think about the issues involved-certainly some parents will actively work at promoting this. The converse, however, is also true and it is to this that we must direct some attention here. For a moment's reflection will reveal that the school itself also contributes in a number of ways to this process of unreflective learning that we are describing. A lot of learning of this kind goes on as a result of the experiences pupils have at school, even though those experiences are not always acknowledged by teachers as having this kind of moral import. It is not only when teachers are deliberately setting up projects in moral education or extracting moral lessons from their work in literature or history that moral learning is going on. As much, if not more, is learnt from the way in which they organize the work of their pupils, react to the behaviour of individuals, use punishment, exercise discipline, achieve control and, in general, approach their pupils, handle their classes and manage their classrooms. Moral attitudes are caught from every interaction of teacher and pupil since these again, like all human interactions, are moral interactions.

It will be apparent that the school will contribute to this kind of unreflective moral learning both by its deliberate attempts to ensure the acceptance by children of certain values and through this kind of unconscious absorption of the values implicit in its pattern of working and its structures, in short, though what has been called the "hidden curriculum".

For, in the first place, teachers will often for a variety of reasons attempt to establish certain habits of behaviour or attitudes in their pupils without concerning themselves too much or at all with the question of whether their pupils come to hold these attitudes or adhere to these habits reflectively or unreflectively. In other words, they will actively work to promote moral learning without considering weather at the same time they are forwarding the task of moral education. This is particularly likely to be the practice of teacher of young children, especially if they take too seriously or too naively the suggestion of the developmental psychoplogists that at this age children cannot be expected to be critical or reflective on such issues.

The reason for such behaviour may often be a quite legitimate concern to establish and maintain order or to protect some pupils from the excess of others, so that "Be quiet when I tell you to!" or "We mustn't talk when we're in the classroom" or any other such straight injunction may be justified in such utilitarian and pragmatic terms. Or they might be prompted by a genuine, if misguided, urge to promote "good" habits, as is true of a good many new-style school assemblies. But all such injunctions provide the wrong kind of basis for morality, since they all suggest that the prime reason for adopting such habits or beliefs is respect for, or even fear of, the authority of a superior. To that extent, therefore, they are not conducive to moral education and, as we have seen, may even, if they are too strong, positively inhibit it. It is this kind of moral teaching that, as we saw in Chapter 2, has been described as indoctrinatory and, as we also saw there, it can only be avoided by offering reasons for any injunction so that, even if the precise reason is not understood at the time, the relevance of reasons to behaviour is always made clear (Hare 1964). If teachers are not aware of the dangers, therefore, they can in this way through their own deliberate attempts at moral teaching contribute to the kind of unreflective moral learning we are discussing here and thus perhaps effectively inhabit moral education. On the other hand, if teachers are conscious of the potential dangers, the way to avoid them is not difficult to find and they can very easily use such situations to lay the right kinds of foundation for moral education.

Much less easy to deal with are the hidden sources of moral learning in the school, those values, attitudes and resultant habits of behaviour that are assimilated by the pupils in a largely unconscious manner. There are several sources of such learning and it will be helpful if we can look at each of them in turn.

We shall see in Chapter 6 that there is a moral dimension to most, if not all, areas of the curriculum. In many cases, as, for example, in the teaching of history, literature and the humanities generally, this moral dimension is explicit or at least can and should for the most part be made so. One cannot go very far in introducing pupils to the plays of Shakespeare without recognizing that one is presenting them with important moral dilemmas and thus contributing to their moral education. This is also true, as we have seen, of the kind of literature that we might introduce quite young pupils to, so that he or she would be a strangely insensitive teacher who did not appreciate that at any age there exists this dimension to the work children do in school in these areas of the curriculum.

What is less readily apparent is that similar valve positions are implicit in other material that we present to children in contexts where it is not our intention to encourage such critical reflection and response, and that not all the values residing in such material can be made explicit in this way. Some are woven into the very fabric of the material and this creates especially difficult problems when our concern is not to promote debate and discussion but to achieve rather more mundane goals. Thus those texts which are used as basic readers for young children and whose prime purpose is to effect a fluent and steady development of reading skills must have a content and that content will inevitably be based on some kind of value structure. This is why many such reading schemes are currently under attack as sexist, as promoting a hidden and unconscious acceptance of sex roles, or as reflecting a middle-class ethos-Janet in the kitchen helping Mummy, John in the garage helping Father to clean the car (and Rover, good dog, Rover, coming and going between them). Indeed, attempts have been made to use this phenomenon of unconscious assimilation of values to promote particular kinds of attitude, political, religious or social. The readers written for use by young children in some countries have a content that is quite overtly and blatantly political and/or religious, for example, and several attempts have been made recently to produce reading schemes for use in the USA and the UK that would by this method promote such social virtues as racial and social harmony and tolerance. Much moral learning, then, takes place in this largely unconscious manner through the content of materials that teachers might regard as having no such wide-reaching purpose, function or significance.

Secondly, there is no way in which children can avoid "catching" moral attitudes, beliefs and habits from their teachers. This is a further implication of that claim of the Newsom Report with which we began that "teachers can only escape from their influence over the moral and spiritual development of their pupils by closing their schools" (1963, &160). The moral views that teachers hold and the manner in which they hold them will be communicated to their pupils whether they wish it to be so or not, As we noted above in considering the role of the parents in moral development , moral learning comes from every kind of human interaction, the interaction between teacher and pupil no less than any other. The individual teacher's values will be plain from the way in which he sets about his business in the classroom, the kinds of relationship he develops with his pupils, the way he organizes their learning, the way he reacts to their mistakes and misdemeanours, his use or abuse of punishment and in general his whole approach to the job of teaching. The teacher who without question or explanation requires a pupil who has not done his homework to write it out ten times by the next day is clearly promoting a different kind of moral learning from the one who asks whether any circumstances at home made it difficult for him to do it. (He is also, incidentally, fostering a very strange notion of education.) Similarly, the teacher who was once heard telling a class of boys to take particular care of a set of books because they had paid for them themselves was encouraging a moral attitude that he himself, one suspects, would have been horrified by if he had thought seriously about it. Which of us has not been guilty of the same kind of thoughtless remark? A good deal of unreflective moral learning, then, goes on through the ordinary day-to-day business of every teacher's classroom.

Furthermore, pupils will also learn from the manner in which teachers hold their value positions and this is a more serious problem because it has direct implications for their moral education as well as their moral learning. If it is apparent from what a teacher says or does that many of his moral beliefs are held unreflectively or have been accepted uncritically from other sources, if, in short, he reveals that he is not himself morally educated and morally autonomous, then pupils are likely themselves to settle for an authoritarian form of morality and remain at the stage of heteronomy or socionomy, so that their moral education will in this way way be impaired and retarded. To absorb in this unreflective way an attitude from someone who himself holds that attitude as a prejudice, unreflectively, is likely to be more detrimental to moral education than to imbibe it from someone who holds the view because he has thought it out. What we are discussing in general here is that accidental indoctrination or miseducation we examined in Chapter 2. However, we are now taking the issue a step further and suggesting that it is likely that our influence will be more seriously miseducative or indoctrinatory if we ourselves hold views in such a manner as to indicate a response to moral issues at the level of heteronomy or even socionomy.

Thus both the matter and the manner of every teacher's moral code, its content and its form, will be communicated to his pupils through all of his contacts with them and will contribute, for good or ill, to their moral development

Lastly, we must note that the organization of the school is a further source of moral learning. Just as the way in which the individual teacher organizes his class will reveal certain values that the he holds, so the way in which the school as a whole or even the school system is organized will display the same kind of hidden value structure. For implicit in any kind of organization is a set of values and those values will be absorbed, for the most part unconsciously, by those who are the objects, even the victims, of that organization or system. Moral learning, then, is as much a function of the way in which we organize our schools as of any deliberate provision we make for it within them. It has become apparent in recent years that the way in which the school is organized will determine to a large extent the kinds of relationship that are possible within it; it will also govern the kind of moral learning that goes on and, indeed, the kind of moral education that is possible.

Again, this can be used quite deliberately to promote moral education. The use by many schools of "councils" of staff and pupils is not only a device to ensure the smooth running of the school, it is also an attempt to create an organizational structure that will itself contribute to the moral education of its pupils. Again, however, it is what happens in an unrecognized and unacknowledged way that is more important, since its effects, because they are "hidden", are more influential and difficult to control and those effects may well be positively inimical to moral education. It is for this reason that many people have condemned all forms of selection in educatin, secondary school selection and streaming in particular, because it reveals attitudes of mind that children exposed to such a system will absorb, attitudes that are based on a competitive ethos and a notion of differential human worth and which are felt by many to be as reprehensible when they lead some pupils to regard themselves as members of a superior race of human beings as when they lead others to develop feelings of inferior value. Conversely, it is this that in part explains why the introduction of mixed-ability grouping with its corresponding assumptions of human quality and collaboration has invariably led to improved social relationships in the school (Barker-Lunn 1970,Ferri 1972, Newbold 1977). For it represents a change in the infrastructure of values within the school, a different kind of "hidden curriculum".

It is also worth noting that in some cases, where the ethos of the school is in too direct an opposition to that of the homes from which the pupils come, the effect can be not only detrimental to moral education but also to education of any kind. This was, for example, posited as a major factor in the failure of pupils from "working class" homes to achieve the success they seemed capable of in the school system, especially after they had obtained admission to grammar schools (Jackson and Marsden 1962). The values, the ethos of the grammar school were too much at variance with those of the homes they came from. The notion of a corporate school spirit, for example, is not one to which children and young people from such backgrounds too readily respond. Nor is this phenomenon confined to grammar schools, as Barry Hines in *Kes* reveals plainly and sensitively.

We must again note, therefore, the many kinds of danger and threat to moral education that reside in the kind of moral learning that is promoted by the way in which the school is organized. We must note too that it is not just a matte of getting the "right" kind of organization. What is important is to realize that, whatever kind of organization we adopt, this kind of hidden learning will result, so that again we need to take account of it in considering what steps we should take to further the moral education of our pupils. It is probably true that a looser, more fluid, more flexible, "democratic" form of organization will ensure that pupils are encouraged to think more deeply about such matters, but the important thing is that they should be so encouraged and that again unreflective learning should not be allowed to inhibit or impair their moral education. If we were concerned only with socialization, in the structural functionalist sense of coming to accept the social values of the group, it might be enough merely to ensure that our organizational structure reflected the value structure of our society (if, indeed , any one such structure could be identified). But, since we are concerned with education, this is not sufficient.

From all of these sources, then, both inside and outside the school, children will acquire moral attitudes, beliefs and habits of behaviour. All of this moral learning must be converted into moral education. Indeed, this is the only realistic way in which we can approach moral education. We must accept that every pupil will have a content to his moral learning and that we must ourselves contribute to that content as well as being concerned with the form of moral education. It is to some of the problems of providing that kind of content and building a moral education on that kind of foundation that we must now finally turn.

Providing a content to moral education

Let us first of all remind ourselves why we need to provide a content for the developing morality of our children. There seem to be at least three reasons for this. The first of these is that children from the earliest age need rules, norms criteria of choice, standards of behaviour, since from the beginning they need to make choices. They may not yet for the most part be faced with the big moral issues that come with adolescence and that widening awareness of the world that accompanies that stage of human development, but moral choices still have to be made. Should I, to avoid being punished, tell mother I have not been at the jam?Should I eat my friend's sweets while he or she isn't looking?Should I use my greater size and strength to bully someone smaller and weaker? Should I tell lies about someone or, in circumstances where it will get them into trouble, should I tell the truth about them?And so on. We must not see moral problems as always being on the grand scale. For most of us they a usually much more mundane.

From the earliest age, then, children need criteria to appeal to in making such choices. This is probably one of the reasons why they do absorb values, norms and standards from all aspects of their environment in the ways we have just tried to outline. For this reason, then, teachers must not only recognize that they do acquire their values in these ways, they must also acknowledge the need to help them to acquire the "right" kinds of value.

Secondly, as we noted in Chapter 4, children need to develop settled habits and patterns of behaviour if they are to have the self-discipline to carry out the rational moral choices they may later come to make. They can only develop such settled dispositions if they are provided with or helped to acquire some standards and norms of behaviour from earliest times. As Aristotle said, we become virtuous by acting virtuously. This raises the problem of what Richard Peters, echoing Aristotle, has called the paradox of moral education. We shall shortly be suggesting that this is not a paradox but rather the very essence of moral education, although we must consider some of the difficulties it raised for teachers

For, thirdly, children need a content of this kind to provide the raw material of their moral education. Even if our concern is primarily with form or manner, this can only be taught, as Kohlberg argues, through content. Moral education, as we have had cause to note on several occasions, cannot be planned or practised in a vacuum. There is a content on which it must work and, in turn, it needs such a content to work on. It is essentially the process of converting moral learning or even moral training into moral education. It is not, therefore, something different from moral learning; it is something more than moral learning. It must start with moral learning and go on to something very much more sophisticated. We have to accept that there is a continuous interaction between moral behaviour and moral education at all stages and that, in the end, moral education will be the product of the individual's moral experiences as well as those deliberate attempts that we are suggesting teachers should make to promote his moral education. To put it differently, before a moral education that has the *form* we described in Chapter 1 can be achieved, the individual will need and, indeed, will possess a *content* to his morality, a system of values of some kind, however acquired. Not only, then, can we not, as moral educators, ignore the existence of this kind of moral learning, we must also recognize and accept its necessity both for the individual's continuing behaviour and actions and as the raw material of the education we are hoping to offer. Moral education - again perhaps like all education - can only be effective if it starts from what the child brings to school with him and every child needs to be helped to develop moral values and not merely to be able to reflect rationally about them. In short, the moral educator must be concerned with the content as well as the form of morality, a truth that much that has been written on the subject of moral education has been inclined to ignore.

The existence of moral learning acquired in these informal ways therefore, provides the teacher with a basis for moral education. It also, however, creates a problem for him, since essentially the moral educator is in a business where his pupils must use the tools and skills he is trying to help them to acquire long before they have acquired them. It is as though we were trying to give driving lessons to pupils who travel to and from school in their own cars or train fighter pilots who, in between lessons, take up their planes and engage in dog-fights, or give lessons in the use of a lathe to pupils who are endeavouring, outside school hours, to make a living as machine-tool operators - a crazy and seemingly impossible task.

This problem manifests itself in different ways according to the age-range of pupils we are concerned with. In the case of the younger child, for example, it is this feature of moral development that gives rise to those fears of indoctrination that we mentioned in Chapter 2. For it appears that children are acquiring a content to their moral beliefs, a content to which their teachers themselves, as we have just seen, must contribute, and are requiring guidance from their teachers in the development of such content, long before they appear to have the mental and intellectual capacity to achieve the level of understanding necessary for them to think for themselves on such issues. It would be a mistake, however, to assume that this problem does not arise with older pupils. Certainly, the onset of puberty does not bring more important moral problems for the individual to resolve; it also brings with it a greater awareness of moral issues, a greater consciousness of their importance and a wider view of their significance, so that it is at this age that the horizons widen and the young person suddenly takes an interest in the cares of the world and adopts all kind of idealistic views on them. He is thus at his most impressionable and, therefore, at his most vulnerable stage. It cannot be assumed, however, that, unlike the younger child, he has now the understanding to think for himself and to be autonomous, that his moral education is almost complete. Certainly he should be further on in his moral development but he is still highly susceptible to influence, as the incidence of religious "conversions" at this age indicates, and, as we suggested in Chapter 2, we are flirting with danger as moral educators if we assume that indoctrination is a problem that only the teacher of young children need be concerned with.

For all of these reasons children need to be helped to acquired moral values and all teachers must accept that they have a share in the responsibility for offering them such assistance. We must now turn to a consideration of what this implies for the practice of moral education and some of the ways in which teachers might aim to fulfill this responsibility.

The first problem we face in approaching the task of providing a content to the moral education of pupils is that which we discussed at some length in Chapter 2, the impossibility of establishing a universally valid or acceptable basis for any particular set of moral precepts. However, this problem is not peculiar to moral education. For judgements of value are as difficult to substantiate in other spheres too and the problem that we are identifying is one that is common to all education, the problem of finding the middle road between leaving children entirely alone and imposing our views and values on them. This is well brought out in the words of John Dewey, "There are those who see no alternative between forcing the child from without, or leaving him entirely alone. Seeing no alternative, some choose one mode, some another."

The solution Dewey himself suggests here is summed up by the word "guidance". "Guidance is not external imposition. It is freeing the life-process for its own most adequate fulfilment."It is precisely this kind of guidance that the child needs in the sphere of morality.

Children and young people need and have a right to expect guidance with the day-to-day choices they must make. Like most education, moral education is best forwarded when it begins from the first-hand experience of the individual pupil. Opportunities for discussing far-reaching moral issues of the kind the Schools Council's Humanities Curriculum Project has directed its attention to, as we shall see in Chapter 7, have a great deal to offer to moral education, but they do not always have the direct personal relevance that the most effective moral education will require. It is for this reason that the teacher in the context of this kind of discussion can remain neutral and get away with it. He cannot, on the other hand, take a detached view of the real problems children and young people are endeavouring to solve. This is why the development of counselling services in schools has to be seen as one aspect of moral education, a point we must return to in the next chapter.

The difficulty, however, remains. For even if we see it as our task as teachers to guide pupils rather than to impose upon them, we still have to resolve the problem of attaining acceptable criteria upon which to base such guidance. There are two points to be made that have a bearing on this problem, the first of which can be dealt with quite briefly; the second will require the rest of the chapter to answer.

A good deal of basic, commonsense guidance can be offered to upils in a largely uncontroversial manner. There are certain broadly accepted social norms concerning such matters as respect for human life, for truth, for honesty, upon the basis of which one can suggest that pupils should not kill, steal. lie, cheat, harm or hurt other people and a lot more besides. The more one looks into this question the more it appears analogous to questions of freedom in education generally. There is a lot of "interference" in the lives of pupils that we can justify in terms of protection of others, to use J.S. Mill's famous criterion, and there is a good deal more that we can justify if we are prepared to appeal to the concept of education as embodying respect for persons, for knowledge, for truth, for freedom of thought and so on. Furthermore, if there is any value in what we said at the end of Chapter 4 about the need to promote in our pupils a feeling of concern, empathy, even love for others, then that will take us some way towards establishing a positive content to the moral advice we can offer. We must not assume because there are no valid or universally accepted arguments for ultimate moral value positions, that our hands are tied as moral educators and that we must not be positive in the moral guidance we offer our pupils.

The second point that needs to be made here is a little more complex and one that we must be careful to explain clearly to avoid misunderstanding. It is important that we provide moral guidance but, in a sense, the exact content or our moral teaching or moral guidance does not matter overmuch if the manner of it is right. If our approach to moral teaching and guidance is always such as to be conducive to moral education, if our concern is that pupils should be brought as soon as possible to think for themselves and to make their own minds up on these issues, if we are concerned always that they should be developing self-control and so on, then, within reason, the exact advice we offer, the precise precepts we encourage them to adopt are not as crucial as they would be if our approach was an intentionally authoritarian one and we were aiming to implant certain beliefs unshakeably. John Dewey's solution to the problem of finding a basis for educational guidance generally was the notion of the "experiential continuum"; that experience is to be encouraged which appears of all the possible alternatives to be likely to be productive of the most fruitful further experiences. It is a notion that would appear to be at least as useful in the sphere of moral education, since it would suggest that our approach should always be such to promote the continuing moral education of the individual or, perhaps more importantly and more usefuly, such as not to block this continuing development. In other words, we must have constantly before out minds the basic principles of moral education if moral learning is to be converted into moral education, however slow a process that might be, and if pupils are to be brought to the inside of this form of life. This is not perhaps so different here from other subjects.

Nor is it necessary to assume that if we get our pupils' moral thinking onto a sound and autonomous basis they will go off in all directions when it comes to establishing their own moral principles.

In fact, the reverse is the more likely. Just as an education in English. literature is unlikely to result in a preference for the *Beano* above all other works and an education in music will seldom produce an addict of the bagpipes, so a moral education is unlikely to lead to a rejection al all human valves. It is probable that a concern for the manner of moral education will lead to that respect for persons, that belief in the importance of treating others as ends in themselves and never as merely a means to the satisfaction of our wants and desires, that Kant and others have seen as the supreme principle of human morality.

To say that, however, is not to say that there is a rational or logical connection between the two nor is it to argue that anyone who did, after due and proper reflection, reject this principle would not be entitled to do so or would be behaving in an irrational way. The connection we are arguing for here between a proper form of moral thinking and human valves is contingent rather than necessary, but it is perhaps sufficiently firm ground upon which to base the positive guidance that our pupils will need. Provided that we do not lose sight of the crucial importance of manner, both the manner of our pupils' moral thinking and the manner in which they come to hold their moral beliefs, an content can be established upon which real moral guidance can be given.

In the end, however, as is the case in education generally, the teacher's main task as so often may be avoid doing positive harm. It may be more important for him to recognize the ways in which he can inhibit the moral education of his pupils than to seek for ways in which he can positively further it. What are the main dangers here?

Undoubtedly, the first of these is that which derives from an overdogmatic approach on the part of teachers or, indeed, of any adult. If it is to be possible for a child to think for himself at some later stage about any particular moral issue, the guidance he is offered at an earlier stage must not be too heavy-handed or dogmatic. A light and easy touch is essential if autonomy is ever to be possible. For if any moral precept has been forced upon us in early childhood in an aggressive manner, perhaps accompanied by severe punishment for any misdemeanour in this area,it is unlikely that we will ever be able to come to a detached, objective view of it. Whether it remains embedded in our value system or we later kick against it and reject it, a proper appraisal of this particular attitude will always be very difficult,if not impossible, since either of these reactions will give a "twist"to our moral thinking and will involve our emotions in the wrong way. Thus the child whose infantile explorations of sex are dubbed as "dirty"by his parents, and perhaps accompanied by severe punishment, will always find it difficult to divest himself of such an attitude, no matter how hard he might try to hold the issue up to the subsequent test of rationality.

For the dangers of fixation here are immense. This is exactly the kind of experience we suggested earlier might lead to such fixation and thus cause the individual to "get stuck" at an early stage of moral development. Most of us are so stuck in relation to some aspect of our behaviour. We all have our "hang-ups". Too dogmatic an attitude on the part of teachers or parents, too severe a reaction to certain kinds of behaviour will be likely to lead to such fixations and will thus be counter-productive to the cause of moral education, since they will make subsequent rational, objectives appraisal very difficult, if not impossible.

This in turn highlights the need for teachers themselves to be morally educated, autonomous persons . For only then will they find it easy to be non-dogmatic and non-authoritarian in their approach to moral issues, since only if they have given a good deal of thought to the matter themselves will they realize how little basis there is for being dogmatic about anything and how slender are the grounds for any kind of moral authoritarianism. If, on the other hand, they themselves have fixations and" hang-ups", if the basis of most or all of their moral views is heteronomous rather than autonomous, they will convey this to their pupils and will thus make it very difficult for their pupils to get beyond that stage themselves. As we suggested earlier, if pupils "catch" not only the matter but the manner of such beliefs from their teachers, their hopes of becoming morally educated may have gone beyond recall. Just as it is difficult, if not impossible, for a teacher of mathematics to take pupils beyond the level of his own attainment in mathematics, so is it impossible for the teacher to help his pupils towards a morally educated state if he has not reached such a state himself.

Moral education is essentially a matter of accepting the moral views that pupils already have and helping them to become conscious of what these are and to subject them to some kind of critical evaluation in order to raise and improve the quality of their thinking. This is one of the things that the Humanities Curriculum Project sets out to achieve, as we shall see in Chapter 7. In offering pupils help and guidance with what to believe, we must always stress and establish within them respect for the quantity of their opinions. We must remain always aware of the need for them to appreciate that they must take full account of all relevant information, that they must be objective, rather than selective, in their interpretation of such information, that they must attain the highest possible level of understanding, that their views must be rational in the sense of being coherent, consistent and so on and that they must avoid double standards. Whatever content we offer, whatever particular views they have or are encouraged by us to have, the most important thing is that our approach to their moral upbringing must be such as to further, and certainly not to inhibit, the ultimate attainment of moral autonomy.

Particular problems are raised here, of course, for the teacher of very young children. For at this age children are particularly malleable and susceptible to the influence of adults as well as being at a stage when it is unlikely that they can attain the conceptual level of thinking necessary if they are to make their own minds up on moral issues. There would seem to be at least three things for the teacher of young children to bear in mind in this connection. The first of these is that some children from a very early age do reveal the beginnings of really critical thinking about morals. Comments like "That's not fair, miss" are indications of this. We must not too readily assume that stages of development are closely linked to chronological age. Secondly, as we have suggested before, it will help towards the ultimate achievement of moral education if, even when children cannot understand the reasons for certain moral precepts, we still give the reasons so that they begin to get the idea that morality is not a matter of the authority of those with greater power that oneself but of reasoned consideration and argument, that reasons are relevant to moral decisions. In particular,

as we noted in Chapter 3, if their moral education is to be forwarded, we must offer them moral advice and guidance couched in terms "one stage above"the stage at which they are currently operating. Lastly, if reasons do have little effect at this early age,as it has been suggested, this is all the more reason for trying to adopt a light and easy touch with young children, for not being too dogmatic or authoritarian. What Freud has told us about fixation, about unconscious motivation and the resultant loss of control and autonomy suggests that it is in the earliest years of life that we are most at risk in this respect. The message thus seems to be clear. At this stage, more than at any other, teachers should be concerned to avoid doing positive harm. If they can achieve that, they may have contributed more to moral education than by any positive steps they might take.

The crucial thing is that whatever content there is to our pupils' moral learning and wherever it comes from, our own contribution to it as teachers should be such as to forward its conversion into moral education. In other words, we should, on the one hand, avoid doing anything that will militate against that process and, on the other , we must do all we can to raise their attitudes and beliefs from the almost unconscious level of unreflective acceptance to that of fully conscious critical awareness, to encourage a fully rational approach to morality and to help our pupils in their progress from anomy to autonomy. This we must do in respect of values they acquire from sources outside the school. We must also, therefore, see to it that from the outset the values they acquire from us and from the school as a whole are of such a kind and are presented in such a manner that they at least do not inhibit this process but rather promote and forward it.

Summary and conclusions

In this chapter, we have tried to suggest that no attempt at moral education can be successful unless it begins from a realization that a good deal of moral learning goes on in many informal ways both inside and outside the school. We have discussed some of the sources of such moral learning outside the school, considering in particular the contribution of parents, the peer group and the media. We them examined some of the "hidden"ways in which the school through its organization and the teacher through his approach to the day-to-day business of the classroom can also contribute to this kind of learning. We also noted that as well as being a factor to be considered by the moral educator, this is also a necessary part of moral development since pupils need to make moral choices from the earliest age, that, in fact, such moral learning is the very"stuff',the raw material, of moral education. We finally looked at some of the problems that face the teacher in his attempt to make a reasonable contribution to this learning and to covert it into moral education. In doing so, we recognized the importance of providing positive moral guidance but suggested that it is not so much the matter as the manner of what we have to offer here that is crucial and that, as so often in education, the important thing is for us to avoid doing positive damage.

It is one thing for all teachers to be aware in general of what harm they can do in this area or of what positive steps they should be taking to promote moral education. There are also, however, very specific contributions that can be made by teachers in particular subject areas and there are projects in moral education that have been specially designed to help us to meet some or all of the problems we have considered here and in the earlier chapters of this book. It is to a consideration of these that we must now turn.

6

Values For Education

"What a piece of work is a man! How noble in reason! How infinite in a faculty! in form, in moving, how express and admirable! in action how like an angel! in apprehension How like a god! the beauty of the world."

- Shakespeare (Hamlet)

Mankind has been constantly striving for emancipation i.e. freedom to choose its own destiny. During its long and chequered history, mankind has developed three forces to control its group destiny viz. social, political and economic, and evolved some sort of value system to provide life and blood to the individual and society. Every known society has a value system-a set of rules and goals that guide its conduct and judgements. The business of social life proceeds on the assumption that the values established in the groups are the ones that must be respected and enforced. With this end in view, every cultured society has developed some educational system to operate within its socio-economic and political system because education is one of the potent factors most likely to influence and modify one's behaviour. If we ask the syllabus makers, " which domain are you working in ?" the answer surely is-the affective-although this is not clearly recognised or stated and is frequently disguised by superficial emphasis on the cognitive and psychomotor domains. Basically, however, it is attitudes, sets of socially correct beliefs and behaviour based on socially accepted norms that the syllabus is trying to reach or indoctrinate.

Both, attitude and behaviour, being the functional aspects of one's personality are apt to be greatly influenced by education. In a broader sense, education, formal or informal, is a means to one's awareness to some information, knowledge or facts. It broadens one's mental outlook, influences one's belief structure and modifies one's attitude towards an issue, object or class of people. Further, the process of educating a person enables him to think in terms of right or wrong, true or false, reasonable or unreasonable. And thus, in turn, it invariably influences a person's overt or covert behaviour in varying degrees, depending on various other factors also. From a sociological viewpoint, all education proceeds by the participation of a person in social consciousness. According to the common notion illiteracy or lack of education is generally associated with conservatism which connotes rigidity to change and inability to discern pros and cons. But education has been called the third eye "*Gyanam tritiyam manujasya netram*". It is associated with modifiability, susceptibility to progressive views and rationalism. It contributes in liberalising one's attitude. Therefore forming attitudes or imbibing certain values is not an idle matter. It means one is no longer neutral to the issues. They are value laden for him in a positive or negative way. Psychologically, no one is born an *Arya Samajist, Vaishnava, Shaiva, Shwetambari, Digambari, Shia, Shunni, Protestant, Catholic* or so, but in each case he becomes one. His becoming any one of these means his forming appropriate attitudes.

From where does an individual evolve his or her values and form a set of attitudes towards objects and issues? Certainly from the family, the school, the mass media and a host of voluntary associations involving the individual. How far the schools are responsible and to what extent the teachers should make a deliberate effort to inculcate the values? Some may sincerely point out that children should be left free to form their own attitudes and choose their own values and that we should respect moral autonomy and differences in beliefs. But we should remember that respect for autonomy ought not to deter schools from providing occasions in which individuals seek attitudes and values. In fact it is one of the major responsibilities of the school to expose to the young minds the diversity prevalent in the society. A true teacher never says, "Do as I do";he like the *Rishi of Taittiriya Upanishad* says, "Do whatever you deem right. If you are in a fix, follow men of character and righteous persons." Such freedom must be given to a person.

Values are nurtured in a particular society and hence are governed by its outlook. A conservative society will develop parochial values while a liberal society will evolve magnanimous value system. Though the ages, ours has been a multiracial hence liberal society. Therefore the values which this society evolved are also liberal encompassing diverse outlooks of various communities. Ours has been the first culture of the world, "*sa prathma sanskritih vishvavarah"(Yajurveda);* that is why human begins all over the world came here to learn practical lessons of character, "*aitad desh prasutasya skashathagra janmanah. Swam-svam charitram shiksharen prithivyam sarve manvah." (Manusmrti. 2/20).* All these factors go a long way to make its character international. The values it evolved knows no limits of geography, history or sociology. These are cosmopolitan in the true sense of the word, not meant for citiens of a particular state only, but for human beings as such; hence are "human" in essence.

Unless I have misread Indian history and literature, what is constantly emphasised in it is a high standard of conduct, "a*charah paramo dharmah shrutyuktah smrita eva cha*" (*Manusmriti* 1/108). This appears to be radically different from the western ideal which at the moment concentrates on a high standard of living. But what I would like to underline is that these two ideals should not be viewed as contrary to each other, rather these are complementary; I repeat complementary. Kanad has rightly defined *dharma* as a proper blending and synthesis of the material prosperity and spiritual upliftment, "*yato abhudaya nishreyas siadhih siadhih sa dharmah.*" Material prosperity is indispensable for our mundane needs. It is no use preaching homilies to a hungry person because hunger and want deprive one of all idealism. Therefore material prosperity the primary requirement of human beings. " *Wayam syama patyo rayinam* (Rigveda, 10/121/10).

In order to preserve the humanity of human begins, spiritual upliftment is equally important. Material prosperity is necessary to enable a person to perform one's duties so that one could maintain a high standard of conduct. Spiritual upliftment provides a framework within which efforts must be made for material prosperity. Thus these are the two sides of the same coin. Their simultaneous presence presents a balanced view and absence of either of them culminates in lopsided development. The present crisis has emerged just because of such development. As Lord Todd has rightly said, "While science and technology have been bringing about vast changes in our material existence at an ever increasing pace, we have failed to match them with appropriate social and educational change." such a state needs to be remedied.

We have been experiencing a rising spiral of lawlessness around us. Law-breaking, and catch-me-if-you-can attitude has led to erosion of authority as a pastime. It is a story of guided missiles and misguided men, creating a lucrative market for muscle men and informers. In the words of Vinoba, "bhrashtachar" wants to wear the garb of "shishtachar" and "vishishtachar". It is interesting to quote the results of experiments done on the behaviour of apes in this respect. Kept under control, the apes divide themselves into a central group commanding power and privileges, and a peripheral group devoid of them. A similar situation is seen in human society also with a few differences. In the peripheral human group, there are many who try to enter the central group through traditional channels of education and training, while others, who are either physically, physiologically, psychologically or circumstantially incapable or uninterested, wield the danger or *danda* with cloak to share the privileges of the dominant and reigning central group.

Let us consider very briefly why such a stage has come and what we can urgently do about it. One main reason is that the gap between what we think, what we say and what we actually do, has been increasing. It will serve no purpose to criticize the government, which may be the Highest Common Factor, rather than the Lowest Common Multiple, of our behaviour. Often, we talk of getting good results without developing the requisite courage to give good results owing to our aberrant behaviour. We talk of Raman, Pasteur, Einstein, Flemming and Khorana; rush to gulp medicines while lying on death-bed; but slump thereafter into our superstitious behaviour without trying to imbibe the scientific spirit of the great souls. An honest person must quietly sit down, and understand the implication of the law of *karma*. Honesty is not a permit to be arrogant. On one side, you may see a Ravana-like person, drowned in his misdeeds all the day and, may be, dreaming some plot even while sleeping. On the other hand, you may notice an honest person, draped in his linen of saintliness but lethargy. According to the law of *karma*, the one who has invested more energies must get more material fruits at least. Therefore, true wedding to truth, honesty and love is possible only when we invest more energies in what we do than the crooks around.

Secondly, there has been a sudden ecological disbalance, both on the material and spiritual planes. On the material plane, we know fully well that we had the system of *ashramas*, where mother Nature had full freedom of wearing any garments of its choice in the form of minerals, vegetation or animals. Even the king had to take permission of the *Rishi* to enter such holy precincts of nature. In our domestic functions, we put "*bandanwar*", a representation of the trees, so that they may not be annoyed. Such was our participative, ecological joy, which has now diminished. Now we want to denude the forests, and blast the mother earth recklessly for our selfish short-term goals. We will have to learn to recognize that man is a component of this ship - the mother earth - with limited resources.

Denudation in the spiritual sphere has been still more miserable. Main difference between a saint and a normal human being is that a saint always sows goodness, without even expecting returns or dividends. A normal human being, on the contrary, expects that the acts of goodness done by him are duly reciprocated and the pool of goodness continually replenished. With the increase in the speed of our life, the time gap between the moment when an act of goodness continually replenished. With the increase in the speed of our life, the time gap between the moment when an act of goodness was done by somebody, and the time when that noble act is reciprocated, is being diminished or even eroded completely. In the good old days, a man could continue to disburse nobility all around without expecting dividends in his life-time. The right hand did something good which even the left hand did not know. This was the real *gupta-dana.* Later, somebody could reciprocate his acts to his sons and daughters. In short, there was a gap of one or two generations between the seeds of nobility sown, and the saplings of reciprocity growing.

This was a sweet gap, nurturing our social roots. The speed of life has demolished this gap; and we expect an immediate return of whatever little good act we do. There is a lurking fear that our good act may go waste. This is the level of distrust. We will have to meditate and realize how important it is for our happy and healthy survival, that we rejuvenate this divine pond of goodness, and ensure that it does not dry up, and that the forest around it ever remains lush green. If we desire to preserve such a garden, we will have to preserve our core of goodness first and strengthen the principle of "purity of means".

Another very important ecological component which affects us tremendously, is the increased speed of our life. We can understand it by taking a few examples. Upto the year 1859, we were burning coal at the rate of 33,000 million tons per century. Now this rate has become ten times. In other words, half of the total energy consumed in the last 2000 years has been consumed in the present century. Our knowledge is now doubling in 5-6 years; 80 per cent of the total number of scientists born since Plato are alive and kicking today; more than 1000 books are being published in Europe per day; we are changing our place of work very fast; our industrial houses are busy reducing the life-span of their products; the filament in a bulb burns faster now; in short, speed around us is on increase. Load on all our sense organs is multiplying. The increased stress is bringing in several unhealthy components, e.g. anger, agony, despair, cruelty and fear. Even the endocrinologists seem to agree on the effects of anger, leading to a kind of conditioning, followed by disturbed memory, decline in intelligence and loosening of our objects.

All available indications are that the speed of our life is adapting to it. Till now, we have seen the effect of speed in the form of increased stresses on our senses. Let us now observe a beautiful facet of its effects by conducting a simple experiment. Take a cup of tea while sitting on a balcony, and look at the traffic flowing through the market. Nothing unusual strikes our senses. Now drive a vehicle through the market. Increased speed has a peculiar effect on us. All the minor-most defects of the transport system become noticeable now. Faster our speed, the more the efficiency in the transport system we expect. Such an effect of increased speed on our body, mind and intellect is amazing.

We can make another experiment. Observe a scooterist carrying a person on the back seat. You may notice that he not only drives but also talks and in fact conducts a seminar all through. The few exceptions, which may be noted, are usually due to a significant social, economic or cultural gap between the driver and the pillion rider. As soon as the vehicle comes to a halt, the meteoric agility of the body, mind and intellect fades. A million dollar question is whether we can adopt, imbibe and assimilate this healthy dynamic component of the effect of increased speed of life around us. Simultaneously, can we minimize its ill-effects, e.g. stress, anger and agony? if the answer is yes, then how? In the resolution of this puzzle lies the golden secret of human potentialities. Let us see how rationally we can use these keys to lay strong foundations of happiness and bright future.

We will have to believe that effort in a reflection/mirror image of the life-spark. What is the aim of our life?In my opinion, it is a holy journey towards independence. Unlike a leo, human-child is born with physical dependence on the mother. Slowly he comes out of the mother's lap, and learns to sit, crawl stand and run. This is his journey of physical independence. Then begins his sojourn of economic independence. Thereafter, the phase of consciousness and independent intellect may or may not come. It is a common sight these days to meet such young men, who are physically, physiologically, and economically round. Many of them, however, cater such conditioned reflexes by smoking, drinking or drugging that they droop and wither before beginning to blossom.

Shelley has said that a man is like a burning coal, gathering ash; and once in a while a breeze comes and it glows. The important question is: what is this glow? Can we consciously control and modulate it? My answer is, yes, we can definitely do so. In order to understand it, let us take an example. There is a vast bulk of millions of people, who have a tiny spark of life in them. This spark represents the sum total of the energy of their life-time. This energy is apparently so little that their living or dying does not significantly affect the course of human evolution. Then, there is a second category of people, who have consciously or otherwise blown this spark into a tiny or big flame. Those who are intelligent, and have the requisite power of perception, can experience the light and warmth of this flame. Such people with a flame are fewer in number, but contribute a lot in the process of human evolution.

There is a third category of persons, who are very few in number but matter the most; the persons who have converted this flame into fire. I do not know how to describe this process of metamorphosis, after which body becomes a mere formality. Power of words is usually limited, although a right word, uttered at the right time in a right manner, changes into a *shabda brahma*. Till a better expression is available, let us use the words "Time transgression" to understand the metamorphosis of the flame into fire.

How would you define that moment, when Albert Eistein discovered that memorable relation between matter and energy? After this moment, it did not matter very much whether he lived or died. His body was nearly a formality thereafter. Without this moment, the course of human history would have been very different. In that moment, he transgressed time. One of the brightest querries for us is to know whether we can consciously move from the spark towards the flame/fire. In my humble opinion, this journey is consciously possible. In order to do so, there are two essential prerequisites : extreme level of concentration and power of observation. In other words, an effort to merge with what one desires to do. It is surely in this path that many of our seers had distinctly experienced the moments of timelessness (*shunyata*).

When the speed of change around us is increasing it is not easy to concentrate. Biologists have given us techniques of filtering the galaxy of external impulses. Neurophysiologists have given us the golden threads to hold and ride the chariot of time. It is scientifically possible to store the selected impulses in the huge "ocean" of instincts. The journey beyond this milestone is more to be experienced than expressed. The truth is that a man can thus hone his intellect to be ready to catch a miracle, which is sure to happen. When an exceptionally bright intellect is wedded to a pure and free "soul" or the linen spread into the moments of timelessness, time can be transgressed. Human efforts and potentialities are tremendous. It is biologically possible to increase our tensility, despite the increased speed of change around us and the multiplicity of impulses. The number of scientists struggling with these problems is increasing. The flow of investigations gives us an indication that we are going towards those paths which were possibly known to our seers. This is the path joining the lame knowledge through *manan, shraddha, nishtha* with "blind *karma*", i.e. the path of *yoga*. In this path can be sought the secrets of divine merging with the aim, i.e. "*Satyam-Shivam-Sundaram*". This alone can brighten the rainbow coloured tapestry of Indian culture and civilization.

7
Scientific Ethics

In this address on the principal types of ethics, I purpose to speak to you of what may be characterized as modern or scientific ethics, and then to set forth a few practical considerations in conclusion.

By modern ethics, I mean those conceptions of ethics that are peculiar to modern thinkers. Needless to say that Hellenic and Christian ideas still flourish in present-day civilization; following on the Renaissance, however, there have sprung up, along with them, doctrines that are alien both to the ancient doctrines we are now about to consider.

I

Scince is the principal creation of the moderns. Appearing in the sixteen, and seventeenth centuries, with Copernicus, Galielo, Kepler, Descartes, and Netwon, it spred in all directions in the eighteenth and reached its fullness of expansion in the nineteenth.

At the present time, it is by science that we live; for it reacts on the mind that creates, it and which it seem to be engaged in utterly transforming. What, then is science? Or rather, what is that scientific mind which has become an essential element inm modern thought?

Science has for its object the knowledge of nature. Of course, antiquity and the Middle Ages studied nature: but antiquity set out to find in her that order and harmony in which human reason delights; and the Midle Ages, considering nature in her relations with moral being, inquired more especially how man must deal with her in advancing towards his eternal destiny. Modern science examines nature in and for herself, Exclusive of the tendencies and desires of th ehuman soul. It regreds the world as a mechanism whose first cause is unknowable, but from which all idea of an end, particularly a moral end, is absent. The scientist start with observable facts, and reascends, liks by link chain of natural cause, without knowing where he is going. He has not the fainstest idea him; his mental state is what is generally known as scientific impartiality.

Science, thus understood, was at first applied only to inorganic being, celestial bodies, minerals, forces of the physcial and chemcial worlds, in which are manifested neither life, thougth, nor will. then it extended its domain, the dream of Descrates was realized, and science took possession of living bodies. Later on, the manifestations of sensibility, intelligence, and will fell beneath its sway. Ethics provided no exception, for Descartes had already hinted at the possibility of dealing with it as a science. In Spinoza, this idea takes on a precise form, and since then, many philosophers have attempted to carry it into effect. It the present time, it would appear as though it were indeed on the way to realization, and that the broad lines of scientific ethics had been laid down once for all. Let us see in what this work of the human mind has considered, and what results seem destined to be the issue thereof.

In truth, the task of setting up a scientific system of ethics is strange and paradoxical. Ethics, as thus understood, will have to be based on facts alone. To follow nature will be the fundamental rule. This is the motto even of the ancients; but they regarded nature from an esthetic point of view, seeing in her that intelligence and harmony to which human activity aspires. What the moderns have to do is to evolve ethics, i.e. the determination of what ought to be, from a reality stripped of all kinship with the intellect and the will.

Nor is this all. Modern societies, in fact, possess a whole assemblage of acknowledged ideas regarding the ideal after which man must aim: mankind has acquired these ideas in a spirit altogether different from that of modern science. Traditional ethics, both Hellenic and Christian, was established freely and spontaneously. The Greek sages heeded neither theology nor science; they simply asked themselves what it was that constituted supreme, beauty, the one sovereign boon. Christianity created its type of moral perfection even more freely, liberating itself from all exterior necessity and taking account of none of the conditions of earthly life.

Science, which finds itself faced with these moral traditions, Hellenic and Christian, and sees them incorporated in human nature, as it were, does not, at the outset, think of challenging their legitimacy; instead of that, it purposes to find their bases in the necessary laws of nature. And so this is the problem it has to face: how is it to adapt the strict employment of scientific methods so as to justify ideas whose special characteristic is that they sprang from the free development of human consciousness? Can the link be made, and the scientific method applied in all its rigour? Is there any fitness or propeiety between such a methos and such an object? We shall be able to judge by ht eresults.

II

There are several kinds of methods that are strictly scientific. Let us first consider the employment of mathematical demonstration in the sphere of ethics.

Mathematics and ethics have this in common: they are sciences of the necessary; both lay down principles which they afterwards develop by a process of reasoning. Mathematics determines the relations necessarily realised in matter; ethics investigates all that ought to be done by a free and intelligent human being. Might not he mathematical method therefore be applied to the demonstration of things ethical?

This was Kant's point of view. He dealt with ethics as a geometrician, believing that it was possible to apply to ethical dogmas the kind of certainty that applied to mathematical truths. He starts with the principle that the idea of duty has for each of us the same evidence as mathematical axioms. It is impossible for an honest, self-examining conscience to doubt that it has a duty to perform. If we pay attention, we find this belief implied in all the moral judgements that observation has brought to our knowledge. On this foundation, Kant builds up the whole of his system of ethics. With the utmost rigour, he establishes the reality and dignity of the human person. He shows how man ought to respect both himself and his fellow-beings, how the person ought always to be treated as an end, never as a means; and how sincerity, self esteem, and attempts to procure the happiness of others constitute fundamental duties. Duty for duty's sake, the effort to improve oneself and to contribute towards the happiness of others: such is the resume of his doctrine.

We see that ethics, as Kant interprets it, lost nothing by being subjected to mathematical discipline. This ideal is not one whit behind the Christian ideal, as regards purity and loftiness of purpose. The only fault we can find with it is its excessive severity.

But though ethics, in its essentials, remains intact in this system, such is not the case with the mathematical method. The latter has shown itself very complacent, and this ethical mathematics only apparently resembles mathematics, properly so-called.

For instance, it is true that the idea of duty possesses for us the same evidence as a principle of geometry? We know only too well that such is not the case. We cannot affirm that duty exists as we affirm that a straight line is the shortest distance between two points. Beneath the combined influence of the facts of observation and the exigencies of thought, mathematical axioms obtrude themselves upon us: it is not so with moral truths, which outstrip the given reality and are not bound down to the necessities of thought.

Again, things ethical are, in any case, unfitted for restriction within exact definitions, like those of geometry. They do not admit of mathematical proof and exactness. And perhaps it is better so, for, were belief in duty as unavoidable as adhesion to mathematical truth, it would not be meritorious at all; it is just because it involves voluntary effort that there is something generous and noble in it.

The practical conclusions, then, which Kant reaches along a line of well-directed deductions, possess, in reality, no mathematical value. To tell the truth, the results were assumed at the outset. The philosopher has demonstrated what he meant to demonstrate. As for the scientist, he does not know where demonstration will lead him.

III

It may be said of all philosophers and moralists who deduce the rule of our conduct from our natural feelings, that, in ethics, they follow the methods of the physical sciences. In the observation of our psychic nature they try to discover the law which, in fact, governs human actions, and they convert this law of fact into a maxim of conduct.

Some of them, such as Adam Smith, regarded sympathy as the principle of our actions.

Others imagined the primitive character of our nature to be rooted in egoism, not in sympathy, e.g. La Rochefoucauld and Bentham.

Stuart Mill endeavoured to reconcile the two great doctrines of interest and duty, by showing that such actions of ours as we call distinterested and explain by sympathy, or the idea of moral law, may in the final analysis, like the others, be reconciled with or brought within the scope of personal interest. certainly it seems to me that I can perform actions that are disinterested, devote myself to friends and country, sacrifice advantage to duty. Certainly we sometimes pursue the general interest without thinking of our own. This, however, it because experience has taught mankind that this kind of action usually ensures the good of the individual. To keep faith with one's fellow-beings, serve one's country or devote oneself to some noble cause, are all actions which were originally inspired by personal interest, though at present they appear to be ends in themselves. Here we have an application of the law of habit. The idea of certain actions has, in the course of time, become so intimately united with the idea of the pleasure to which they lead, that it has finally come to take their place and to be itself regarded as a principle of conduct. Man has forgotten the original and true end of these actions; it is the means he now regards as the end. Thus the miser loves money for itself, without remembering the purpose it is intended to subserve.

The utilitarian ethics of Stuart Mill, the perfect type of ethics dealt with by the physical science method, no longer offers, it would seem, that conformity to the judgements of conscience which we found in Kant. This system of ethics may seduce the intellect and produce learned books, but no one, strange to say, would advocate it before an open assembly. Men, in a meeting, will never acknowledge that pleasure and personal interest are the supreme and sole end of human activity. The public conscience, which Aristotle, not without reason, regards as superior to the sum total of individual consciences, would rebel against such language. Stuart Mill exhausts all the resources of his ingenious dialectic in an attempt to include under utilitarianism the morality of dignity and disinterestedness, but without success. Here it is ethics that suffers from the use of the scientific method.

After all, is the method followed strictly analogous, as it is believed to be, with that employed in the physical sciences? It is not an easy matter to admit that this is so. Scientific observation bears upon what is, upon observable phenomena and the relations between these phenomena. And this observation comes about by means of the senses. The scientist, then, proceeds blindly, urged by facts onward to conclusions he cannot foresee. The utilitarian moralist, for his part, observes within himself the workings of the soul. Now, the data of interior observation are neither definite nor primitive. In those feelings and opinions, those habits and infinitely complex phenomena we find within ourselves, how can we distinguish that which properly belongs to human nature, and is primitive and fundamental, from that which is variable, accidental, and derived, contingent, it may be, and determined at the outset by a free will? Besides, interior observation of the principles of our actions makes us acquainted not precisely with facts, but with ends. Even were the object proposed universally desired to the extent that pleasure is, it is still a mere idea, conceived as exercising attraction over us. Now, as we have said, science knows no ends in nature. It knows only purely mechanical causes and effects.

And so, in the utilitarian system, on the one hand, ethics has lost its greatness: it cannot, without defective reasoning, maintain the higher elements of the code of morals. On the other hand, the scientific method is not strictly applied. Not yet then, have we come into possession of the scientific ethics for which we are seeking.

IV

Science, as we conceive it nowadays, suffices into itself; it no more needs to submit to the laws of ethics than to take into account those or religion. Of all the sciences, however, is there not one that contains within itself what is ordinarily called ethics?

Amongst other objects, science includes the study of living beings; and this study, biology as it is called, comprehends, so far as the higher animals are concerned, both physical and moral manifestations. There may, then, be an ethical science: that portion of biology which deals with the ethical nature of man. Ethics is only one branch of natural history.

Here, the idea of scientific ethics is very clearly outlined. We shall not attempt to find, in prejudices and moral traditions, previously imposed solutions of scientific investigations; nor shall we set up as imperative maxims the confused and suspected data of the individual conscience: from without, we shall observe the general laws of life and of the world, and from these laws deduce those which, whether men know it or not, necessarily govern their conduct. Herbert Spencer and Darwin offer us this latter type of ethis, an ethics dealt with after the method of the natural sciences.

Life, according to Spencer, is the lasting adaptation of an individual or group of individuals to its environment. On this basis, what can ethics be? Not, as Bentham and Stuart Mill would have it, the recommendation that man should seek after what is useful to him, directly or indirectly, according to his feelings or the dictates of his individual conscience. Apart from the fact that the ethics of Stuart Mill was but a finalistic and esthetic ethics, devoid of scientific authority, it set before us an object that contradicted itself.

To seek after pleasure by taking the interior sense, the subjective opinion, as a guide, is a sure way to miss it altogether. Pleasure, indeed, is the end which the individual pursues, but the latter, by his feelings, cannot know what procures it. Nine times out of ten, his desires are a delusion and a snare. The task of making us happy is one that we must entrust to nature, *i.e.* to science, which discovers the laws of nature. If we obey the universal laws, including the law of adaptation to environment, of which life itself consists, we may be certain that, sooner or later, pleasure will be ours. Nay, what we call obedience to the laws of nature is really only a metaphor. We ourselves are nothing else than a part of nature, and so the adaptation of each individual to his surroundings and to the whole, the harmony between individual happiness and universal happiness, must gradually and of necessity come about. Such is the ethics of Herbert Spencer: the science of the conditions of human happiness, deduced from the general laws of life and from the conditions under which the human beings is question exist.

However remarkable be its scientific character, it is possible that this doctrine may not yet be the perfect type of ethics as a science. Indeed, it contains some traces of finality. This law of the adaptation of the individual to his environment, assumed to be absolute and supreme, is not a direct result of the observation of nature: it still implies the idea of harmony, as the end of universal evolution.

Darwinistic ethics is more strictly scientific. Darwin himself does not trouble to draw up a system of ethics, but when some objection to his system is sought in ethical ideas, he examines them and explains them from his point of view. He lays it down as a principle that the general law of the living world is the effort of each organism to continue to exit; and also the preservation and increase of those particularities useful in the struggle for existence. Vital competition and natural selection are the only causes of organization and change which nature brings into play. Now, in the struggle for existence, ethical feelings do play an important part. Sociability, love of family and country, honour, are all special forces added on to our physical and intellectual powers. What goes under the name of ethics can only be the study of the ethical factor which mankind introduces in the struggle for existence.

Here, the idea of scientific ethics is very nearly realized. Even in Darwinism, however, do we not meet with an ultimate memory of finality? Is not that individual development, that triumph in the struggle for life which, according to Darwin, the innate tendency of every living being has for its object, is not that also an end? Is the love of life indisputably that inevitable, universal law which Darwin takes for granted? One fact, at all events, seems to provdie the contrary: suicide, and the distaste for life, of which man is capable.

If the last word on scientific ethics was not spoken in Darwinism strictly so-called, we find it in many recent works in which evolutionism and Darwinism have developed in a scrupulously naturalistic direction. Taking it literally, the true naturalistic ethics is nothing more than the natural history of morality, without any hypothesis set up as an imperative rule interfering with it. The natural sciences try to discover what laws govern the formation and changes of the various beings in nature. They enable us to see, without our forming the faintest preconceived ideas, along what successive phases these beings have passed in reaching their present condition. This method of research is applied, purely and simply, to the study of the moral being. It is proved that our moral feelings, which appear simple and innate, are really complex and derived; and an attempt is made, both by synthesis and by analysis, to connect them with the general mechanical causes of the universe.

Thus we see that the method is absolutely scientific, and ethics, as a science, has a veritable foundation. The result, however, at which we arrive, is evident, and it is given by naturalism itself: there is no longer any ethics. Already disfigured and mutilated in the systems constructed after the method of the physical sciences, ethics altogether disappears in those that deal with it after the method of the natural sciences.

Take, for instance, the notion of right: how could this notion continue to exist? The idea of right is based on that of freedom; and naturalism cannot see in freedom anything but illusion. Science will explain historically the genesis of the idea of right, and the result of its explanation will be the resolution, purely and simply, of the idea of right into the conditions of existence in which human communities find themselves.

And how is charity to be defended? It is absurd in a system where the destruction of the weak by the strong is the only social law known to nature, the only principle of what we call progress. To practise beneficence, that is, to interest oneself in the outcast, the weak and the wretched, to spend one's time and strength in keeping them alive, is the same as to attempt, from ignorance and superstition, to oppose the inevitable march of nature: a foolish, barren task.

And so the naturalistic system fully satisfies the conditions of science, but it annihilates ethics. That was bound to be the case. At the first blush, the idea of setting up a scientific system of ethics may have proved extremely fascinating, but ethics and science march in opposite directions. Science studies what is; ethics, what ought to be, what is fitting or obligatory. It is impossible to bring the later within the scope of the former.

But then, it will be said, though a little science unsettles ethics, much science reestablishes it; for, when studying things closely, we note that the traditional moral ideas are not arbitrary inventions but necessary phenomena, based on the nature of things.

My reply is that I cannot continue to attribute authority to ideas, the origin of which is shown, to lie in the mechanism of brute forces. Why should I respect them? Nature has made them, I am told. Yes, but she has made many things that are not respectable. These ideas, which, it is imagined, ought to guide me in the search after pleasure, actually hinder me: wherefore sacrifice the certain for the uncertain, the clear for the obscure, the present for a future that does not concern me? Consequently, I put aside derived laws and indirect means, to consider the one fundamental law. This law, science tells me, may be formulated: life for life. A strange formula, if it is supposed to given my conduct. For if life has no other end than itself, it has no value whatever in my eyes. The man who kills himself is precisely the man who believes that his life cannot any longer serve him for any other purpose than to live.

GENERAL CONCLUSION

From this study, which has been mainly historical, we must see if we cannot draw a few practical results.

The rights of science are indefeasible: of all the powers before which the human reason finds itself, science is the one which obtrudes itself most irresistible upon the reason. But if science cannot establish ethics, can it really abolish it?

The scientist is a spectator, and science is a mirror wherein reality is represented, epitomized. Now, does the spectator exclude the actor? On the contrary, he calls for and demands him. There would be nothing for science to observe, were there not an activity which is ever producing phenomena. Can I not apply this principle to my moral life?

Science, shall I say, applied to man, cannot prevent me from believing myself someone and acting as such, since it awaits my actions so as to have an object to analyse. We must not ask of science to give us the rules and regulations of our acts, nor must we fear that it will prevent our adopting any particular rule that it has not sanctioned. Science cannot order us to do anything, not even to cultivate itself; we are free to choose some external principle of action. Our only obligation with regard to science is that we take care that the rule we adopt shall not contradict its fundamental conditions and acquired results.

But where is this rule to be found? In Hellenic ethics? Or in Christian ethics?

These two combined seem to comprehend the entire human ideal; the one is the ethics of the intellect, the other that of the will Harmony and love, good and duty, beauty of form and sublimity of spirit: these sum up all that man can wish: all our ethical conceptions, then, must come under Christian and Hellenic ethics.

It is no easy matter, however, to reconcile these two doctrines. The one deals with the present or temporal life, the other with the future or eternal life.

Hellenic ethics sets before us, as an end, that state in which nature is in harmony with spirit, without therefore abdicating its own distinctive essence and value. The term of this wisdom is the serenity resulting from the perfect harmony between corporeal and intellectual perfection. Certainly, Hellenic ethics is idealistic: its object may even be regarded as the raising of man above instinct and animality. But what it has in view is the coincidence of form with idea: it is the realization of idea and the idealization of nature. Its object is to find the point where matter meets spirit, to unite the latter to the former in the most harmonious fashion. Not too much of anything, either in the spiritual or in the physical order of things: such is the Greek maxim.

Thus, Christian ethics is far from being the ethics of moderation. Far rather is it the ethics of a passionate love, an infinite desire. It insists on our being perfect as God himself is perfect. It orders spirit to free itself from matter as the butterfly leaves behind its chrysalis; for finite nature cannot contain infinite spirit. Is this transcendent ideal, in which nature is sacrificed to spirit, capable of being reconciled with the Greek ideal, which, whilst maintaining both within strict limits, unites them in one harmonious whole?

We must resign ourselves to the fact that we can regain neither the serenity of the Greeks nor the joyous enthusiasm of the early Christians. To the ancients, ethics is a doctrine; to the Christians, a belief. By reason of the conflict between Hellenism, Christianity, and Science, ethics is to us a problem. Let us not, however, be unduly depressed on that account, for, because it is a problem, it is therefore the very leaven of life. The attempts we are incessantly making to solve this problem invigorate the soul:

Ce n' est qu'en ces assauts qu'ec late la vertu,
Et l'on doute d'un coeur qui n'a point combattu.

Are we, moreover, to believe that we are reduced to the necessity of seeking and doubting?

If the question seems insoluble in theory, it may be possible, in practice, to come nearer to a reconciliation. According to this view, let us see how the role of Hellenism, Christianity, and Science may be interpreted.

Science, as we have said, does not allow us to form moral conceptions incompatible with the truths it pre-supposes or establishes. But whilst it makes us more and more thoroughly acquainted with reality, it places the forces of nature more and more at our service. It is for us to use them well. Science can supply us with the instruments of morality.

Now, this very morality may be inspired both by Christianity and by Hellenism, if each of these two systems makes certain concessions to the other.

Hellenism desires that man should spiritualize nature : cannot Christianity consent to this? To transcend nature, is it necessary to do away with it? The lesson to be learned from Greek ethics is that nature is not only a collection of atoms governed by blind forces, but that, in everything that is, the intellect can discern an esthetic and ideal element. The Greek will teach us to add on an idea to all reality, to unite reason to force, reflection to instinct, joy to work. He will show us how the humblest occupations of human life may be regarded as beautiful.

Strangers once came to visit the illustrious Heraclitus. They expected to find him in most imposing surroundings, whereas he was actually engaged in preparing his food with his own hands. As they were amazed to see him engaged in so menial an occupation, Heraclitus remarked: "Here, too, gods are to be found".

Thus the Greek idea ennobles the meanest and lowliest existence: it causes life to be esteemed and loved. The spirit of harmony delights in our world, everywhere finding itself at home therein.

A joyous, serene life, however, no longer proves sufficient for those brought under the influence of Christianity. The man who has become conscious of his will and his power to love will have nothing to do with the peace and calm of wisdom. In particular he is unable to find quite and happiness in the mere contemplation of visible harmony. And so he will give a welcome to that ethics of in-tention and spirity, of love and scarificewhich orders him, by means of his will, to do what nature with her loftiest instincts and forces could not do: to create within oneself an invisible, superior nature: in a word, to aim at that indefinable perfection which is the dream and aspiration of the human consciousness.

Is such ethics compatible with Hellenism? It would appear to be so, provided that, whilst assigning to man a supra-sensible destiny, it recognizes natural life and the legitimacy of natural life, and refrains from setting up renunciation of the world as the condition of this higher life.

Man is a traveller seeking his home. Science walks by his side, offering him the various powers of nature he happens to desire; but science, indifferent to the path he is to take, is incapable of serving him as a guide. And yet, there before him appears a beautiful young genius: the genius of harmony, the genius of Greece herself. He takes man by the hand and goes with him through the most enchanting lands. They reach the summit of a mountain: all around stretches a marvellous picture, radiant with grace and light. Heaven and earth blend in one, nor is it possible to discern the line that separates them. "Behold, here thou wilt find happiness", says the genius. And the traveller is tempted to, exclaim:. "This is my home at last." And indescribable thrill, however, passes through his frame; a feeling of uneasiness is aroused, and he begins to question himself. Is there no other destiny for him than thus to contemplate the various beings of nature, from without and in their *ensemble*? He wishes to have a close view of all these beings which, seen from above, blend into the harmony of the whole; to know their nature and activities. He descends into the valley and looks. Alas! they are beings that toil and suffer and destroy each other, burdened with physical and moral infirmities of every kind. Then he has a presentiment of another destiny for himself: the communion of feeling, *i.e.* of suffering, with all these wretched creatures. The invisible world, the world of souls stands revealed before aim. To help his brethren and love them, to employ every effort in making them good and happy; is not that the ideal after which he aspires? "Thou art indeed beautiful, my visible home, abode of harmony and serenity. But thou, my invisible home, hast all the sublime mystery of the infinite and the divine. It is not my destiny to strive to attain the latter, all the time I am living in the former?"

SCHOOL AND LIFE

I

The question of the relations that exist between school and life has stirred the imagination of moralists of all ages. The ancients long ago denounced thc tendency of the school to assume to be, not a means, but an and in itself. *Non schole,* said a famous maxim, *sed vitoe discimus.* Rabelais and Montaigne heap ridicule and sarcasm upon the school that turns out only scholars and not men; Rousseau gives a new lease of existence to school-teaching, by definitely assigning to life, not instruction, as its end.

In our days, people have vied with one another in maintaining, developing, and applying these principles. And yet the same criticism is still heard on every side. The school, it is urged, is a preparation for competitive examinations and the exhibition of a bookish science, rather than for life itself. Book at this child who has most creditably repeated his geography, arithmetic, or history lesson. Take him when he has left school and is brought face to face with living realities in front of him stretches a country the description of which he knows by heart; an arithmetical problem is set him, similar to those he has learnt theoretically; events take place that are connected with those dealt with in his history classes. And in this very world, the key of which he is supposed to possess, the child finds himself quite out of his element; he cannot recognize, as they really are, the persons and things whose pedagogic symbol he has mastered. What has he learnt, after all? A number of words and ideas, but very few facts of like nature with those to which life introduces him. Load him with prizes, diplomas, and certificates, but make no attempt to utilize him: he is a good pupil, but he is not a man in the true sense of the word.

The result is the same, our censors allege, as regards moral education. In spite of the vigorous efforts made by the school to spread its influence beyond the sphere of understanding and really to reach the soul, feelings, and will of the children, what the syllabus calls moral education too frequently degenerates into lessons just as abstract as the rest, and of which the pupil rids himself by learning them by heart; obtaining, as the reward of his zeal and application, good marks or exemption from certain tasks.

Is all this, moreover, add these worried critics, the mere result of neglect on the part of the masters? Is it not rather a fault inherent in the school, as such? In a word, is not everything which the school takes in hand destined to become, in a greater or less degree, an imposition to be written out, or a lesson, to be learned and repeated without a mistake? This is the meaning that a great number of parents give to the word: learn. They think that a good school is one in which the pupils have answers ready for any question they may be asked in an examination. The subject matter, in itself, is of little importance; the official syllabus is everything. Contemporary history, for instance, now that it is one of the subjects of instruction, possesses, for many children, no more actuality than do the wars of Rameses II., no more reality than the rule governing the participles; its sole interest consists in being rewarded by a mark expressed in figures varying from zero to ten, with a certain multiplier.

Such complaints are frequently heard, even in these days. Doubtless this criticism is anything but universal; there are numerous cases to which it applies but slightly, or not at all. Still, how can we affirm that language of this kind merely confuses the past with the present; that the evil in question need not be dreaed in the future; and that the school, as at present constituted, is certain to become increasingly linked and blended with real life as the years advance?

The matter is one which must be looked into; for it is not the master's fault alone that causes a tendency for the school to remain aloof from the facts of life. That is a natural tendency, which man may try to check, though he cannot suppress it altogether. Everywhere, and at all times, the school has produced what is called scholasticism, *i.e.* the transformation within abstract formulae, shut in and regarded as absolute, of the living, untrammelled creations of the man of genius. The latter draws directly from nature herself, continually endevaouring to lay hold upon and interpret ever more faithfully some of her true characteristics. The scholastics lay hold of thought in the throes of labour, and fasten it down in the form of inflexible, imperative rules, which they convert into substitutes for things. This phenomenon is a general one; it is seen alike in the history of art and low, of philosophy and literature, and actually constitutes a kind of law in itself. Every period of original activity is succeeded by one of scholasticism, of attachment to academic forms.

The reason is that, in order to maintain and spread some particular intellectual acquirement, we naturally set ourselves to teach it; that we do this by means of concepts; and that the concept-that marvellous invention of human understanding whereby the products of thought become capable of being apprehended and communicated-possesses a dangerous fascination. We look upon clarity as synonymous with truth: this is the snare into which the intellect would entrap us.

If man, in general, is so readily a dupe of the concepts and words into which he translated his intellectual creations, how would it be possible for the teacher, in particular, not to have a predilection for that which is preeminently the instrument of instruction?

Consequently, it is not simply a matter of chance, it is by virtue of the general laws of the human mind that the school, which ought to be a preparation for life, is constantly in danger of becoming a substitute for it.

And yet there can be no doubt but that this tendency is an evil one. It is not only from the practical point of view that we look upon a system of instruction which eliminates all thought of reality as being defective; it is also a serious defect for the intelligence itself, if it is unable to connect together idea and reality, science and life. This evil which, as though of necessity, threatens school life, is one that should be energetically fought. What is the best way to oppose it?

II

In their desire to eradicate the evil, many modern thinkers feel disposed to adopt the very contrary of all abstract, intellectual methods, and since our aim is to fashion children for practical life, in their opinion, life itself ought to be the sole foundation of education and instruction. Life by means of life, not of books and regulations: such appears to be their motto.

In accordance with this way of looking at things, moral education, in school, should consist essentially not in filling the child's head with rules and precepts, but rather in developing habits of life.

Now, action and repetition of action are the main factors of habit; consequently we are to eliminate such abstract reasonings and principles as claim to obtrude themselves on the mind before it has established their realization in facts. Moral experience and intuition must be the starting-point of every attempt to formulate moral rules; even to these very rules we are to attach but little importance, since it is action, after all, that is the end; and habits that have become like instincts are a far more sure and powerful motive than the most cunnigly deduced abstract principles.

The master's role is to consist in utilizing all the conditions of school life, and even, if need be, in calling forth appropriate incidents, so as to bring into being and develop in the children the very habits he purposes to impress upon their minds.

And we find the same revolution in matters of instruction, strictly so-called. The exclusively concrete method which is here constrasted with the scholastic may be called the pragmatistic method.

If consists in eliminating didactic books and formula, theories and rules, as far as possible, and bringing the pupil directly face to face with facts. To demand a knowledge of facts from intuition alone, to acquire practice by means of practice, to bring to the mind no other rules or laws than those we have ourselves been able to elicit from phenomena: such is the ideal. Is it the pupil's object to learn a foreign language, for instance? Then, according to this method, the language already known should be altogether left out of account, and the pupil should revert to the state of a child who is learning to speak for the first time. No dictionaries, grammars, or translations are to be used. The master speaks to the pupil in the language he purposes to teach him, and, at the same time, gets him to perceive, by means of the senses, the objects whose names he mentions. Or again, he explains, in the foreign language, complex ideas which have no corresponding sensible image. In this way one's ingenuity is taxed in enabling the pupil to grasp the realities of each subject of study direct, not through the medium of notions and abstractions, which, it is considered, can be nothing else than distorting media.

A clear, plausible, and all the more seductive method in that it is the very opposite of the bookish system, that primitive vice of school instruction.

Still, is such a contrast, in itself alone, a guarantee? A witty writer was wont to say: "Beware of opposing a fool with the same exaggeration he himself shows, or you run the danger of being as great a food as he is himself".

In a word, the pragmatistic method is the very one that Socrates denounced in the sophists of his own day, and which he regarded it as his mission to refute, viz., practice by means of practice, all theory having to be looked upon as an ineffectual shift or subterfuge. Now, are we quite sure that Socrates was engaged in a useless task, and that it is the sophists who were right?

I remember a phrase often used by my friend M.Chantepie du Dezert, the librarian of the Sorbonne: "It is only in geometry that a straight line is the shortest distance between two points". In the concrete world of reality, the shortest distance is the one which most speedily leads to the goal, and this is what the straight line, speaking generally, does not do.

So far as moral education is concerned, the idea of getting life itself to contribute towards the formation of youth is assuredly a most fruitful one. It must be borne in mind, however, that, in school, this idea can be applied but imperfectly. The master's very presence prevents the children from being under the ordinary conditions of real life. Life implies man left to himself, in his relations with his equals and with the rest of mankind. Is this the system adopted in school?

Sports organized and carried out by the pupils themselves, apart from extraneous control, as in England and the United States more particularly, constitute with tolerable accuracy the conditions of education by means of life.

And indeed, this apprenticeship to real life, as distinct from the school, is a very genuine and useful one. The school neither can nor should absorb the entire human being. Children and young people, when left to themselves, give one another lessons in dignity, courage and co-operation, loyalty and obedience both to traditional rules and to the common will, that could not be replaced by the intervention of any master, however clever he might be.

Still, this education of children by the children themselves is assuredly insufficient.

However real it be, it is empirical in its nature, nor is there any guarantee that it will, conform in all respects with the moral ideas and the requirements of society. Every particular community or caste is liable to foster prejudices. Children and young people, when isolated, as it were, from society as a whole, may form a very erroneous conception of life.

Besides, the more children live with one another and suffice unto themselves, the more they risk losing connexion with preceding generations and taking no interest in the tasks which these generations have handed down to them. If we want a bond of continuity to be maintained between successive generations, they must, to a certain extent, come in contact with and know each other, as well as live together.

Free, open-air games are excellent and necessary, though insufficient. The school- without speaking of the family- has also a part to play in moral education.

If the master, simply because he is a master, finds it impossible for him to place children under conditions of actual life, at all events, he is able to give them moral instruction of the utmost value, such as they could not acquire of themselves; now, what he is able to do, that he ought to do.

It is a mistake to believe that a human being's actions are never determined by anything else than his instincts, passions, or habits; and that ideas and theories can have no effect upon him. Indeed, every man possesses, stored away in his mind, maxims, principles, and reasonings which he is constantly saying over and over again to himself and to others, and which, at any given moment, influence his actions. Doubtless, the mind, like a cunning sophist, is ever finding reasons for attributing honest motives to base or violent actions- *after the event.* But even sophistry is an act of homage that passion pays to reason. Not only is it in conformity with human dignity, it is also beneficial to morality that a man be treated, not as a well-trained animal, but as an intelligent being, amenable to instruction and persuasion.

The master, by virtue of his position, is rather a teacher than a trainer. Let him beware lest he despise his special province: it is devoid neither of beauty nor, of efficacy. Instead of confining himself to working out the various incidents of school life, or artificially arousing so-called natural reactions, let him not be afraid of teaching clearly, methodically, and rationally. Definite, well-connected ideas still constitute what the mind retains with the greatest fidelity; it is they that are best calculated to direct a man's judgement throughout life.

Similar remarks may be made regarding instruction, strictly so-called. The pragmatistic method is not the shortest, as one might imagine, even for the man who aims only at practical results. It consists in doing without rules, formulae, and theories. Formulae, however, are nothing but past experiences generalized, i.e. the means of learning, once for all, what is taking place or what it is prudent or fitting to do in a multitude of different instances. The rule, when thoroughly understood, dispenses with an endless series of observations, comparisons, and tentative methods; it is the experience of centuries, condensed and placed at our disposal. The rule, then, is a short cut, not a roundabout way. Leibnitz said that all mathematical theorems are nothing else than tachygraphies, or abbreviatory methods of thinking.

Not only is the rule the shortest way, it is also the one that leads farthest and highest. To regard abstractions as merely, *impedimenta*, cumbersome objects to be brushed aside, is to deprive oneself of the opportunity of conceiving the reasons of things, as well as of the means of rationalizing and mentally assimilating them. Man wishes not only to have power, or even knowledge; he wishes to have understanding. This latter ambition, indeed, can never meet with full satisfaction; it may be satisfied, however, to some extent, and it is concept, abhorred by pragmatists; that is the means by which this satisfaction may be obtained.

And so no good purpose would be served by proscribing or denouncing the printed word, the book,- as we see a tendency to do in certain directions,- that treasure store from which men like Rabelais, Montaigne, Rousseau, of whose names we are so proud, have drawn so abundantly. Naturally, it is the master's province to direct the pupil along this line of development. But the book, in itself, is nothing less than the best of acquired science, expressed in the clearest, the most logical and exact way. It is by mediating on the book, with the master's help, that the child learns to fit the various details in the whole, to acquire knowledge of things with the utmost exactness, link them to one another, trace their profound, philosophical meaning, and engrave them forcibly and intelligently upon his memory.

After all, what object have we, as teachers, in view, except to enable our pupils to do without our assistance, and to instruct themselves, when they come to be deprived of the ordinary school teaching? It it not the greatest advantage that can be gained from study, to have the consciousness that what one knows is but a beginning, an initiation, and to be capable of undertaking and carrying through, alone and at any age, such supplementary or fresh studies as are deemed either necessary or desirable? Now, it is by teaching men to make use of the book, that this independence, this possibility of being sufficient into themselves, is assured. The book represents their true enfranchisement.

To sum up, we may say that, even as applied to modern times, it is Socrates who is right and the sophists who are in the wrong. Practice by means of practice alone, the end converted into the means, the suppression of idea as the medium between impression and reaction: all this represents animal routine substituted for human thought and action. Now, quite apart from the distinctive worth of science and intelligence, the practice which is at once prudent and expeditious, certain and productive is that which is illumined by theory.

III

Is this equivalent to saying that we must take no account of the ever-recurring objections to bookish instruction, to the substitution of words for things, and of the school for life itself?

Far from being worthless, these objections are of the utmost importance; but they are directed against the abuse of theory, against an erroneous interpretation of the role which theory has to play, not against an intelligent use of abstract knowledge and rules.

The human mind has two ways of interpreting the meaning and the role of concepts. One may suppose- in fact, one is inclined to acknowledge-that certain concepts are so well established, so clear and comprehensive, that they may legitimately be set up as substitutes for reality. In that case, instead of beginning over again to make slow and painful observations of facts, we think we are entitled to start with some of these concepts and, by means of that infallible instrument called logic, deduce therefrom the consequences they involve, purely and simply.

Now, it is concept, when understood and employed in this fashion, that renders instruction abstract and alien to life, dogmatic and frequently barren of results.

But this way of interpreting the meaning of the abstract, this way of looking upon rules, is not the only conceivable one. In reality, it is erroneous and should be rejected. Formula and concept, science itself in its totality, is never anything but an inadequate and perfectible expression of the real. It is the store or supply, in a workable, communicable form, of such observations as we have been enabled to make on the recent past of our world. Of this past itself we know but little; whereas we can form nothing but conjectures about the future.

Rules, therefore, should be regarded not as perfect, inviolable types of being, but rather as instruments of orientation and research. When thus understood, it is evident that they are by no means opposed to- but rather invite- a consideration of concrete realities, and a broad, frank introduction, of life into the school.

Nor is this everything, for clearly the word, life, implies not only the exercise of activity, strictly so-called, of sensibility and will, but also that of intellect. To neglect thought and attribute value to impulsive action only is not living as a man. Now, ideas and words, when regarded in their true nature as imperfect, living, and flexible symbols of real things, are, strictly speaking, both the expression and the stimulus of the life of the intellect.

In practice, the means to be employed in order to enable concepts and rules to play the part which really belongs to them is constantly to set them face to face with realities. We must bring it to pass that there are established and retained in the mind associations of ideas which carry it at once from the sign to the thing signified, and *vice versa.* Concept should always suggest intuition, just as intuition should call for concept.

Thus one of the most necessary practices of instruction, the indispensable condition of its efficacy, is what is strictly called exercise, or the concrete use of rules, whereby the mind actually acquires a very lively, and, as it were, instinctive sense of the connexion between abstractions and realities.

Finally, what is of supreme importance is not, that such or such a process or method be used, but that it be used in manner really active and instinct with life. It is easy to reduce into scholastic, mechanical routines the very methods that are designated as active and direct; just as, on the other hand, the most abstract and uninteresting book may be made a thing of life by the comments and explanations of a master animated by a love of childhood and of science.

Whilst condemning the use of purely pragmatistic methods, we can and we ought to insist upon the necessity of introducing into the school the utmost possible amount of life and activity.

There arises one question, however, of the greatest moment: what is this life, strictly speaking, with which we are here dealing?

The expression, "Life in school," has really two significations.

The phrase may means that anxious thought or preoccupation regarding real life, the social life which awaits the child on leaving school, should be ever present in the master's mind; that the school, in the case of the child, should take the future human being into consideration and help him to mould himself.

And assuredly this meaning is a perfectly correct one. To educate children is to endeavour to make men of them, to cultivate and develop those faculties which they will find necessary in adult practical life.

There is another way, however, quite as interesting, of regarding the life which ought to prevail in school.

Childhood is not merely the preface of mature age; it has its own value and beauty, its right of existence *per se.* Why live always in the future and never in the present? Let children enjoy their childhood, let them manifest the qualities of their age, for their own sake, and delight in the pure joys that nature showers on them.

Nor let it be imagined, either, that in living their own lives, children are neglecting to prepare themselves for adult life. Of a certainty, the child ought to fit himself for man's estate, which he will subsequently be called upon to take up. But then, has man, on his side, nothing to learn from the child? Would it not be to the advantage of the former if he were to be influenced by the latter? Childhood stands for idealism; it stands for faith, artlessness, spontaneity, rectitude, freedom from reserve confidence, optimism, mental sprightliness and curiosity, flexibility, infinite aspirations and ambitions. It is good for the, child to be put in a position to realize and develop these precious qualities and virtues of his age, so that adults, when brought in contact with him, may quicken into renewed life somewhat of these virtues within themselves, and that the child also may subsequently have the opportunity of retaining some traces of them, amid the disillusionments of the life of this world.

Let the school, then, be a living one in this second signification also. Let it live the life that is fitting to childhood and youth! Let it be a charming, a privileged sport, where children may have the joy of learning for the sake of learning, of studying in quiet and faith, of seeing justice and goodwill all around, of working and playing in common, the while they are linked to one another by the precious bonds of comradeship. It will fill their imagination and memory with dear and charming recollections which, some day, they will discover to be a source of strength and blessing.

In this way it will fill the role- which it is so well calculated to fill- of acting as a medium between the past and the present generations; it will enable the latter to share in the virtues of the former, and *vice versa*; and it will procure, between successive generations, that continuity in change which constitutes the condition of the existence, might, and greatness of a human community.

A society that is sane and youthful, justly confident in the future; such is the offspring of a school that is truly living.

8
Habits and Values

Habit, change, and illusions of change form the procession of the events of conscious life. Habits may be instinctive and congenital or acquired; but they are always automatic in their operation. I Changes may be accidental or voluntary; they may be either enforced by circumstances or originated in the choice of the individual. The greatest lives are those at once most controlled by choice and furnished with the most habits . To acquire new habits and to eradicate older habits, which may or may not have been useful in their time, is as much the purpose of education as to control instinctive activities and already established habits.

"Communities,"said Daniel Webster, "are responsible as well as individual." For communities are free to acquire habits, to make changes by choice, and to modify their characters in accordance with new truth. Both the responsibility of the community, though vastly greater than that of the individual, is abstract and secondary, while that of the individual is primary and concrete. In a material sense, there is no such reality as a community: there is only an aggregation of individuals. Educating a community, enlightening, benefiting, informing, directing, degrading, debauching, robbing a community: each of these phrases is but a figure of speech. Yet within the figure of speech is an idea; and this idea is a reality of the spirit, a reality many times stronger than the reality of the human body of the individual.

> By "consciousness of kind, "to use the phrase of Giddings, groups, classes, societies, communities of men are brought together to reinforce their sense of likeness and agreement. The stranger introduced among associated men and the variant born within their number have but the choice, to agree or to oppose "the social mind." The history of these agreements and oppositions is the material for all sociologists, - Gumplowicz, Tardes, Le Bon, Spencer, Bosanquet, Giddings. This history contains the mechanical explanation of all wars, strifes, concords, councils, events movements, since men first dwelt in villages by the ancient mid-earth sea.

The community moulds the individual even to the extent of transforming him into its own image, - unless he resists the process. Even so, it moulds him into its opposite. Thus, oppression produces the hero from among the meek oppressed; sordidness, the generous benefactor from among the sordid; and every evil and, alas! every good, its opposite. And why? Because humanity, seeking completeness and universality, is ready for every experiment and for every variation.

It is useless to try to understand the reason or the nature of many things. Before the final problems, the human mind sinks abashed. Is this universe finite or infinite? If finite, is there an infinity of finite universes? How do other worlds, differ from this? What am I? How does grass grow? What is evil? Why does the good God permit or cause it? Is He good? Is He onnipotent? These and a thousand other questions that children ask, and we all ask, are useful only to stir the soul from self-content and to enforce the truth that the world is a school for education, not for acquiring final concrete knowledge. We can no more carry facts into the life beyond death than we can carry silver and gold.

These eternal questions have their greatest value in that they are not yet answered: therefore, they serve to stir the souls of the millions of each generation. The child discovers them; and wonders. Each new question is to him a new mountain-top with vaster outlook upon life. Each one of us, over and over again, rediscovers them when facing new vistas of experience. In a sense it is the same with the petty questions of life that may be answered. We think that we have gained new wisdom when very often we did the same thing in the same way with the same contentment, last year, ten years ago.

Before birth, as Lotze remarked half a century ago, there proceed astonishing, unaccountable physical changes, - recapitulations of the past, vital experiments, outlived or abandoned, - whose issue is the new-born babe, prepared to live in the air upon the surface of the earth, eager to grow in bulk many times and in strength yet more, but never to change greatly in any essential feature save in that which is to be associated psychically with the new birth twelve or fourteen years afterwards. Before that new birth of puberty into adolescence, there proceed other and still more astonishing changes in the soul. When we remember that one babe in five is still-born or dies within ten days after birth, and that two in five die within a year of birth, we can see how severe Nature's first examination is[2]. Yet no child of normal mentality ever goes insane. Tyler calls adolescence "Nature's second examination. "Not only is it accompanied by insanity, but the entire sex-life, both physical and psychical, seems to constitute a predisposition to insanity and to suicide. Before adolescence,sex is quiescent, prepotent rather than potent, discoverable rather than aggressive, Before adolescence, the boy and the girl display racial, ancestral, ancient heredities, In adolescence, more immediate paternal and maternal traits struggle for mastery, the boy trying to put off the general human qualities and to devote himself to what is typically manly and the girl to become womanly. Often it is a battel royal. Of the changes proceeding now, few are illusory; illusory; most, indeed, are more serious, more recreative, more profound than they seem, cutting clean into the marrow of life.

Stronger than the habits of communities, far stronger than the habits of individuals, are the habits of the social institutions, which indeed, when cross-sectioned at any particular time, appear to be all habits, pure conventions without any 'voluntary intellectual processes. This, too is illusion. One who imagines that the social institutions are permanent and changeless is deceived as much as one who imagines himself a voluntary agent, freely choosing and changing his course in life. The working doctrines of Property and of Family, the basic theory of what the State is and for what it is, the conception of what Business may rightly undertake, the very psychology of the race changed when a man could no longer give his own body as pledge for a debt. These all will change again when a man cannot give the homestead of his family as a pledge for debi.

For ideas construct, destroy, and reconstruct the world. The notion that men are the sons of God and therefore equal brothers has overthrown monarchy and aristocracy, established democracy, severed church and state, and subordinated religion to politics . it will yet establish equality of opportunity in economic affairs and make education and culture the chief business of life. To use the phrases of Lord Acton, it has been "a doctrine laden with storm and havoc," and is "the secret essence of the Rights of Man and the indestructible soul of revolution." It will make impossible starvation in the midst of plenty and ignorance in the midst of knowledge[3].

In its degree, every idea, great and little, is a transformer of habits and a converter of wills. And yet in individuals, in communities, in the institutions of society, habits have been, are, and forever will be nearly all of life. The human body in its myriad processes, the human soul with its fathomless memories, the human crowd with its intricate maze of opinions, the social institution with as many historical origins as a mighty river has tributaries and sources, could not be operated from moment to moment by independent acts of will. Therefore, the past lives in the present, and indeed is nearly all of the present. What we in our pride call "the present," "modern times,," "the new idea, "is but the edge of the difference by which the limits of a particular recent past and of the now are parted. The sum of these differences through the ages is vast. I and my ancestor of ten thousand years ago would find our thoughts incommunicable and one another incomprehensible. I and one who has grown in entirely different surroundings from different ancestry may find ourselves complementary and agreeable, or we may find ourselves so antagonistic that our only relief from the strain of juxtaposition is battle. Two likenesses and two differences unite me with and divide me from my fellows. What I know and desire that he does not know or desire, and what he knows and desires that I do not know or desire, set us over against one another. The masses of similar knowledge and opinion and the forces of similar habits and motives bring us together. We may associate for mutual help because of our differences; we may collide and struggle; or we may part in peace; we may collide and struggle; or we may part in peace: but we may never be of one and the same mind.

From the separation of men by differences in ideas, this age apparently suffers less than any other because of certain of our inventions, of our discoveries, and of our social institutions. Type, press, mail, periodical, books, typewriters, telegraph, telephone, school, library, university, theatre, opera, church, lodge, ballot, council, legislature, horse, bicycle, automobile , electric railway, steam railroad, lecture, mill, factory, mine, store, office building, - all conspire to acquaint men with common ideas and to train them in common habits. Yet the separation is greater in reality than in appearance, because men differ from the extreme of many opportunities to get knowledge to the extreme of none, and from the extreme of surpassing ability applied industriously to great opportunities to the extreme of dullness indifferent to small opportunity. In ideas and habits, Caesar differed not more from the Roman slave than Grant differed from the American slave.

One man looks out upon the world and sees particular things in isolation, sees fragments, not whole; another looks out and sees the same things in their modern comparative relations to groups communities, social institutions, and also in their historical relations, knowing stages and processes and motives by which they have come to be what they are. One has all the instincts, intuitions, innate ideas, categories, grounds of sufficient reason that the other has; but the first exhausts his resources in the simpler psychological processes of sensation, perception, memory, while the other, without fatigue, runs all the gamut of thought. The latter understands, can stand up under, the burden of knowledge, bearing it easily, moving it freely. Such were Kepler, Newton, Leibnitz, Comte, Helmholtz, Spencer, Darwin, Agassiz. And such, as Plato taught, should be the rulers of men, because they are their leaders .

For several reasons, the School does not respond readily to new truths, is peculiarly conservative of the past, is governed by habits that have perhaps been discarded years ago by adult men living in the modern regions of the world. To an exposition of the first reason, the foregoing passages of the present chapter have been devoted. Every social institution changes slowly, painfully, reluctantly. Property, Family, Church change even less than does the School. Every particular family, church, school has its own traditions and customs that give it a characteristic atmosphere. The new member usually surrenders soon to its ideas and sentiments. But the cultural, the political, and the economic institutions change more freely. The reason is not far to seek. Most of them are as yet in the processes of formation; and, therefore, they best display the activities of the modern age.

In the School, kinesis proceeds slowly because of certain characteristics peculiar to it. The School like the Protestant Church has passed over into the mood, if not the actual control, of women. Even the Catholic Church finds most of its workers and active members among women. That women is more conservative than man is a commonplace of psychology. Nearly all the actual teachers of the classes of pupils of elementary schools in the cities, towns, and villages are women.

The textbook is a factor making for conservatism. The history of the publication of new truth is this. It is discovered and discussed. Accounts appear in monographs. Synthetic minds incorporate in treatises the teachings of the monographs. University lecturers study the treatises and expound them in their class-rooms. Their pedagogical disciples finally present these views in practical texts, which the boys and girls study. Even in an age of steam-power and of rapid printing, the process takes a generation when no controversy delays the progress of the new idea within the schools . Sometimes, for want of controversy, the new truth is ignored and almost forgotten.

Another factor making for the undue preservation of the past in the education of the present is the persistence of men of average talent and of gentle character in the few positions not occupied by women. Though teaching is still the most attractive, honorable, and dignified, if not the most lucrative, of all the vocations opon to women, it is by no means so in the case of men. But men of average talent and of amiable character are not the leaders of the race, the builders of institutions, and the reformers of society.

Still another factor is the undue importance of laymen in the political offices that control the public school and as patrons of the private school. The layman and the laywoman remember their own educational experience and, of course, have no adequate knowledge of professional progress since they went to school. Sometimes, these lay persons are discontented with their own schooling and desire something better for the children of the present generation. But these instances are few. Only men and women either of unusual natural gifts, of mind or of later and larger educational advantages ever know that the educational processes by which they came to be what they are may not be the best possible processes. It is as hard for a man to imagine what he would have been if he had been instructed by different teachers as it is for him to imagine what he would have been if he had been born of different parents. He is as incredulous, even as scornful, of the one idea as of the other.

Again, many of the teachers and some of the supervisory force are really but lay persons, often without even a veneer of professional knowledge.

Unfortunately, these several factors conspire together, in the strong-willed, ill-informed layman confronts the lonely, gentle schoolmaster and the crowd of schoolmistresses and overcomes them often by his very faults.

Another factor is poverty. Changes in schoolhouse architecture and increase in equipment, changes in textbooks and additions to grounds, and improvement and enlargement of faculty, cost money. They involve diversion of wealth from present habitual uses to new uses: whether to do this and how best to do this require consideration, consideration requires time, and the time of the lay ruler in worth money, and he refuses to give the thought required to understand the situation.

Apparently, for the maintenance of the past in the present and for the shutting-out of the new with the blind or necessary continuance of the old, a vicious circle has been established. This is certainly true in the case of the public school.

9

Moral Behaviour

'What is morally acceptable behaviour?' as the medical expert might give one the answer to the question 'What sort of factors are conducive to heart failure?' Not is it my intention to 'prove' that a particular moral viewpoint is incumbent upon us, if we assume 'prove' to mean 'demonstrate in some incontrovertible manner'. My purpose rather is to put forward an argument for a particular point of view and to appeal to the reader to consider the argument as an argument. Naturally it is my view that the argument is convincing and that it consequently leads us to accept a particular moral viewpoint. But at the same time I am aware and it is important that the reader should be too, that this argument, which is not in essence original, and this viewpoint, which has been held by various people throughout history, has never yet met with universal acceptance. Some people evidently do not find the argument convincing. All that is asked of the reader is that he should examine it for himself and accept or reject it be references to the argument rather than by reference to such consideration as whether he happens to like it, whether it leads to conclusions that he has been brought up to accept, or whether it coincides with what most people think.

I shall proceed by examining two concepts that have long been widely valued: 'freedom' and 'equality'. I shall try to argue that regardless of what we may *casually* think about these concepts - what we think they mean, whether we think them morally important and what relative importance we attach to them - if we think *carefully* about what is meant by such claims as that 'Men ought to be free' or 'Men ought to be treated equally' there are certain conclusions that cannot be avoided. To be precise I shall argue that there is a sense in which 'freedom' and 'equality' are to be valued, but that their value is subordinate to the value of happiness. In other words I shall be arguing for a modified form of the utilitarian view of ethics,pioneered most notably by Jeremy Bentham and John Stuart Mill, which claims essentially that the measure of goodness or of the rightness of action or rules is the extent to which they promote happiness, and the measure of wrongness or badness is the extent to which misery is caused. (See Chapter 6 for a more detailed presentation of utillitarianism.)

Since I shall be arguing that there is good reason to adopt this particular moral viewpoint or that utilitarianism is a more reasonable ethical than any other, for the remainder of this chapter I shall make some general comments about the sort of considerations that would lead one to regard a particular view, explanation or argument as relatively reasonable or unreasonable. I shall do this by first considering an example from the sphere of aesthetics.

Suppose that a teacher, who prefers the novels of George Eliot to those of Ian Fleming, and who regards them as superior or better works of wishes to justify that value judgement. (This wish to justify is not, of course simply an academic exercise. If the teacher has no criteria whereby to justify his selection then he has no criteria whereby to select at all, and the teacher generally does need to make some kind of selection.) Why George Eliot a better writer than Ian Fleming?

The realm of aesthetic value judgements is no less tricky than the reals of moral value judgements, and on many views of aesthetics it is more or less impossible to lay down fixed rules or criteria for assessing the aesthetic value of a work of art. Certainly there is as much disagreement and uncertainty about what criteria count for evaluating works of art as about what criteria count for assessing the goodness or rightness of actions and behaviour. One can, of course, pin-point features of various works. One can say, for example, that George Eliot has an ironic touch, that she is good at developing characters, or that she shows respect for unity of design. To pin-point such featurs in a particular writer may not be an easy task for instance, one might argue for a long time about precisely what constituted good character development in a novel, about how one judges whether characters in a particular novel had been well drawn, and whether in point of fact a writer like George Eliot did develop her characters better than a writer like Ian Fleming. But in principle it is not an impossible task and indeed it would seem to be the sort of thing that most literary criticism is about. However, to say that George Eliot has certain features that Ian Flemings lacks, or that she does some specific thing better than Fleming, one thing - to say that she is a better awriter, or even that she is more worth reading, is quite another.

If one had certain specific ends in view - for instance, if one wanted children to study character development in novels - then, of course, one could say that Eliot was better for that purpose. But then the question of the value of the end or purpose one had in mind would arise, and one could only claim that Eliot was more worth reading than Fleming in some general sense, if one could establish that to study character development was relatively worthwhile thing to do. And unless one could establish that the features that Eliot's writing was agreed to have were the necessary features of good writing, one obviously could not conclude that Eliot was a better writer than Fleming.

In other words, although in principle we can agree on the features exhibited in the writing of a particular novelist, it is always open for someone to say that he does not see why those particular features are relevant reasons for judging a novelist to be a good novelist. He might say, and it is not obvious that it would be absurd to say, 'Eliot develops character better than Fleming, but Fleming is more exciting, and therefore Fleming is a better writer. The problem here is that, since it is not clear what count as good reasons for judging a novelist to be a good novelist, since it is not clear that one could rule out 'being exciting' as an irrelevant consideration, it is not clear that one could describe any view as unreasonable, provided that it did offer some kind of reason. Does it follow that, if I were to say that it seemed to me more reasonable to regard George Eliot as a good novelist than to regard Ian Fleming as a good novelist, I would effectively be begging the question and assuming that the sort of reasons I produce for valuing Eliot are good reasons, whereas the sort of reasons that others might produce for valuing Fleming are bad reasons? Yes, I think it does follow: I would be begging the question. What are we to say, then? Is any assessment of any writer as reasonable as any other? Not necessarily.

What is clear is that, insofar as it is agreed that one cannot 'prove' that good novelists must have certain specific qualities, one cannot 'prove' that one novelist is better than another. It follows that, whereas in some spheres such as science one can say that certain theories are unreasonable because they fly in the face of the evidence and can be shown to be false, one cannot simply assert that some value judgements about particular novelists are unreasonable on the grounds that the values appealed to are false values. Nonetheless, although we have to concede that we are not in a position to lay down the law about what count as good reasons for evaluating novels highly, it does not follow that any view is as reasonable as any other. There are at least four ways in which a person's assertion that a particular novelist was a good novelist might be regarded as an unreasonable assertion, even though one might concede that one could not prove that the assertion was false.

1. In the first place a person might simply make such an assertion and refuse to produce any reasons for his judgement. One could scarcely regard it as reasonable for a teacher to insist that Eliot was a brilliant novelist, while refusing to give any reasons for that claim.

2. Secondly, although we may disagree about what sort of reasons count as good reasons for regarding a particular novelist as a good one, it does not follow that *any* reason will do. There are surely *some* reasons that none of us would accept as relevant reasons and which, if somebody were to use them, we should regard as a clear indication that the person in question had not got the faintest idea of the sort of thing that we were trying to do in evaluating novels. If somebody were to argue, for instance, that Ian Fleming was a better novelist than George Eliot because more of his books had been turned into films, because he wrote more novels, because he was a man, or because his books were more attractively printed, we should just say - an I don't see why we should not say - that he clearly did not grasp the sort of thing that we are trying to do. These kinds of reasons just are irrelevant to the question of whether a novelist is a good one or not. At the very least, reasons put forward in defence of the quality of a novelist must relate in some way to his writing.

3. But suppose that somebody were to argue that Fleming was a better writer because he was more popular or more generally enjoyable? Would that be an unreasonable criterion? Although most people seriously concerned with literature would probably foam at the mouth at such a suggestion this seems to me a much more tricky question. It is true that the popularity of a novelist need not be related to anything to do with his style of writing. He might simply hit upon a popular theme, or become a cult figure by whatever mysterious process people become cult figures. But one might argue that the essential criterion of a good book was that it should provide enjoyment, and that, therefore, writers who were popular obviously were good novelists, since by definition they had the talent for writing enjoyable books. We may think it odd to make writing books that people enjoy the sole criterion of good writing. We should probably *feel* that this was unreasonable (and I am sure that most of us would *say* it was). But is it?don't know. But what does seem to me to be quite clear is that, if somebody were to insist on the claim that this is a good reason for judging a novelist to be a good one, we could not rule his suggestion out as absurd (as we could if he evaluated by reference to the attractiveness of the printing),

and we could not prove that he was wrong.

I have introduced the example of someone who proposes the enjoyment a book gives as the sole criterion of literary worth in order to draw attention to the third way in which an argument about the worth of novelists may be unreasonable. Although the claim may not *in itself* be obviously unreasonable it would be unreasonable of somebody to put forward this argument if they were not prepared to accept the consequences of their argument. If the suggestion is put forward seriously that this is the sole criterion or literary worth, then we should expect the person who put it forward to accept, consistently with his argument, not only that Ian Fleming is a better writer than George Eliot, but that Agatha Christie is better than both of them and, interestingly, that the Bible, being the best seller of alltime, is the best book ever written. In the same way, if somebody were to put forward the suggestion that books were better in direct proportion in their length, crazy as this may seem to us, I do not see how one could prove that it was a bad criterion. But we could say that it was an unreasonable suggestion unless the individual concerned was prepared to accept the consequences: for instance, that by and large Victorian novels, written as they generally were in three volumes, were ipso facto better than twentieth century novels, or that I can turn this into a good book by going on writing for three thousand more pages.

All this may seem pretty absurd, but it has a point. The observation that for a view as to what constitute good reasons in this sphere to be reasonable its consequences must be consistently accepted by the holder of the view, in fact does a great part of our job for us. We may not be able to prove that a particular view is unreasonable in some objective manner, but very often, by pointing out the consequences of the view, by getting its proponent to think more carefully about what he is committing himself to, he will himself come to agree with us and reject his original view as unreasonable. One thing that would clearly be unreasonable would be to claim that such and such was a good reason for valuing a writer in one instance, but then to say that it was not a good reason in another instance.

4. Finally, and most obviously, a view or an argument might be regarded as unreasonable if the reasoning offered to support it was in some way fallacious or inconsistent. For example, one might encounter some variant of the notorious argument 'All cows are four-legged. This is four-legged, therefore it is a cow'. Thus somebody might try to argue that a particular novel was obviously a good novels on the grounds that it had unity of design and on the assumption that it was agreed that good novels had unity of design. But from the agreed premiss that good novel have a unity of design, it obviously does not follow that all novels that have a unity of design are good novels, unless it is also agreed that unity of design is the *only* criterion of a good novel.

Here, then, are four ways in which arguments about the quality of a writer may be unreasonable, even though we concede that we are not sure precisely what kind of reasons are good reasons for evaluating a writer highly. We shall not regard as reasonable suggestions that are put forward without any attempt at all to back them with reasons, arguments that make use of reasons that seem totally irrelevant to the question at issue, arguments the consequences of which the proposer will not himself accept, and arguments that are inconsistent or fallacious.

These same considerations enable us to dintinguish between reasonable and unreasonable arguments in the moral sphere, as I shall now illustrate.

1. Suppose that somebody were to suggest that everybody ought to commit suicide - that this was the right thing for us all to do. Such a suggestion no doubt seems odd, like most examples that philosophers tend to drag up. But the fact that it seems odd, unlikely, even preposterious, is no objection to it. It is conceivable that somebody might say it, and if we are really keeping an open mind at this stage about what ought to be done we cannot simply dismiss suggestions that we would not ourselves propose. The question is, if somebody were to make such a suggestion, could we say that it was unreasonable?

For all we *know* to the contrary, it may in some sense be true that we ought to commit suicide. We certainly cannot dismiss the suggestion are obviously false, simple because we do not like it, we think it silly, or only one in a million people would take it seriously. To do that would be equivalent to arguing that George Eliot is obviously an inferior writer to Ian Fleming, because we prefer Fleming. We would be being unreasonable because the mere fact that we do not like a suggestion is not a good reason for concluding that it is false. So what do we do, when faced with the bizarre suggestion? We take it seriously.

'Right,' we say, 'you suggest that we ought to commit suicide. This does not strike us as either obvious or true. As it stands it is obviously not particularly reasonable suggestion, since you have offered no reason whatsoever to support it. But we are willing to listen to your argument for this point of view. What reasons have you for assuming it to be true that it would be a good thing if we all committed suicide?"

Now, the proponent of the view in question might reply simply by saying that he has no reasons to offer - he merely intuits it. Can we say that he is wrong to intuit it? We certainly cannot. But there are a number of thing that we can say: we can say that there is no reason to suppose that his intuition is correct. We can say that it would be unreasonable to expect that world to act in accordance with his intuition, when it does not share his intuition. We can say that there seems no reason why we should place the claims of his intuition before the claims of anyone else's intuition. But above all we can point out that if he believes that we ought to act in this way, and therefore, presumably, wishes to convince us that we ought, he will have to produce some kind of convincing reasoning, and that is all there is to it. Proof we do not ask for; but some reason to share his conviction, we naturally demand. If he sticks both with his conviction and with his acknowledgement that he has no reasons to offer in support of it, then the question of whether he is right or wrong in some metaphysical sense becomes it practical terms irrelevant. We cannot be expected to regard as reasonable a point of view for which we have no intuitive sympathy and for which there is apparently no argument. Now, of course, it may be that on close scrutiny all moral viewpoints will be seen to end up with some fundamental assumption that has to be accepted on intuition and which is, as a matter of fact, only intuited by some. If this turns out to be the case, we are indeed in a mess. The suicide ethic would be no more unreasonable than any other. But at this stage, when we are embarking upon the search for a reasonable moral viewpoint and when it is an open question as to whether there is one or not, we may fairly say that here, at any rate, is one that does not appear to be reasonable.

Of course the man we are concerned with might offer some kind of reason. He might say, for instance, that the reason that we ought to commit suicide is that God demands it. That is certainly a reason, but clearly it does not really escape the problem of the simple intuitive view, for it merely pushes the question of what reasons there are to accept the view one stage back. Instead of asking what reasons there are to accept the claim that we ought to commit suicide, we should natural ask what reason there was to suppose that God exists, or, more crucially, what reason there was to suppose that a specific idea of a God, who amongst other things made this demand for suicide, corresponded to any reality. How do we know, what reason have we for supposing, that God, even if he does exist, does indeed make this demand? Evidently we shall soon be back with the intuition of the person in question. Even if he could produce some religious texts, allegedly the work of prophets who knew the will of God, we should only have his intuition to support the claim that these texts were indeed the work of people who knew the will of God.

Here then we have an example of a moral view that we can see no reason to accept at all. It involves either a naked assertion, backed by no reasoning whatsoever, or else bases itself on a premiss that is itself merely asserted and is very obviously open to question. This does not stop those who do believe from beliving. Contrary to one popular opinion it does not even show that they are wrong or necessarily foolish so to believe. But it does stop anyone from legitimately claiming that it is reasonable to believe and unreasonable not to. It is neither reasonable nor unreasonable; reason does not come into the matter.

2. Consider now an example of a moral viewpoint that does make appeal to reasons but where the reasons given are simply

irrelevant. As with the aesthetic sphere, despite the problem of deciding precisely what reasons do count as good reasons in this sphere, there are nonetheless some sorts of reason that evidently do not count at all. Let us assume that somebody claims that it is morally objectionable to spit. We ask him what his reasons are for asserting that we ought not to spit. There are a number of replies that we can imagine that he might give, some of which it would be difficult to dismiss as obviously absurd. He might say that we ought not to spit because spitting was a hazard to public health and we ought to be concerned about maintaining public health. On the assumption that it was empirically true that spitting spread germs, this would be a reasonable *kind* of argument. One cannot dismiss concern for the health of others as obviously irrelevant to the question of how we ought to behave. But suppose instead that he had said that the reason one ought not to spit is that spitting causes one to purse one's lips in an ugly manner. In this case there is no need for us to quibble about whether or not it is true that spitting is ugly, since, even if it is true, such a consideration seems entirely irrelevant to a moral question. It is the wrong kind of reason.

Again, suppose that a man objects to adultery an claims that it is immoral. Suppose also that we disagree with his judgement, but recognise nonetheless that his point of view deserves to be taken seriously and therefore ask him for the reasons that lie behind his conclusion. He might argue along a number of different lines: that adultery involves deception, that in general it leads to the breakdown of marriage and hence is detrimentalto the welfare of children, or that sex is not something that should be indulged in ecept within wedlock and with a view to procreation. Now these are very different arguments and our attitude to them might well vary from person to person in respect of each argument. Furthermore, if unconvinced by them, we might wish to counter each argumentin a quite different way As against the first argument it might be objected that deception is some times justified or, perhaps, that adultery need not necessarily involve deception. As against the second it might be argued that there is no necessary reason for adultery to lead to the breakdown of a marriage, or that, even if it did, it is not true that broken marriages are detrimental to the welfare of children. With regard to the third argument we might simply say that we do not agree with his view of the role of sex, and demand some further argument from him to substantiate his claim.

But what is clear is that, however much we disagree with this man, all these attempted arguments of his are prima facie plausible. That is to say that, although we may not accept his arguments, he is at least appealing to reasons that seem related to the moral sphere: his reasons for condemning adultery are that we should avoid deception, that we should refrain from causing suffering, or that we should not sin, and these are recognisable as moral reasons. He and we are at least talking the same language.

If on the other hand he had argued that we ought not to commit adultery because adultery involves taking off one's clothes and we ought to take of our clothes as little as possible, we should regard him with bewildered astonishment. A man who argues in this way clearly does not have the first idea of what morality is about. Such reasoning would not simply be silly and unbelievable - it would be absurd and irrelevant, because a consideration such as that people take off their clothes just is not a moral consideration. He is not offering the sort of reason that could count as a moral reason. And despite all that has been said about the difficulty of 'knowing' anything in the moral sphere, we all *know* that.

It may be felt that the point that I am making here is a as mall one, since surely nobody actually would offer reasons of this sort. But it is a crucial point. For if the reader accepts that making ugly faces and taking off one clothes, however fanciful such examples may be, cannot in themselves constitute moral reasons for acting or refraining from acting in various ways, then he has conceded that only some reasons count as moral reasons. If that is so, then clearly moral rules or moral commands must be backed by moral reasons, and our job is to discover in more detail what reasons do count as moral reasons. I shall be arguing in Chapter 6 that ultimately there is only one kind of reason that can count as a moral reason.

3. Thirdly, we may regard it as unreasonable for somebody to

claim commitment to a particular moral viewpoint unless he is prepared to accept all the consequences of that viewpoint. In my view a number of those who commit themselves to emotivism as the correct view of ethics when first introduced to it, may be regarded as unreasonable on these grounds. For, as we have seen, if one accepts emotivism (at least in one form) one commits oneself to the view, in Ayer's words, that in saying "Stealing money is wrong" I produce a sentence which has no factual meaning - that is, expresses no proposition which can be either true ot false.....I am simply evincing my moral disapproval of it'. To which we may add that, in saying it, I am trying to `create an influence' of disapproval amongst my audience. But if this were so, if this was all there was to be said, it would follow that I could not meaningfully make the remark `Stealing money is wrong' in the company of people who shared my disapproval (for how could I be trying to create what already exists?); that one could not meaningfully distinguish between making this remark and making a propaganda film to discourage stealing (for both would involve evincing one's own feeling and attempting to create an influence); that the way to assess the quality of a moral argument would be in terms of how effective it was in creating an influence; and above all that there would be no recognisable distinction between a remark such as `Bullfights - ugh!' and `Concentration camps are wicked'.

My point here is not that these consequences are unacceptable, although I believe that they are, but that some people who might claim to be emotivists will nonetheless be found saying that stealing is wrong, even in the company of those who agree with them, assessing moral arguments by criteria other than their persuasive power, and even distinguishing between what they merely do not like and what they regard as morally wrong. In other words their practice is inconsistent with their preaching. They do not give evidence of accepting the consequences of their view. And *that* is unreasonable.

Finally, there is the most common way in which a moral viewpoint may be unreasonable, namely when the argument for it is fallacious. Obviously arguments may be fallacious in a number of different ways, and we cannot review all the various forms of fallacious reasoning here, but perhaps the single most dangerous form of fallacy in the moral sphere is the assumption that the fact that something is the case constitutes a good argument for concluding the it ought to be the case, to which attention has already been drawn in Chapter 2. Another kind of fallacy that has to be guarded against is the use of reasoning, to support a particular viewpoint that is prima facie relevant reasoning, and that is not in itself inconsistent, but which is not obviously sufficient to establish its conclusion; reasoning in other words, that is not strong enough to do the job required of it. It seems to me that the standard argument for a relativist theory of ethics is of this kind. It is, of course, absolutely true that different societies have had and have now different moral values - some societies have even lacked a concept of morality, as we should understand it, altogether; furthermore, it is true that this is a pertinent consideration for the individual trying to inquire into the problem of morality to take into account. But this consideration is not sufficient to establish the validity of a realativist position. It is not true that it proves that morality is a purely conventional game and that there is no more to be said on the matter. It is unreasonable to assume the truth of a conclusion based on the strength of such a selective consideration alone.

Perhaps the most notorious (and anyway an excellent) example of an argument riddled with fallacy is provided by Hitler's argument in *Mein Kampf* for Aryan supremacy, which is well worth exposing once again Hitler wrote:

> 'In opposition to the bourgeois and the Marxist-Jewish worlds the folkish philosophy finds the importance of mankind in its basic racial elements.... It be no means believes in an equality of races, but along with their difference it recognises their higher or lesser value and feels itself obligated to promote the victory of the better and the stronger, and demand the subordination of the inferior and weaker in accordance with the eternal will that dominates this universe. It serves the basic aristocratic idea of nature and believes in the validity of this law down to the last individual......
>
> All the human culture, all the results of art, science and technology that we see before us today, are almost exclusively the creative product

of the Aryan. This very fact admits of the not unfounded inference that he alone was the founder of all higher humanity....For the formation of higher cultures the existence of lower human types was one of the most essential preconditions... The Aryan gave up the purity of his blood and therefore lost his sojourn in paradise: blood mixture and the resultant drop in the racial level is the sole cause of the dying out of old cultures.'.

Notice the different kinds of suspect argument that Hitler manages to pack into these brief extracts that serve so admirably as a text for fallacious reasoning. First the simple falsehood (or stupidity) of asserting as fact what is palpably not fact, namely the assertion that 'all...human culture' is 'almost exclusively the creative product of the Aryan' or that 'blood mixture' is the 'sole cause of the dying out of old cultures'. Secondly, what on earth is meant by the phrase 'the founder of all higher humanity' and why would the fact, if it were a fact, that the Aryan was responsible for ` human culture' imply the inference that is drawn that he is the founder of all higher humanity? Thirdly, where is the link between this claim about cultural superiority and the conclusion that the Aryan is therefore superior in some general sense? Even if it were true that the Aryan was culturally superior and the founder of all higher humanity, why would it follow that the Aryan counts for more, as Hitler evidently assumes. But above all on what grounds does Hitler identify the better with the stronger?Could there be a more glaring instance of fallay than to argue that, because the strong dominate the weak as a matter of fact (an observation dressed up by Hitler as the product of an eternal will and a law of nature), it is right and proper that they should?

One might worry the less if this type of argument were confined to the brain of a Hitler. But unfortunately it is not. Quite apart from the fact that thousands accepted this particular argument, this type of argument is still to be found, as it has been since the time of the ancient Greeks. Plato, for instance, put almost the same argument into the mouth of Callicles:

'Nature demostrates that it is right that the stronger should prevail over the weaker...Right consists in the superior having the upper hand.

> By what right did Xerxes invade Greece? By right of his natural superiority....just as Hercules drove off the cattle of Geryon without paying for them or being given them, because this was natural justice: that all the possessions of those who are weaker and inferior belong to the man who is better and superior. That is the truth of the matter, Socrates, and perhaps you would realise it, if you wasted less time toying about with philosophy and turned to something more important.'

I imagine that the reader does not require me to point out in detail the arguments used by certain modern states to justify racial discrimination that essentially merely repeat this fallacious argument of Callicles.

My conclusion is that there are various ways in which a point of view may be classified as unreasonable even if it is not known to be false. We have looked briefly at some of these ways and some ethical positions that apparently are unreasonable. We are looking for a reasonable ethical view, which is to say one that is argued for, that is not fallaciously, irrelevantly or inadequately substantiated, and that above all is supported by reasons that count as moral reasons.

10
The Free School and Values

What is a 'free school'? What is meant by the demand for free schools or for more freedom in schools? Clearly there is not some single ideal pattern of a free school, to which all schools that claim to value freedom conform. In order to proceed, therefore, I shall take as an example of a school that appears to value freedom highly, and which most would regard as a free school, A.S. Neill's Summerhill. What exactly is the nature of the freedom provided at Summerhill?

The distinguishing feature of Summerhill is that children there are to a large degree free from rules and restrictions that have been imposed upon them by adults. This means in particular: (i) The day-to-day government of the school is provided by a council that consists of all the children who wish to partake in it and the staff.Each child and each menber to staff has one vote numerically the childern are therefore in aposstion to over-ride the staff. (ii) There is very little that the children are forbidden to do except by a vote made by themselves in council. (iii) Specifically, attendance at lessons is voluntary for all children at all times.

These are aspects of Summerhill freedom. But to describe these aspects it not to give the kind of answer that we want to the question, What is the nature of Summerhill freedom? This tells us in what respects the children are as a matter of fact free. But we want to know why they are free in these respects. In other words, on what principle or principles does Summerhill function? What good reasons are there for giving children these freedoms? Only when it is clear what the reasoning is that lies behind these aspects of Summerhill life can we be in a position to assess for ourselves or meaningfully argue the merits of such a free school.

The first thing that we need to know is precisely what kind of a claim is being made by those who want free schools along Summerhill lines. For one might argue in favour of the type and amount of freedom to be seen at Summerhill in two logically quite distinct ways, either by making an empirical claim or by making a simple evaluative claim. (Or, of course, one might attempt to combine the two kinds of claim.) Thus champions of Summerhill might argue from the assumption that weall hold certain broad values in common, and make the empirical claim that as a matter of fact if schools provide children with the sort of freedom they enjoy at Summerhill then certain desirable consequences are likely to follow. For instance, it might be said, we value happiness and self-reliance, and children brought up in this kind of a school become happy and self-reliant as a consequence of the freedom they are given. Alternatively, the direct evaluative claim might be made that children ought to be given these freedoms, regardless of the consequences, because it is wrong to deny children such freedoms. On this view, although one might still value happiness, self-reliance or anything else, and hope to promote

them as well, nonethelese the point world be that childern should have this freedom. even if it could be shown that they were not in fact very happy, self-reliant, etc., as a result.

In other words, Summerhill freedom might be commended either as an end in itself or as a means to some other end or ends, rather as the manager of a small firm might accept workers' representation on the management board either because he believed that it was right that they should be represented or because he believed that it would have desirable consequences such as promoting harmony in the firm or, more cynically, causing him less trouble in the long run.

Although nobody, I imagine, would accuse a man such as Neill of granting various freedoms to children in order to avoid trouble for himself and his staff in the long run, there is nonetheless a real question as to which of the two types of claim he was making. Did he assume certain educational aims, certain objectives that ideally should be met, and believe that the free situation he provided was an effective means of promoting those ends and achieving those desirable consequences? Or did he say to himself 'To hell with all this desirable consequences stuff; this is the morally right way to treat children?' Was his argument of the form:'It is desirable that people should acquire a love of leaning and that they should learn certain things. A school that provides the sort of freedom that Summerhill does promotes such learning and love of learning better than a more restricted traditional school does'? Or was it of the form: 'Giving children the freedom to decide whether they want to learn anything is more important than seeking to ensure that they do learn anything. We therefore ought to give children that freedom even if as a matter of fact the result is that relatively little learning takes place?"

In my experience most students and disciples of Neill take the view that he stood for the latter, immediately evaluative, position. And it is certainly true that he was not apparently much impressed by the specific aim that I have taken as an example - that of promoting learning in the traditional sense of becoming competent or knowledgeable in some sphere, subject or discipline. He was not saying that the freedom at Summerhill is desirable on the grounds that it is an effective means of producing good scholars and academics. But although learning was not one of his aims, it was by no means clear that his argument for freedom was not of the empirical type, and that he did not advocate freedom for the sake of some further end. For Neill not only talked and wrote a lot about freedom. He also talked a lot about happiness.

More than once he wrote of his desire to promote happiness and we therefore come to the specific question: is the freedom provided at Summerhill desirable because it leads to an increase in happiness, or would Neill have claimed that, though he valued happiness, it would nonetheless be right to provide the sort of freedom that Summerhill provides even if as a matter of fact it could be shown that such militated against happiness? Neill, who at the best of times had a certain contempt for fine argument, would probably have replied that it was a bit of both: his school treats children as they ought to be treated and happens thereby to promote happiness. End of argument. Exit hair-splitting philosophers in confusion. So, at any rate, many of Neill's supporters would hope.

But why should we give up so easily? There are matters of real importance here. The answer that I suggest Neill might have given simply avoids the interesting question of what we are to be do in specific instances where granting freedom to children can be seen to militate against concern for promoting happiness. And we still have to consider whether it is *true* either that children ought to be treated in this way or that such freedom does promote happiness.

The latter question, precisely because it involves an empirical claim,is not strictly speaking a philosophical question. It can only finally be answered by carrying out some empirical research, some kind of survey, is an attempt to discover whether it is or it not the case that schools run on Summerhill lines do more to promote happiness than schools that are markedly less concerned with freedom.

Sad to relate, no such research has ever been undertaken, so that all we can say for certain at this juncture is that if this was Neill's claim (or part of it) it stands only as a hunch. However, certain observations may be made on this hunch. In order to attempt to verify it-can surely ideally one would like to make the attempt-one would need to do some preliminary conceptual analysis on the the concept of happiness, so that one knew what one was looking for. I have not set a very good example here by the way in which I have confined myself to making a few general points about happiness sufficient for the argument I was trying to outline in Part Two. But we can see, from the confusion caused by attempts to test 'creativity' without first analysing the term clearly, the sort of mess that we would get into if we attempted to assess the amount of happiness around without a clear idea of the concept. A survey that contented itself with remarks such as 'It was my impression during my two-hour visit to Summerhill that the children were happy' would be pretty unsatisfactory to anybody concerned with precision and truth. Secondly, and more importantly, one would have to do more than establish whether or not the children at Summerhill were happy. For if happiness is of importance, then, presumably, ideally our concern ought to be to ensure a community then, presumably, ideally our concern ought to be to ensure a community in which people are happy and contribute to the happiness of others; it would not be enough that children should be happy at school. (I have made this point before in reference to utilitarianism; but it applies no less to those who are not utilitarian, but who nonetheless feel that happiness is *one* important value.) Just as free-schoolers (and deschoolers) have rightly criticized some traditionalists for forgetting that childhood is itself a part of life to be enjoyed rather than something to be seen only as a preparation for adulthood, so we may legitimately criticize free-schoolers if they ignore the fact that childhood is *only* a part of life and *does* lead on the adulthood.

Ideally, of course, anybody who values happiness at all would want to see happy children and happy adults. But it is an unfortunate fact of social life that if we want all adults to be happy there are certain ways in which we cannot allow individual adults to pursue their happiness. And if we wish to promote the happiness of all as much as possible, then we are bound to attempt to lead individuals to find happiness in certain necessary features of social life, or at least not to find such features irksome. It is surely not patently absurd to suggest that if all children were educated along Summerhill lines, enjoying that degree of freedom (I am thinking here particularly of the freedom to opt out of all lessons, or, to use a less old-fashioned term, deliberate teaching activities), the community would be a less happy body. I do not say that this is so. I say that it is a contention that deserves to be taken seriously. I am merely drawing attention to the fact that, if the justification of Summerhill-type freedom is supposed to lie in considerations of happiness, then the argument is about nine times as complex as some people would have us believe. It is not clear that the tradtional, relatively unfree school has to be miserable as an experience: it its not clear that childern necessarily grsain in term of happiness from self-goverment and the freedom to out of lessone; it is not clear that the community does not benefit, in terms of happiness, from an attempt deliberately to cultivate a high level of competence in various sphere: it is not clear that children cannot be more happy as a result of being initially directed into the pursuit of knowledge and understanding than if they are given the freedom never to begin the pursuit. It is not clear that deliberate (call it enforced, provided that one remembers that enforcement does not have to be harsh or brutal) initiation into various complex fields such as history, English literature or science cannot lead to a positive gain in happiness both for the individual and the community, taking the long term view.

Bantock has written that utility, by which he means essentially an emphasis on happiness rather than specific commitment to the ethical doctrine of utilitarianism, is the curse of our age. 'A supine acquiescence in the notion that happiness is the ultimate vale has led us to underestimate the importance of achievement, even at a temporary loss of personal content. Child-centered education has been much imbued with the desire for happiness.'

My reply would be that it is not the aim but the practice of much progressive education that is questionable. If the claim is that the sort of freedom that Summerhill provides and any other so-called progressive aspects of education are desirable because they promote happiness, in the sense of contribute to the sum of human happiness, then the utilitarian must in principle approve of the progressive ideals. He must side with Neill, as against Bantock, to the extent of saying that if excellence does not in any way contribute to happiness, it is of no worth ; it is not its own reward. But this, I stress, is a conditional claim. *If* free or progressive education *does* this, utilitarianism is its justification. But does it do this? As I have already indicated, that is a question of stunning proportions. In keeping with my general desire not to sit on the philosopher's fence,I will merely add that I suspect that by and large it does not, and that the objection to many of the moves to increase freedom in schools is that they will finally result in a less happy society. (I 'suspect,' I do not 'know.)

At any rate, the claim that the sort of freedom provided at Summerhill is desirable on these grounds is at least coherent. What of the other kind of argument, the direct evaluative claim that it is wrong to control, direct and manipulate children and that therefore it is right for children to be free?

As we have seen, the suggestion that we have no 'right' to impose anything on children or to coerce them into doing anything, or that children have a 'right' to freedom, although it looks like an appeal to some kind of fact, is in reality no such thing. It is only a way of making the claim that in the speaker`s opinion, we ought not to impose anything. we should not therefore be misled into thinking that we may not quite reasonably ask on what grounds the claim is made. why have we no right to impose? why ought children to be free?

We have also seen that it is meaningless simply to assert that people ought to be free: some specification is needed as to what they ought to be free?

From to or to do before we can bgin to make sense of the claim. Now there are some educationalists who would argue that children should be free to determine all aspect of their life for themselves and hence their own development, Selfi-regulation, which seems to be sysnonymous with self-determination,is in fact an ideal advocated by Neill. what is there to be said about this claim? three things:

1. In respect of young children at least, it is surely meaningless to talk of the child "determine" his life or developement. To :determine" anything involves asserting one`s control over it, rather than merely automatically responding to it and it therefore involves at least a degree of cognitive ability. The 6-year-old child who walks out of lesson because he feels bored is not "determining" anything (At least there is no necessary reason to suppose that he is.) he walks out in response to his feeling of boredom. He is not in a position

meaningfully to determine his life and his development because he lacks (relativety, but to a marked extent) the information and the reasoning capacity to structure that information that are necessary to determining the course of events. If one does not know what options are open to one, if and does not know how to evaluate them, if one dose not know what means are most appropriate to selected ends, if and does not know what demands are going to be made on one in the future, if one does not know what the fconsequences of various courses of action are likely to be, how can one 'determine' the future course of one's life? To describe young children as determining their lives or development, therefore, is simply a misuse of language.

2. whatever anybody *says*, we none of us in fact literally leave children to determine their own development. we all do impose on children's freedom to some extent and cannot help so doing. That we all do so does not constitute a good argument for concluding that we ought to (no 'ought' direct from an 'is'), but that we cannot help so doing obviously makes the claim that we ought not to a trifle absurd. (Another little philosophical aphorism runs:'ought' implies 'can.') The mere fact of sending a child to school is a limitation on his freedom to determine his own development, and this is so regardless of the nature of the school.

Rousseau has often been thought of as one who championed the complete freedom of the child, because he insists, in *Emile,* that the tutor should leave everything to natural consequences and do nothing. But to make the positive effort to create a ' natural environment', as Rousseau would have Emile's tutor do, even going to the lengths of keeping Emile away from other children, not to mention adults, who for some reason do not count as part of the natural world, is fairly obviously to interfere: one cannot really claim to be giving complete freedom to an individual to determine his own development and pattern of life if one first of all structures his environment to one's own ideal. In the same way schools in which adults refrain from overtly interfering with the freedom of children cannot sensibly claim that each child thereby acquires complete freedom to determine his life. All that happens in such a situation is that the limitation on the freedom of the individual now comes for the most part directly from his peer group rather than from adults, and that this should be so was decided by and imposed by adults. This may be a desirable state of affairs, but it does not amount to refraining from imposing on children's freedom, and therefore it cannot be desirable simply on the grounds that children's freedom ought not to be imposed on. And it is simply untrue to pretend, as some have done, that such a school does not impose values: it imposes (or attempts to impose) the values enshrined in that kind of school. To set up a school, however "free" or to join the staff of one, is to have already made a deliberate move to structure a particular kind of environment, presumably with the avowed purpose of having some kind of effect on the development of the children within it.

3. older children are, of course, capable of determining the course and pattern of there lives. Are we to conclude that they should be given the freedom to do so? Are we to accept that, notwithstanding the fact that the nature of the school will inevitably have constituted a source of various pressure on the child in his formative year, which may or may not materially have influenced the course of his development, once he is technically in a position to determine the course of his own, he should be free to do so? (So that we have something firm to hold on to, let us say that children are technically capable of determining their own life at least by the time they enter secondary education.)

There is really nothing for me to add to the argument of part two. There I tried to show that one cannot accept that anyone, whether child or adult, should simply be free to determine his life in all respect as he sees fit. The consequences of taking such an absolute position are just unacceptable. All of us must concede, or so I argued, that there are some things that people should not be free to do. Once that is admitted we are obliged, unless we do not mind proceeding in a totally arbitrary fashion, to attempt to formulate some criterion or criteria whereby to assess the limits of freedom . My criterion was the utilitarian one, and I am sticking to it, unless such time as somebody gives me good reason to drop it. Therefore I say that the sort of freedoms that children should be given has to be decided by reference to the tendency of specific freedoms to contribute to the happiness of the community. If we have reason to believe that the involvement of children in running the school contributes to the general happiness, that is a good reason for encouraging the practice. But, in this case, let us remember that *this is* the reason for advocating the practice. Consequently we are off the point if we drone on about a right to freedom, and we may quite consistently add that there should be certain limitations to the power of a management body or council thus constituted. There are certain things that we will not let children decide to do, whether individually or by vote in a council, because we cling to our belief that they will be to the detriment of the happiness of society. For example, they certainly may not vote to encourage bullying. Well, perhaps they never would, but the point is that we need to do some thinking about precisely what are the limits of the power of such a council to be, before we set it up. Can the children, for instance, be free to decide that all lesson should be voluntary (assuming that that is not a freedom that they have already been specifically given)? I can think of nothing more likely to spread resentment and disillusion, and hence unhappiness, than inviting children to participate in school management, without specifying the limits of their competence, and then using one's authority to over-ride half of their decisions. And yet, in my experience that is precisely what most schools that countenance some form of council do.

I am aware that the sort of view I am here putting forward is one that is abhorred by many radicals. They point out, correctly, that the sting is in the tail: all this talk of freedom, giving the children the freedom to decide about the running of the school - and then, wham, bam, the limits come down : they are free to decide, provided that they decide as I do. Yes; that is what I am saying and I have given my reasons for saying it. Nothing that I have heard yet has persuaded me that I should subscribe to the view that children should be free to do precisely what they want nor, specifically, that they or anyone else should be free to behave in ways that militate against the long-term happiness of the community. I have indicated my feeling - and admitted that it is by no means a proven contention - that in terms of happiness the community will lose if all attendance at lessons, or whatever you want to call them, is voluntary. Suppose the children in a particular school sincerely feel that I am empirically mistaken? I can only say that there seems to me good reason to claim that as a general rule adults, in view of their greater experience and knowledge and reasoning ability, are better equipped to make such judgments than children. And it is important to note that we are and concerned with *value* judgments at this point, but empirical judgements. Therefore we should adopt the rule, in the interests of the long-term welfare of the community, that teachers remain the *final* arbiters of the limits of freedom. To a certain frame of mind such a pronouncement is intolerable; I only hope that it will be discussed and considered with the seriousness due to what is after all the most complex aspect of the debate about freedom in schools: who decides?

Finally, having acknowledged the difficulties in my view, let us turn once again to a rival view. What did Neill actually have to say about the limits of freedom? - for he certainly imposed limits on the freedom of children at Summerhill. Despite his talk of self-determination or self-regulation, there are clear examples of things that children may not determine to do. He argued, with scathing scorn for people who do not appreciate that his solution is the correct one, that the answer lies in a distinction between liberty and license. But we must weather the scorn, for we have already seen that such a distinction solves no problems at all. It merely restates the problem: how do we decide what freedoms are licence and hence unacceptable? After careful consideration of the examples that he incidentally gave of various freedoms that are and are not allowed at Summerhill, I can only conclude that he committed himself, whether he knew it or not, to the utilitarian criterion. For he said that children should not be free to jump out of windows, jump on sofas, smash pianos or kick doors; they should be prevented where possible (bars on windows), and corrected where prevention is impossible. Now on what grounds could he cite these examples, except that they constitute behaviour that either harms the child himself or annoys other people? But this notion of harm, whether physical or psychological (i.e. causing annoyance), whether to the individual or others, is merely another way of expressing the utilitarian criterion. But if this is so, if Neill, or anyone else, would argue that children ought not to smash pianos because to do so involves causing harm to others, then we may surely reopen the question of whether all the freedoms that he would have granted to children are in fact desirable on his criterion. As ever, all we are after is consistency: if 'harm' is the criterion, then the only remaining question of interest is whether more or less harm is caused, taking individual and community into account, by self-government for children to the extent that Neill advocates and complete freedom for children to decide whether or not to attend any lessons.

I have not been concerned either to dismiss or accept Neill's view of education. I am concerned with the way in which we should approach the sort of issues that a school like Summerhill raises. Presented with the example of such a school, we ask 'Why do you do this and that?' My own view is that Neill was not actually very clear why. He seemed to proceed to a considerable extent by intuition and he was not in fact entirely consistent. But that is not the point at issue, which is rather that we do not want talk of 'rights', 'self-regulation' and unqualified 'freedom', so much as some coherent account of the criteria necessary for determining rights and the limits of freedom for children. The most interesting issue seems to me to be the question of voluntary attendance at lessons. I conclude with a question: surely on the assumption that we have something to offer, on the assumption that our schools are attempting to initiate children into worthwhile activities, it must by definition be worthwhile to take steps to ensure that children are initiated into them?

Educational Distribution

Independent sector

Argument about the independent sector of education is often confused by forgetting that there are many different types of independent schools and by failing to distinguish between three different types of argument. Within the independent sector there are schools as disparate as Summerhill and Eton; there are religious and secular foundations; boarding and day schools; schools where the emphasis is on a traditional academic curriculum, schools which could only fairly be described as progressive and experimental; besides the well-known public schools, there are schools for the handicapped, for the blind and so on. It is conceivable that there might be good reason for adopting a different attitude to different kinds of school within the private sector. The three different questions (and hence types of argument)that must not be confused are: (1) Are independent schools good schools? (2) Are independent schools in principal acceptable? (3) Are independent schools in practice acceptable or desirable in our society? The first of these questions is about the schools themselves, the second about the system of private education, and the third involves consideration of both the previous questions in relation to other features of our society.

Of the many points that have been made at one time or another on one side or the other of this argument I shall single out five that are commonly put forward in justification of an independent sector and three that are put forward by way of objection. It is argued that an independent sector is desirable because: (1) It provides a good education, not otherwise available. (2) It caters for certain specific needs that some children at least may have, such as the need for a boarding school. (3) It serves various minority interests. (4) It provides the opportunity for experiment that is lacking in the state system. (5) A principle of freedom justifies an independent sector. In the words of Walter Hamilton,

> 'To take away from such parents as at present have the means to exercise the right to educate their children at their own expense would be an invasion of liberty unheard of West of the Iron Curtain, an act of tyranny which would not lose its tyrannical character because it was exercised by a constitutional majority.'

As against these points it may be argued (1) that the independent sector provides a bad education, (2) that it leads to social division, and/or (3) that it is in principle unacceptable that the education in question should be the privilege of the few.

Clearly whether the education provided in the independent sector is good or bad is an exceedingly complex question that depends for its answer on such factors as what one's view of a good education is, which of the great variety of schools in the sector we are talking about, and, in some cases, what children we are talking about (for example, there may be certain children for whom distinctive schools such as Abbotsholme or Gordonstoun would provide a good education and others for whom they would not). In any case, since the question of the quality of education provided is a question about the schools, whereas we are primarily interested in the principles that may or may not justify an independent sector, and since any blanket assessment of private education will obviously be a ludicrous oversimplification, it seems best to concentrate primarily on that part of the independent sector that people generally seemed concerned about - namely, the traditional public schools. Now although there is certainly a wide difference of quality in the education provided, on any criteria, by the various public schools, and although there may be some whose objection to the public schools is that they deny their pupils a good education, it seems best that we should proceed by assuming that a public school education is in some sense a good education. That, at any rate, would seem to be the view of those who pay large sums of money to obtain it for their children and the view of those who resent the fact that it is confined to the few. The people concerned may have very different reasons for regarding it as a desirable education (some may see it simply as a passport to a better job, some as a good training ground for character, some as academically stronger), but that it is generally regarded as desirable can hardly be doubted.

On the assumption, however, that the public schools provide a good education, what we are being presented with here is merely the beginnings of an argument for certain features of the public school education being brought into the state system. If, for example, boarding be singled out as a desirable feature of education, for whatever reason, for at least some children, that is an argument for boarding facilities being provided by a good educational system, whether it be private or state controlled. Neither of the first two points put forward above as possible arguments for the independent sector, therefore, are in fact any such thing. They do not justify the system in principle; they merely offer possible reasons for admiring specific schools.

The next two points (that an independent sector caters for minorities and allows of experiment) are about the system, as opposed to being merely about specific features of specific schools. Furthermore it is as a matter of fact true that within the independent sector there has been considerable experimentation and that minorities have been catered for. But these truths are only contingent truths. That is to say that, although it is as a matter of fact true, there is no necessary reason why it should have been true or should be true in the future; nor is there any necessary reason why there should not be experiment and a catering for minorities within the state system. There obviously has been, and is, experiment within the state system, thought perhaps it has a less distinguished record for catering for minority interests. So even if we accept the need for continued experiment and for some concern for minority interests, and even if we acknowledge the contribution of the independent sector in these respect, we cannot conclude that therefore the independent sector is justified.

We thus arive at the only argument that could hope to establish that an independent sector of education is in principal justifiable-an appeal to freedom.

The question before us is whether it is right that a desirable education should be available and reserved for those who can afford it. One does not have to be a philosophical genius to see that opponents of the independent sector are obviously correct in their assertion that the wealth of parents is not a relevant criterion for differential educational treatment. It has nothing to do with education. It is as bizarre as the claim that having red hair is a relevant reason for being provided with a distinctive kind of education. Furthermore they are probably right that the existence of a private sector is one factor that may contribute to social division. However, it seems to me that we should not make too much of this, since it is at worst only one factor, and it is difficult to believe that the abolition of a private sector of education is going to make very much practical difference. The whole question of the independent sector is therefore finally seen to rest upon the question of freedom. Do we accept that justification is to be found in the principle of freedom?

Obviously we do not. Hamilton's argument simply will not do. Passing over his emotive hysteria about iron curtains and his question-begging reference to a 'right' as rapidly as possible, let us nonetheless not that one point he makes is true: to take away this freedom from those who can afford it would indeed, by definition, be an 'invasion of personal liberty', and those who are in the habit of ranting on in other contexts about the importance of freedom without qualification or substantiation are of course hoist on their own petard in the face of Hamilton's impassioned cry. But we, I trust, do not have this habit. As we have seen, talking about freedom without qualification is meaningless. The question must be whether there are reasons that can be given to defend this specific freedom of the few who can afford it. Is there any reason why those who are rich enough to afford it should be given the freedom to acquire preferential education for their children? Any such reason, to be acceptable, would, I have argued, have to appeal to the ultimate consideration of equal concern for the welfare of all. Beyond question, I suggest, in principle there can be no such reason. A private sector of education is thus, in ideal terms, indefensible.

However, before leaving this topic, we should not allow a concern with principle and abstract theory, such as philosophy predominantly displays, to blind us to practicalities. It would not be at all unreasonable to suggest - although the suggestion will irritate those who expect a revolution to build Rome in a day - that in practice we have to take into account a number of other factors, and that as things are it would be worse in terms of the welfare of society as a whole to sweep away the independent sector than to retain it. Two reasons in particular might be given to support this suggestion: (1) Given that the distribution of wealth in our society is as a matter of fact unequal, a private sector of education is a useful means of taxing the rich and effectively increasing educational resources for the rest of us. (2) Given that the private sector provides a good education in some sense, the community as a whole may be thought to gain from the existence of such well-educated people.

I am not personally convinced by the second point, and in any case I should have thought that the idea of calculating whether in fact the community gains from the existence of ex-public school individuals constitutes in impossible task. As for the first point, one can think of a variety of other ways of taxing the rich and increasing educational resources if that is what one wants to do. (Since we are dealing with practical considerations it is worth adding that if all parents had their children at state schools this might serve to bring a certain amount of influential pressure to bear on the demand for increased educational resources.) However, this is a point of view which it would have been churlish not to mention.

What we surely have to conclude from this discussion is that ideally the state system of education should incorporate whatever of those features of the private sector (be they features of individual schools or of the system) can be shown by reasoned argument to be desirable and offer them to all or to all whom they would benefit, rather than simply to those who can afford them. The independent sector is not to be justified in principle, but, if at all, as a practical expedient prior to the self-sufficiency of a universal state system.

The state system

The suggestion that ideally a state system should offer the good things to be found in the independent sector to all conveniently raises the question of whether this means offering the same kind of school to all children. Does it, for instance, commit one to comprehensive schools as opposed to the tripartite system? It has been suggested to me that to raise this question at this point in time is to be out of date before one begins: the tripartite system is on the way out, whether one likes it or one. I find this suggestion peculiar. Assume that it is true that a comprehensive system is here to stay - is that any reason to stop considering the merits of alternatives? If advocates of comprehensive education had taken the view that since we had a tripartite system there was no point in considering the rationale behind it or of examining alternatives, we would probably never have had a move towards comprehensivisation. I take the view that whatever system we have or will have in the near future has got nothing to do with the question of what system we ought to have, and thing we must resist is any tendency in the next generation of teachers unthinkingly to assume that a comprehensive system of education is obviously an improvement on what it has replaced.

There are, of course, many variants on the comprehensive plan, and many alternatives that might be considered, besides the simple tripartite model of grammar, modern and technical schools. Such variants cannot be examined minutely here, where my purpose is to focus on the simple question of whether it is desirable or acceptable to offer quite distinct types of education to different children on some criterion or criteria other than the wealth of parents, which was, of course,the assumption behind the 1944 Education Act. Conversely, it may be thought, the assumption that it is not desirable on any criteria lies behind the move towards comprehensive education. But does it?

The initial problem is that no two people necessarily seem to mean the same thing by a comprehensive school. To some it means simply a single community in which the interests of children of all types and abilities are catered for; on this view the essence of a comprehensive school is not that the distinctions of the tripartite system are avoided, but that they do not involve social segregation as well. A related view is that a comprehensive school should take in pupils from every social stratum and background. But some would go further and see a comprehensive school as, by definition, also involving a less rigid distinction between practical and academic curricula; at the very least the individual pupil who, let us say, is essentially non-academic would not thereby forfeit the chance of pursuing whatever slight academic interests he might have. Some, it would seem, want to go farther even than this and argue that a comprehensive school should, again by definition, break down the division between academic and practical completely and offer essentially a common curriculum for all. Finally it is not unheard of for the question of streaming to crop up, with some arguing that comprehensive schools are only truly comprehensive if there is no streaming at all.

It is not to the purpose to attempt a philosophical analysis of the notion of a comprehensive school. The term means 'all-embracing', and we simply have to recognise that fact that essential to its use is the idea of a contrast with any system that involves distinctive kinds of institutions for different children, but that beyond that advocates of comprehensives may be committed to any combination of the above demands. What we have to do is to consider each of these demands in isolation and attempt to discover what can be said for or against them.

But let us begin by considering the arguments for and against the tripartite system.

The 1944 Act demanded that such educational facilities should be provided as were desirable for children in view of 'their different ages, abilities and aptitudes'. In practice this was deemed to involve a distinction between three types of pupil: the academically gifted, those gifted in respect of practical skills or in respect of aptitude for specific occupations such as engineering, and those (the vast majority) who, given the implications of the Act, can best, if bluntly, be categorised as simply relatively less gifted in either respect. Corresponding to each group there arose the grammar school, the secondary technical school and the secondary modern school.

Now we surely cannot dispute that in principle differences of ability and aptitude are eminently reasonable criteria for providing different kinds of education. Conversely we cannot accept the simplistic argument that equality demands that people should all experience the same kind of education. Equality, as we have seen, demands impartial treatment, which means similar treatment except where there are relevant reasons for differentiation. The relevance of reasons is judged by reference to the nature of what is being distributed in the light of the ultimate consideration of concern equally for the welfare of all. On these terms it seems absurd to deny that, if one child has an obvious flair for the academic pursuit of mathematics and another does not, that constitutes a relevant reason for treating them differently.

What then are the objections to the tripartite system? There seem to me to be essentially four that are worth taking seriously:

1. The claim that although in principle such distinctions may be reasonable, in practice they are made extremely inaccurately.

2. The claim that whatever the theoretical justification of the distinctions, in practice they lead to social divisions that are

unacceptable.

3. The claim that the specific education provided by one or more of the three types of school is inadequate or unacceptable as an education.

4. The claim that the system presupposes some kind of assessment, which is unacceptable.

Before proceeding to examine these criticisms in greater detail, I should like to put forward, simply for consideration, the suggestion that all of them are to a considerable extent attempts to rationalise a feeling of objection to the undoubted fact that, as a generalisation, secondary modern pupils in particular become second-class citizens in terms of our materialistic culture. In other words the real objection to secondary modern schools is, in the uncompromising words of Rubinstein and Stoneman, that, by being classified as secondary modern pupils, many of our children 'have their future determined as manual workers at the age of eleven. Secondary modern pupils tend, as adults, to lose in the race for secure and well-paid employment, which may have the incidental corollary that some children (or their parents), in their anxiety to avoid the secondary modern, struggle and gain grammar school places to which they are not entirely suited. If there is any truth in this suggestion, then I wish to make one simple but extraordinarily important observation on it: objectionable as this may be (is), there is no purely educational solution to it. I am not arguing, as some have done, that education *should* not concern itself with what are essentially social or political points, but that educational changes or reforms cannot affect them. If, for whatever reason society differentiates between various roles in respect of status and pay and thereby renders some less desirable, then no educational system can get round this and any educational system will be a selective system, whether it wants to be or not. Whatever is meant by a comprehensive system, it cannot prevent an ultimate distinction between those who are better suited for some roles and those who are better suited for others. If some roles are judged to be superior in a society, that cannot be attributed to the system of education. Second-class citizens are the product of a socio-economic structure and not an educational system. One cannot therefore legitimately object to the tripartite system simply on the grounds that some can be shown to gain more in material terms than others at the end of the day.

What one can do, of course, is argue that the wrong people are gaining. This takes us back to the first objection: that the categorisation of children at the age of eleven has been inaccurate. These really seems very little doubt that this is true, and true in two senses. First, it is clear that examinations such as the 11-plus have been far from satisfactory in terms of accurately predicting potentially successful and unsuccessful grammar school material. Secondly, there is the more subtle argument that, in any case, children respond to the expectations made of them, and that therefore there may be many secondary modern pupils who seem to have been well placed but who, had they had the opportunity to go to a grammar school, would have seemed well placed there as well. Taking these points on their merits, it follows that (a) ideally there is a need for a better system of selection - and perhaps there are more suitable ages at which to select than eleven, (b) there is a need for increased facilities for transference at later stages between the various kinds of education, and (c) there is a need to remove the pervading ethos of a particular kind of school with its inbuilt expectations. Now it may follow from these considerations, although it obviously does not necessarily do so, that a comprehensive school in the limited sense of a single physical community is therefore to be desired. This would be an empirical point, but it seems reasonable to suppose that if all three types of education were provided in a single community, wit would be easier to rectify misclassification, and the atmosphere of the school and the expectation that it put over to the children would be considerably less stereotyped. What we do not have here is an argument for anything more than a comprehensive school in this limited sense. However true it is that children's performance can be affected by what is expected of them, it is palpable nonsense to pretend that all children could do well in any kind of school. What one cannot accept is the argument that simply because some children under a tripartite system may turn out to be what they need not have been, therefore nobody ought to be allowed to experience a distinctive kind of education. Though some non-academic children in secondary moderns might have been academically successful in grammar schools, we cannot conclude that therefore it must be wrong to distinguish between the relatively academic and the relatively unacademic child.

That the tripartite system leads to social divisions is an argument that is frequently to be encountered. How pertinent a criticism is it? The first question is what precisely is meant by social division? Mere differences between groups of people are surely not in themselves objectionable; indeed it is difficult to conceive of a society in which a competent sociologist could not rapidly arrive at various criteria for classification such that he could refer to distinct social divisions or classes. If the classless society means a society in which no criteria could be found for classifying distinct groups of people, then the classless society is not going to come. Clearly if social division is taken to be undesirable then what must be meant is either divisions between groups in respect of advantages desired by all or else divisions in the sense of dissension between groups. It seems indisputable that the tripartite system has tended to contribute towards social division in both these latter senses (and indeed that it has actually served as a way of transferring people from one social group to another): the grammar school tends to be a path to advantage, and no doubt dissension can arise between grammar school and secondary modern school pupils. Here then we have another plausible argument for a single physical community and for the comprehensive conceived of as a neighbourhood school. Though it is unlikely that thc mere housing of different kinds of education and pupils from different backgrounds in the same community will solve the problem of social division, and though it must again be stressed that the nature or society and its outlook in respect of the relative esteem to be accorded to various social roles is the key factor in determining social division, it surely is reasonable to suppose that the less children from different backgrounds and of different aptitudes are treated as different species in their own private world, the more chance there is of creating a spirit of homogeneity, which anybody committed to the overriding importance of equal concern for the welfare and happiness of all must welcome.

In a way the suggestion that the objection to the tripartite system is really that one or more of its constituent parts provide a bad education is the most interesting. It is also the most complex of the objections, requiring for its satisfactory resolution considerably more than a book the length of this one to itself. I have already argued that ideally education should be concerned to develop in the individual those embryonic talents that he has which are not anti-social, a sociable attitude, and those abilities which may be of value to him, either directly or indirectly, and of value to the community as a whole - value being assessed ultimately by reference to happiness and welfare. I have also suggested that on these grounds a modified form of Hirst's forms of knowledge should provide the basis of the education of all and that beyond that specialisation in whatever area the child has interest and aptitude is to be desired. On these terms one could certainly criticise all three of the forms of education provided under the tripartite system on points of detail. But it is not clear that any of them deserves to be dismissed as inherently bad education. However, one may well feel that the central criticism to be made is that there has been too exclusive a preoccupation with the academic at the expense of the practical: that grammar schools have ignored the practical completely and that technical and modern schools have in fact, surprisingly, followed suit with an unnecessary emphasis on a watered-down academic curriculum. To solve such problems there is obviously no *need* for a new system of education, but the comprehensive school, still conceived of as essentially merely a single community catering for all types of child, might well in practice facilitate the provision of a more flexible curriculum.

Finally there is the objection to the notion of assessment to be considered. Now let us face this allegedly burning issue coolly. Unless all children are to do exactly the same things or else be left free to do just what they want, then some form of assessment is inevitable. So long as we retain the notion that some people are better at certain things than others, and that some things cannot be done without certain prior conditions being met (as one cannot discuss the merits of Aeschylus' style if one cannot read Greek, or cannot play football if one does not know the rules), then we are stuck with the notion of assessment - although, of course, it may take a variety of forms. Finding the best way of assessing people, if by 'best' we mean that way which is most accurate and causes least anguish, may be difficult, but we cannot avoid it so long as we continue to make reference to people's 'readiness' to do things, or their 'suitability' or competence'. In short, unless we are prepared to drop altogether the idea that things may be well or badly done, that one can distinguish between the quality of various performances, and that there are standards of excellence in various sphere - whatever those standards may be, which is an entirely separate point - we are committed to assessment. For assessment is logically tied up with the concepts of quality, standard and excellence.

Now of course we are aware - who could not be with the recent spate of Penguin Educational Specials to remind him? - that there are some who apparently either do not understand this logical point or are not interested in the question of whether things are well or badly done provided that they are done. (An interesting philosophical question here: at what point is a thing being so badly done that it does not count as being done at all?) They advocate a total absence of streaming and a common curriculum for all in the sense of a curriculum consisting of various options from which the child takes his pick. With such a scheme assessment would, of course, be reduced to a minimum - perhaps age would be the only criterion of qualification.

What is wrong with this view? With the basic idea that a wide variety of options should be available, perhaps nothing. But to adopt this policy in its entirety is effectively to claim either that children have sufficient knowledge of what is involved in the various options, before they undertake them, to make a sound judgement as to which they will most enjoy, which they will undertake with success, and which will in the long run benefit them most, or that it does not matter whether they do enjoy, succeed or benefit. It also involves the presumption that anybody can 'do' anything, if he is so minded, and that it is unimportant how well equipped he is to do it. There may be some things of which this is true: for instance, to take up an example from a previous chapter, it may be unnecessary to discriminate between people in respect of their ability to think of uses for a brick, or in respect for their ability to talk about 'democracy', if 'talk' about' simply means utter points of view. But this merely raises the question once again of whether such activities are particularly worthwhile. I suggest that there is a very limited value in discussing democracy unless one has some inkling of the historical evolution of democracies, the historical facts about various democracies (how they worked, how they arose and fell, what they achieved, what they failed to achieve), the actual workings of contemporary democracies, and some philosophical competence at handling abstract concepts and, in relation to such a topic as this, ethical concepts; it follows that to make the exercise valuable something more than the random decision to undertake it is required. Why should we accept the naive oversimplification of such men as Postman and Weingartner that to question is all that matters? Anybody can question what is surely needed is some competent and informed answering. Similarly if we accept, as I have argued we should, that there is a value in people coming to understand the various forms of knowledge and a value in expertise in the various branches of science, in history, in literature, in art and in philosophy, then clearly it is not true that anybody can 'do' any of the things that we are concerned with in education.

With the empirical claim that within limits the relatively less able may achieve more in the company of the relatively able, I am not here concerned. The evidence, such as it is, seems far from conclusive either way. But it should be noted that to use this argument in favour of non-streaming involves acknowledging that there *are* standards of ability nd competence (otherwise it would be meaningless to distinguish between the less and more able). And if it is admitted that there are standards of competence, which can be judged, there seems no obvious reason why reference should not be made to them. What must be resisted, according to my argument, is the view that because A can gain something from the study of Z, therefore B must be allowed to study Z regardless of the question of his competence to do so.

Attempting to pull the various strands of the section together, I would suggest that there is a fairly obvious middle road to be adopted between the die-hard proponents of the tripartite system and the more extreme of the many different people who have to be lumped together as procomprehensive. Proponents of the tripartite system are surely right in their claim that such things as the study of English literature modern languages, science, etc., at a relatively academic level (though not necessarily in the manner and the extremely departmentalised form often associated with the grammar schools), is worthwhile (evaluative claim); that some people are better suited to these activities than others and some not suited at all (empirical claim); and (probably/possibly) that the task is better done with a degree of streaming. They are therefore right to conclude that we ought to distinguish between children in respect of their ability and aptitude for such an education, and to resist a common curriculum and an absence of streaming across the board. But there is good reason to suppose that they are wrong to insist on the isolated existence of different types of school. For the sake of promoting social homogeneity and of ensuring more efficient consideration of what children's aptitudes and abilities really are, and possibly to allow of a greater flexibility in curriculum, we see the need for comprehensive schooling in the sense of the provision of institution that embrace all kinds of children and, hence, curricula.

Universities

It has been argued that educational provision should be made for all, although the principle of impartiality might demand or allow different kinds of education to be provided for different people. Does it follow that all should go to school for the same length of time and that, turning to higher education, universities should be open to all?

No. I: does not follow. The essence of the argument for universal education is that education is by definition something advantageous. What we actually provide in the name of education may not be advantageous, but what we *mean* to provide is something advantageous. In broad terms, education consists of a concerted effort to help the child enter on paths that are advantageous to him and not disadvantageous to society, and this is so whatever one's view of what is advantageous and hence of what education ought to involve. No relevant grounds can be discovered for refusing this advantageous process to any individual. But, of course, what is as a matter of fact 'advantageous' may differ from child to child. Some things may be commonly advantageous to all such as, perhaps, acquiring the skills of reading, writing and coherent argument; but, thereafter, one child may be drawn to music, another to carpentry - one to studying classics, another to engineering - and so on. Therefore, although education in the sense of advantageous help is due to all, different individuals may benefit to different degrees from different educational programmes. Only if all individuals were identical in respect of their interests and abilities, and if society wished to maintain this identity, would the case be otherwise.

The concept of education, however, has no time element built into it. It is not a condition of being educated that one should have gone through a process or have 'experienced education' for any specific length of time. One can refer to education as something that never ceases, as something that is contiguous with life itself, as something that only ends with death, and so on. But when we are talking about education in respect of the deliberate activities of various institutions it has no specifc time limit. However one judges the 'educated man', it is not by reference to time.

To decide how long a child ought to be at school (or, on deschooling terms, free to take advantage of educational provision) one has to decide, in theory, at what point the 'advantage' he is supposed to be gaining ceases to be provided effectively, or at what point it would be more to the advantage of him and society that he should cease to belong to a specific institution. This will clearly differ from individual to individual and will, to some extent, be affected by the specific nature of the education or schooling being undergone. The unacademic child, for instance, who has no interest in or talent for a continuation of study in much of the school curriculum, but who has a talent for mechanics, may well benefit from leaving the confines of the institution relatively early and becoming instead an apprentice mechanic. Conversely the student of modern languages may benefit from, and may wish to benefit from, continued institutional help.

The principle of equality, therefore, certainly does not demand that universities should be available to all. In fact, as things are, it demands the reverse. For, although the concept of a university may be difficult to define, although historically the concept has come to be modified to some extent, and thought at present it may be thought to be undergoing change, the fact remains that a university is not just a collection of buildings put there for any old purpose. A university, by definition, could only meaningfully be thought to have a certain *kind* of purpose and there are a variety of purposes that it simply does not have. It may be taken to mean some things, and there are other things which it cannot be taken to mean. It is not, for instance, a place in which people are trained to become soldiers or practice nudity.

Whatever precise definition might be given, it is clear that one part of the meaning of a university is that it is an institution for academic pursuits available to people with certain qualifications. That is to say that by definition there are relevant reasons why some should be excluded. Now of course one may criticise the actual qualification in question from a number of points of view: one may argue that A level passes do not in fact accurately measure or predict the relevant competence; one may argue that those who do badly at A level might nonetheless have done well at university; one may argue that the importance of A levels as qualifications puts a strain on children and impairs their performance or that it leads to the wrong kind of teaching; one may argue that luck plays too great a part in the selection of candidates for university places or that too much attention (or not enough attention) is given to other factors, besides academic qualifications, such as subjective impressions of the character and personality of candidates, and so on. But all such criticisms are criticisms of the actual process of selection: they involve the claim that injustices may be done in selection and that there are unsatisfactory features of the system of selection as it exists. They do not amount to an argument to the effect that the business of selecting is in itself unjust. For whatever the faults of the actual procedure for selection, the fact remains that built into our conception of a university, part of what we mean by a university, is the notion that there are in principle certain standards or degrees of competence in specifiable respects that are necessary to the business of undertaking a university course, and which some people do not as a matter of fact come up to or have.

It may, of course, be pointed out that these qualifications are only necessary because of the way we regard universities, and suggested that they ought to be abandoned. But if the notion of qualifications is abandoned, then, by definition, the concept of a university is altered. Carried to extremes (let us say to the extent that no qualifications are looked for at all, so that anybody can go to university), the concept becomes modified to such an extent as to be altered beyond recognition. If anybody can go and, when there, do more or less anything (as they would have to be allowed to do, since not all would be *able* to do the sorts of thing traditionally associated with universities), then a university becomes indistinguishable from a social club. By opening universities to all, one finally destroys universities. This would only cease to be true if as a matter of fact every individual was capable of undertaking and profiting from a university education essentially similar to the traditional idea of what a university education is, which is palpably not the case.

My argument is this: historically speaking a university is to be understood as an institution of research and teaching at a relatively high level in fundamentally academic areas. On this definition there are relevant reasons for refusing to offer such an education to all, and there is nothing inegalitarian about such is refusal. The principle of impartiality may well lead us to say that all people should be able to continue with some from of higher education and that they should not be effectively disbarred from such by factors such as poverty. But that is a different point. There are in fact a number of other higher educational facilities (polytechnics, colleges of education, medical schools, art colleges, etc.) whose function is precisely to provide alternatives suitable for different people. To insist on a university education for all is, in reality, merely to play the verbal game of calling every such institution a university. For one could not meaningfully insist on a university education, as at present understood, for all, so long as all are not capable of undertaking what is involved in it.

Once again we come up against the argument based on considerations of worldly success and status; it is pointed out that a university education provides a passport to better jobs; other higher education facilities are seen as poor relations. Insofar as this is true, and it is obviously true to some extent, I can only repeat the point made above in regard to secondary education: the fault, if it be one, is a socio-economic one. Employers, by and large, are presumably not so foolish as to prefer candidates simply on the grounds that the word 'university graduate' can be technically and correctly applied to them. When a university graduate is selected for a post, it is presumably at worst because he has undergone an education that the employer sees reason to regard as desirable. Employers will not educational background, just because we make their job harder by referring of everything as a university education.

REFERENCES

1 Bantock, G. H., Education, *Culture and the Emotions* (Faber & Faber, 1967), p. 139.